A
TASTE
OF
SAN
FRANCISCO

San Francisco Symphony Cookbook Steering Committee

Danielle Walker, Editor
Marilyn Jacobson, Managing Editor

Rachael Hagner, Design Committee Chairman
Idell C. Donnelly, Finance Committee Chairman
JoAnn Lucibello, Marketing Planning Committee Chairman
Suzanne Parsons, Sales and Public Relations Chairman
Laurie MacDougall, Production Committee Chairman
Mary Chiu, Recipe Committee Chairman
Mary Tilden, Testing Committee Chairman

Dorothy Walz, Corresponding Secretary
Carol Moss, Recording Secretary

VOLUNTEER COUNCIL

Claudette Nicolai, Chairman of the Volunteer Council
Lois Gundlack, Assistant Chairman for Ongoing Projects

Lauren Lopresto, Staff Coordinator
Margaret Simpson, Staff Coordinator
Raina Glazener, Proofreader
Sheila Larsen, Director of Volunteer Activities

CONSULTANTS

Robert L. Iacopi, Publication Consultant
Jacqueline Mallorca, Copy Editor/Consultant

Drawings by Gary Bukovnik

DOUBLEDAY

NEW YORK   LONDON   TORONTO   SYDNEY   AUCKLAND

A
TASTE
of
SAN
FRANCISCO

THE BAY AREA'S BEST CHEFS OFFER MORE THAN
300 OF THEIR TEMPTING, EASY-TO-FOLLOW
RECIPES ESPECIALLY FOR YOU TO
PREPARE AT HOME

PUBLISHED BY DOUBLEDAY

a division of Bantam Doubleday Dell Publishing Group, Inc.

666 Fifth Avenue, New York, New York 10103

DOUBLEDAY and the portrayal of an anchor
with a dolphin are trademarks of Doubleday,
a division of Bantam Doubleday Dell
Publishing Group, Inc.

Library of Congress Cataloging-in-Publication Data

The San Francisco Symphony.
A taste of San Francisco: the Bay Area's best chefs offer
more than 300 of their tempting, easy-to-follow recipes
especially for you to prepare at home/drawings by
Gary Bukovnik. — 1st ed.

p.   cm.

1. Cookery.   2. Restaurants, lunch rooms, etc.—California—San
Francisco.   3. Menus.   I. San Francisco Symphony Orchestra.
II. Title: Taste of San Francisco.

TX714.S27 1990   90-32472
641.5—dc20   CIP

ISBN 0-385-26380-5

BOOK DESIGN BY CHRIS WELCH

Printed in the United States of America
October 1990
5   7   9   11   12   10   8   6   4

Contents

Foreword x

Preface xi

Restaurants and Chefs

Allegro 3

Amelio's 5

The American Baker 8

Auberge du Soleil 13

Bay Wolf Café and Restaurant 17

Bix 20

The Blue Fox 23

Bua Thong Kitchen 26

Butler's 29

Café Beaujolais 33

Café Majestic 36

Café 222 41

Caffé Freddy's 44

California Café Bar and Grill 46

California Culinary Academy 49

Campton Place 52

Chevys Mexican Restaurant 57

Chez Chez 61

Chez Panisse 63

China Moon Café 65

Circolo 69

Cuisine Cuisine 74

Domaine Chandon 78

Donatello 82

Enoteca Lanzone 86

Ernie's 89

Flea Street Café 92

Fleur de Lys 96

Fog City Diner 103

Fournou's Ovens 106

Fourth Street Grill 109

The French Room, Four Seasons Clift Hotel 112

Greens 116

Harbor Village 119

Harry's Bar and American Grill 122

Hayes Street Grill 125

Hong Kong Flower Lounge Restaurant 128

Il Fornaio Gastronomia Italiana 132

Jack's Restaurant 137

Jean Pierre Moullé 140

John Ash & Co. 143

Jordan Winery 147

Ken Hom 150

Kuleto's Italian Restaurant 154

La Lanterna 157

Lalime's 160

The Lark Creek Inn 164

Lascaux Bar and Rotisserie 169

L'Avenue Bistro 171

Le Castel 175

Le St. Tropez 178

Le Trou Restaurant Français 180

Lipizzaner 185

The Maltese Grill 188

Manora's Thai Cuisine 191

Masa's 194

Meadowood 198

Miramonte Restaurant and Country Inn 202

muchacha's 206

Mustards Grill 210

Narsai David 214

Piatti Ristorante 217

Postrio 221

RAF Centrogriglia 229

Regina's 231

Remillard's 233

Restaurant 231 Ellsworth 236

Sante Fe Bar and Grill 239

Silks 243

Square One 247

Stars 250

Tadich Grill 254

Timberhill Ranch 256

Tortola 259

Tra Vigne 262

Trader Vic's 266

Vivande 269

Washington Square Bar & Grill 272

Wu Kong Restaurant 275

Yank Sing 278

Zola's 281

Zuni Café 285

Standard Preparations

Appendix

Alphabetical List of Restaurants 299

Caterers/Chefs/Cooking Schools 304

Acknowledgments 305

Index 307

Foreword

Music lovers are hungry people—on both sides of the stage. And their tastes are just as varied as their palates are sophisticated. But this cookbook offers more than variety. It also brings us together in the pursuit of the exquisite. The great concert requires a good program, well-rehearsed and expertly played. And so does the festive meal.

As *chef d'orchestre* I am happy to invite you all to be my *co-chefs* in finding new favorites in the following pages. Again, sharing has made us richer.

Herbert Blomstedt
Music Director and Conductor
San Francisco Symphony

Preface

The American food revolution that has taken place during the past decade has had far-reaching effects, and not just in the casual acceptance of food processors or the ready availability of foods unknown to most of us even ten years ago. Today, more than ever before, well-informed restaurantgoers in America are keenly aware of what they eat, and have a far greater appreciation of the skills involved in selecting fresh seasonal ingredients and then combining them successfully. (This makes life a great deal more rewarding for the professional chef: An informed audience is a more appreciative audience!) Both men and women are also far more likely to be remarkably competent in their own kitchens, and to enjoy cooking for friends. Sharing good food and wine with congenial company is, after all, one of the great pleasures of life, whether it's in your own home or at a favorite restaurant.

Editing the recipes for *A Taste of San Francisco* has been both a pleasure and a privilege—it has been rather like looking over the shoulders of the Bay Area's best chefs as they work! Time-saving professional techniques have been explained in detail wherever appropriate, and all of the recipes have been tested in nonprofessional kitchens by home cooks.

Listed alphabetically by restaurant name, the recipes are arranged in carefully orchestrated menus that generally comprise an appetizer, an entrée, and a dessert. If a chef has specified a particular brand of ingredient, we have included this information as being crucial to his or her interpretation of the dish.

A symbol is used throughout the book to indicate recipes that are quick to prepare and cook (times do not include chilling or marinating, if applicable):
• 30 minutes or less.

Whenever the name of a recipe is capitalized (Chicken Stock, for example), the recipe will be found elsewhere in the book on the page specified. Unless alternatives are suggested alongside a specific ingredient, substitutions are *not* recommended.

The restaurants included in this book represent the best that San Francisco and its environs have to offer, and reflect a wide diversity of ethnic cuisines. Inevitably, as we go to press, one or two dining spots may disappear—it's the nature of the business. But a permanent legacy will be left behind on these pages . . . rather like a musical score.

A Taste of San Francisco provides a meeting ground for the professional chef and the amateur cook, and makes a wonderful showcase for the Northern California dining experience. It is our hope that you enjoy using the book as much as we have enjoyed putting it together.

A
TASTE
OF
SAN
FRANCISCO

Angelo Quaranta's Allegro at the top of Russian Hill is an intimate, elegant restaurant with a lighthearted, convivial atmosphere. Chef Quaranta is from Taranto in the south of Italy, but his cooking embraces the whole Italian peninsula. He and partner Pamela Berman manage to make this small restaurant feel like a private club or an extension of your own home, and the food is genuine in the best sense: It is simple, unadulterated, and prepared with a light touch.

PENNE ARRABIATA *(Pasta with Hot Chili–Fresh Tomato Sauce)*

POLLO AL MATTONE *(Grilled Chicken with Sage and Rosemary)*

FRESH FRUIT OF CHOICE

PENNE ARRABIATA •

1 cup virgin olive oil
2 tablespoons dried hot chili pepper flakes
4 cloves garlic, peeled and crushed
6 ripe tomatoes, peeled, seeded, and chopped

Salt
8 ounces penne rigati (short, tubular pasta)
1 tablespoon chopped fresh parsley
Freshly grated Pecorino cheese (imported Italian sheep's milk preferred)

Combine olive oil and chili flakes. Bring to a boil, cool, and add the garlic cloves. Marinate for at least 30 minutes, and strain.

In a saucepan, heat 4 tablespoons of strained chili-garlic oil with tomatoes. Add salt to taste. Keep warm over low heat.

Cook pasta in boiling, salted water until *al dente*. Drain well. Toss in saucepan with oil, tomatoes, and parsley. Serve with freshly grated Pecorino cheese.

SERVES 4

PREPARATION TIME: 10 minutes, plus marination time

COOKING TIME: 15 minutes

EDITOR'S NOTE: Chili-garlic oil will keep under refrigeration for a week or more.

POLLO AL MATTONE

*2 broiling chickens, about 2½ pounds
each, split in half
2 cups virgin olive oil
¼ cup chopped garlic
¼ cup chopped fresh sage*

*¼ cup chopped fresh rosemary
Salt and pepper
Juice of 2 lemons
4 foil-wrapped bricks for weighting
chickens when grilling*

Pound chicken halves to break bones and flatten slightly. Mix oil, garlic, seasonings, and lemon juice together. Marinate chickens in this mixture in the refrigerator from 2 to 24 hours.

Build an intense charcoal fire. Oil the grill rack and place chicken halves on it, skin side down. Weight each one with a foil-wrapped brick and grill until cooked through, about 30 minutes.

SERVES 4

PREPARATION TIME: 10 minutes, plus marination time

COOKING TIME: 30 minutes

Proprietor Chris Shearman has maintained the splendid "old San Francisco" opulence of this landmark restaurant. Established in 1926, it still has its original crystal chandeliers, large oil paintings, and big mirrors in ornate gilt frames. Soft lighting, impressive floral arrangements, and a variety of exceptionally beautiful porcelain plates complete the setting for the artistic, imaginative cuisine of French-born and trained co-owner/chef Jacky Robert.

CRENSHAW MELON WITH PROSCIUTTO SAUCE AND FRIED PARSLEY
CHICKEN WITH PEAR-CREAM SAUCE
BRIE PUFF WITH SAUTÉED APPLES AND CARAMEL SAUCE

CRENSHAW MELON WITH PROSCIUTTO SAUCE AND FRIED PARSLEY •

1 ripe Crenshaw melon
¼ pound prosciutto, thinly sliced
1 large egg
1 large egg yolk
1 teaspoon coarsely ground black pepper

½ cup heavy cream
Virgin olive oil for skillet
2 bunches fresh parsley, stems removed,
   sprigs washed and very well dried

Peel and seed melon, and cut into ½" slices. Grind prosciutto in food processor. Add whole egg, egg yolk, and black pepper, and process until blended. With motor running, slowly add cream. Blend, but do not overmix. Strain mixture. Divide this sauce among 4 plates.

Pour enough olive oil into a sauté pan to reach a depth of ¼". Fry the parsley for 10 seconds, being very careful as the oil will spatter. Divide the fried parsley in equal portions and place on top of the sauce. Arrange melon slices in a crisscross pattern on top of the parsley.

SERVES 4
PREPARATION TIME: 15 minutes
COOKING TIME: 10 seconds

CHICKEN WITH PEAR-CREAM SAUCE

1 quart Chicken Stock (page 294) or
  canned salt-free chicken broth
4 ripe pears
4 chicken breasts, halved, skinned, and
  boned
Salt

Freshly ground white pepper
2 cups heavy cream
Juice of 1 lemon
2 heads Belgian endive, cored and
  coarsely chopped

Pour chicken stock into a saucepan and bring to a simmer. Peel pears, reserving the peelings, and cut pears into uniform-sized pieces. Add to chicken stock and poach until tender, about 5 to 10 minutes, depending on variety. Drain pears and reserve stock. Transfer pears to a blender or food processor and puree.

Combine reserved stock and pear peelings in the bottom of a two-part steamer and bring to a simmer. Season chicken breasts with salt and pepper. Place in top of steamer, cover, and steam until just done, about 6 minutes. Keep chicken warm in the stock.

Place cream in a separate saucepan and boil until reduced to 1 cup, about 10 minutes. Add pear puree and lemon juice, and heat. Strain through a sieve. The consistency should be about the same as a medium white sauce. If too thick, add a small amount of the stock.

Divide endive among 4 plates. Top with chicken, and cover with sauce.

SERVES 4
PREPARATION TIME: 20 minutes
COOKING TIME: about 20 minutes

BRIE PUFF WITH SAUTÉED APPLES AND CARAMEL SAUCE

2 tablespoons butter
½ cup water
½ cup plus ½ tablespoon all-purpose
  flour
6 ounces Brie cheese, rind removed, cut
  into 1" pieces
2 large eggs
1 egg mixed with 1 tablespoon water for
  glaze

2 large firm Golden Delicious apples,
  peeled, halved, and cored with a
  spoon to make a circular cavity
Freshly cracked black pepper
2 tablespoons Clarified Butter (page 291)
Caramel Sauce (recipe follows)
4 small scoops best-quality vanilla ice
  cream

Preheat oven to 450°. Butter a heavy baking sheet. Bring butter and water to a boil in a heavy saucepan. Remove from heat and whisk in flour. Set over medium-high heat and stir with a wooden spoon until dough forms a ball and leaves a film on bottom of pan. Transfer mixture to bowl of electric mixer. Add Brie and beat until incorporated. Beat in eggs one at a time.

Transfer dough to a pastry bag fitted with a ½″ plain tube. Pipe dough onto prepared baking sheet in disks 2½″ in diameter by ½″ high. Brush tops lightly with egg glaze, being careful not to let it drip down sides, as this would impede rising in the oven. Bake until golden brown, about 20 minutes.

Meanwhile, sprinkle apples with pepper. Heat clarified butter in a heavy skillet over high heat. Add apples, cored side down, and turn when golden brown, about 5 minutes. Continue cooking until apples are soft, about 5 minutes more.

Pour warm caramel sauce onto plates. Place a warm Brie puff in center of sauce. Place warm sautéed apple half just off center, cored side up, and fill cavity with ice cream. Serve immediately.

Caramel Sauce

¾ cup sugar
1½ tablespoons water

¾ cup heavy cream

Cook sugar and water in a heavy saucepan over low heat, swirling pan occasionally by handle, until sugar dissolves. Increased heat and boil until syrup turns a deep golden brown, about 6 minutes. Carefully pour in cream; mixture will bubble. Bring to a boil. Reduce heat to low and stir until sauce is smooth. Serve warm.

SERVES 4
PREPARATION TIME: 30 minutes
COOKING TIME: 20 minutes total

Jim Dodge, pastry chef, teacher, cookbook author, and columnist, is now the proprietor of a popular new San Francisco pastry shop and café, which, like his recent book, is called The American Baker. While Jim is professional to his fingertips, his carefully thought-out recipes are easy for the home cook to duplicate. The following pastries are perfect for afternoon tea, singly or in combination.

AMERICAN TEA SCONES
SESAME AND LEMON BARS
EMPIRE COOKIES
BROWN SUGAR AND GINGER FINGERS
DATE AND WALNUT CAKE WITH ORANGE
   BUTTERCREAM

AMERICAN TEA SCONES

1 cup all-purpose flour
¾ cup cake flour
2 tablespoons sugar
2 teaspoons baking powder (preferably Rumford)
1 teaspoon kosher salt

¼ pound (1 stick) unsalted butter, cold
1 teaspoon minced orange zest
½ cup currants
½ cup heavy cream, cold
Unsalted butter and jam for topping

Combine all-purpose and cake flours and freeze, covered, for 1 hour or longer before preparing the scones. This is important, as it helps to make the scones flaky and tender.

Line a baking sheet with baking parchment. In a medium bowl, blend together the flour, 1 tablespoon of sugar, baking powder, and salt. Cut the butter into ½″ cubes and toss with the flour mixture, coating the cubes lightly. Turn mixture from bowl onto a clean work surface. With a rolling pin, roll butter into long, thin flakes. Keep butter covered with flour as you roll, to prevent it from sticking to rolling pin. Scrape flour and butter back into bowl.

Add orange zest and currants. Toss until well blended. Add cream and toss with a rubber spatula until cream has been absorbed by flour. Cover your hands lightly with additional flour. Press dough into bottom of the bowl with your flour-covered hands. Turn dough out onto a lightly floured surface.

Dust top of dough lightly with additional flour. Keeping your hands lightly dusted with flour, work dough gently until it begins to hold a shape. Do not overwork dough. It should be slightly crumbly. Dust the top lightly with flour. Roll dough to ¾″ thick. Using a 2″ round cutter, cut as many rounds as possible, dipping cutter in flour between cuts. Press scraps together, roll, and cut as before. Arrange on lined baking sheet. Sprinkle tops with remaining 1 tablespoon sugar. Chill for 15 minutes.

Preheat oven to 400°. Place scones on middle rack of oven, and immediately reduce heat to 375°. Bake until tops of scones are light brown, about 20 minutes. Cool on rack. Serve with unsalted butter and jam.

MAKES APPROXIMATELY 14
PREPARATION TIME: 20 minutes, plus freezing time
COOKING TIME: 20 minutes

SESAME AND LEMON BARS

1¾ cups all-purpose flour
½ cup sugar
½ cup sesame seeds

½ pound (2 sticks) unsalted butter, cold, cut in ½″ cubes

Lemon Filling

4 large eggs
2 cups sugar
Grated zest of 2 lemons
½ cup freshly squeezed lemon juice

¼ cup all-purpose flour
½ teaspoon baking powder (preferably Rumford)

In the bowl of an electric mixer, blend together flour, sugar, and sesame seeds. Add butter. Mix with the flat beater at low speed until a smooth ball of dough is formed. Press into a 10″-×-15″ sheet cake pan, forming an edge around the sides. Chill for 15 minutes.

Adjust oven rack to lower-middle level, and preheat oven to 375°. Bake cookie crust until light brown, about 10 to 15 minutes. (The center may rise slightly.) Set aside while making filling.

Lemon Filling: In a medium bowl, beat eggs until well blended. Add sugar and mix until smooth. Beat in lemon zest, juice, flour, and baking powder, blending only long enough to mix. Pour into crust and bake at 375° until top center is light brown and set like a custard, about 35 minutes. Set aside to in the pan. Cover and refrigerate for 3 hours. Cut into 1″-×-2″ bars. ...ore, keep covered and chilled.)

...S APPROXIMATELY 70

PREPARATION TIME: 20 minutes, plus chilling time

COOKING TIME: 50 minutes

EMPIRE COOKIES

¾ *cup all-purpose flour*
½ *cup cake flour*
¾ *cup confectioners' sugar*

12 tablespoons (1½ sticks) unsalted
  butter, cold, cut into ½″ cubes
1 cup seedless red raspberry jam

In the bowl of an electric mixer, blend together flours and sugar. Add butter. Using the flat beater, mix on low speed until dough comes together. Remove dough from mixer and form into a ball. Enclose in plastic wrap and chill for 10 minutes.

Line 2 baking sheets with baking parchment. Dust work surface lightly with flour. Center ball of dough and dust top with flour. Roll out into a 10″-×-14″ rectangle. Using a 2″ fluted round cutter, cut out as many cookies as possible. Place on prepared baking sheets, spaced 1″ apart. Gather scraps of dough, roll out, and cut as before. Chill for 20 minutes.

Preheat oven to 375°. Using a ½″ plain cutter, cut out centers from half the cookies. Bake cookies on middle rack until tops are light golden brown, about 15 minutes, in 2 batches if necessary. Cool on rack.

Heat jam in top of double boiler only until slightly thinned. Spread the solid cookies with jam. Center the cookies with holes in them on top, pressing gently to fuse together. Keep covered at room temprature until ready to serve. (Cookies will soften if stored airtight overnight.)

MAKES 18

PREPARATION TIME: 20 minutes, plus chilling time

COOKING TIME: 15 minutes

BROWN SUGAR AND GINGER FINGERS

½ cup cake flour
1 cup all-purpose flour
1 tablespoon ground ginger
¾ cup light brown sugar

12 tablespoons (1½ sticks) unsalted
    butter, cold, cut into ½″ cubes
4 ounces milk chocolate

In the bowl of a food processor, combine flours, ginger, sugar, and butter. Pulse machine on and off until dough forms. Remove from bowl and shape into a 6″-×-4″ pad. Enclose in plastic wrap and chill for 10 minutes.

Line 2 baking sheets with baking parchment. Dust work surface lightly with flour. Center dough and dust top with flour. Roll dough out into an 8″-×-14″ rectangle. Cut into 1″-×-2″ fingers. Place on prepared baking sheets, spaced 1″ apart. Chill for 20 minutes.

Preheat oven to 375°. Bake cookies on middle rack (in 2 batches if necessary) until medium brown and firm to the touch, about 15 minutes. Wait for 2 minutes, then transfer cookies to rack; they will become crisp as they cool.

Break chocolate into small pieces and melt in a small bowl over hot water, or in a microwave oven. Dip cookies in chocolate, submerging them diagonally halfway and scraping bottom of cookie across edge of bowl to remove excess chocolate. Place on cold, foil-lined baking sheets to set, which may take a few hours.

MAKES 56
PREPARATION TIME: 25 minutes, plus chilling time
COOKING TIME: 15 minutes

DATE AND WALNUT CAKE WITH ORANGE BUTTERCREAM

6 tablespoons (¾ stick) unsalted butter,
    softened
¾ cup sugar
3 large eggs, slightly beaten
1 cup all-purpose flour

1 teaspoon baking powder (preferably
    Rumford)
½ cup chopped dates
½ cup ¼″ walnut pieces
Orange Buttercream (recipe follows)

Adjust oven rack to lower middle and preheat oven to 350°. Butter bottom and sides of a 9″ round cake pan. Line bottom with a circle of parchment paper.

Place butter and sugar in a medium bowl. Beat at high speed with a hand-held mixer for 3 minutes. The mixture should look light and smooth. Beat eggs into batter one at a time, beating well after each addition. Sift flour and baking powder together twice. Beat into batter at moderate speed. Fold in dates and walnuts. Spoon into prepared pan and bake until top is golden brown, center springs back to light finger pressure, and edge begins to pull away from sides of pan, about 30 minutes. Cool in the pan on a wire rack. Turn cake out and wrap in plastic until ready to frost.

Set cake, flat bottom side uppermost, on a 9″ circle of cardboard. (This makes decorating and handling the cake easier.) The cake should be 1½″ high. With a long, thin knife, cut the cake into 3 equal layers. Set the 2 top layers to one side.

Spoon about ¾ cup of buttercream into center of cake layer. Spread evenly with the edge of a metal pastry spatula. Define the edge of the cake by drawing the spatula upright around the edge. Center the middle cake layer on top and spread with ¾ cup buttercream. Spread evenly and define the edge as before. Center top layer of cake in place, smooth brown side up. Spoon the remaining buttercream on top, and spread evenly over top and sides. Chill cake until required, then let stand at room temperature for 15 minutes before serving.

Orange Buttercream

1 large orange	*1 tablespoon orange liqueur*
2 large eggs	*¾ pound (3 sticks) unsalted butter,*
¾ cup sugar	*softened*

Wash outside of orange with soap and hot water, rinse well, and dry. Grate the zest. Measure 2 tablespoons and set aside. Squeeze juice from orange and measure out ½ cup.

In a medium bowl, or the top of a double boiler, beat together the zest, eggs, and sugar until smooth. Stir in orange juice. Cook over simmering water, stirring occasionally, until mixture has thickened and will coat the back of a spoon, about 10 to 15 minutes. Stir in liqueur and set aside to cool, stirring occasionally. With a hand-held electric beater, beat butter at high speed for 2 minutes. Add orange mixture and continue beating until light and fluffy, 5 to 7 minutes.

SERVES 10

PREPARATION TIME: 30 minutes total

COOKING TIME: 30 minutes total

Situated in a dramatic setting with sweeping views across well-tended vineyards and olive groves to the Mayacamas Mountains across the Napa Valley, this rustically elegant restaurant was designed by the late Michael Taylor. Enormous wood beams, adobe walls, stone floors, and a huge fireplace afford great atmosphere and provide a suitable setting for French-trained chef Albert Tordjman's cuisine, which features strong, clean flavors and liberal use of olive oil, fresh herbs, and lemon zest.

SALADE GOURMANDE
MEDALLIONS OF SALMON WITH FENNEL
GRAND MARNIER MOUSSE WITH
   STRAWBERRY COULIS

SALADE GOURMANDE

10 ounces tiny French green beans
   (haricots verts)
12 asparagus spears
4 leaves red leaf lettuce
4 leaves Belgian endive

4 chanterelles or other wild mushrooms,
   sautéed in oil and cooled (optional)
2½ ounces foie gras, cut into 4 slices
   (optional)

Dressing

1 tablespoon lemon juice
1 tablespoon sherry vinegar
Salt
3 tablespoons olive oil

1 tablespoon chopped fresh tarragon
1 tablespoon finely chopped shallot
1 tablespoon chopped fresh chives
Black pepper

Wash and trim green beans. Snap off any tough ends from asparagus. Wash and dry red leaf lettuce and Belgian endive leaves.

Dressing: In a bowl, combine lemon juice, sherry vinegar, and salt. Whisk in olive oil and add remaining ingredients.

Blanch green beans in boiling water for 1 minute, and drain. Plunge into cold water to stop the cooking and preserve the color, and drain again.

Marinate in dressing for 30 minutes. Blanch asparagus separately in boiling water for 1 minute and drain. Plunge into cold water, and drain again. Marinate in dressing for 30 minutes.

Toss the lettuce leaves in dressing and divide among 4 plates, placing one in the center of each. Toss endive leaves in dressing and place on top of lettuce. Arrange the green beans on top of the endive, crisscrossing them in a lattice pattern. Place asparagus on top of the green beans in a Y. If using optional mushrooms and goose liver, arrange mushrooms between asparagus spears and top the salad with a slice of foie gras.

SERVES 4

PREPARATION TIME: 30 minutes, plus marination time

COOKING TIME: 2 minutes

MEDALLIONS OF SALMON WITH FENNEL

4 salmon steaks, about 6 ounces each

2 cups Court Bouillon (see Editor's Note below)

4 small branches fennel (stalks and feathery leaves)

Sauce

½ cup Cognac

1 tablespoon green peppercorns, drained

1 tablespoon fennel seeds

½ cup dry white wine

½ cup heavy cream

½ pound (2 sticks) unsalted butter, softened

Salt

Garnish

1 cup tomato concassé (peeled, seeded, and chopped ripe tomatoes)

1 tablespoon fresh cilantro (coriander) leaves, torn up

16 sprigs fennel

4 teaspoons salmon eggs (red caviar)

Debone and skin salmon steaks. Separate at backbone to form 2 medallions. Tie medallions with kitchen string to maintain their shape and set aside while making sauce. When sauce is almost ready, combine court bouillon with fennel branches and bring to a gentle simmer. Poach salmon medallions for 3 minutes, until just cooked.

Sauce: In a small saucepan, combine Cognac, peppercorns, and fennel seeds. Warm gently and carefully set aflame. Shake pan carefully. When flame dies down, add wine and reduce by rapid boiling to almost a glaze on the bottom of the pan, about 5 minutes. Add cream and reduce by half, about 5 minutes. Whisk in soft butter, little by little.

To Assemble: Strain sauce and divide among 4 heated dinner plates. Remove strings and place medallions of salmon on top of sauce. Arrange a quarter of the tomato concassé in the center of each medallion and top with cilantro leaves. Place blanched fennel sprigs north, east, south, and west of salmon. Garnish fennel sprigs with salmon eggs.

SERVES 4
PREPARATION TIME: 45 minutes
COOKING TIME: 15 minutes

EDITOR'S NOTE: To make a quick court bouillon, combine 8 ounces bottled clam juice; ¼ cup white wine; a dash of lemon juice; 1 slice onion; ½ stalk celery, sliced; and 4 small branches of fennel. Add 2 cups water and simmer mixture for 15 minutes.

GRAND MARNIER MOUSSE WITH STRAWBERRY COULIS

4 large egg yolks
¼ cup plus 1 tablespoon sugar
2 cups milk
1 package (3 teaspoons) unflavored
  gelatin

2 tablespoons water
1 tablespoon Grand Marnier
1½ cups heavy cream

Combine egg yolks and sugar in a large bowl. Beat until the mixture thickens, becomes pale in color, and forms a slowly dissolving ribbon from a lifted beater. Meanwhile, bring milk to a boil. Stir half the hot milk into the egg-sugar mixture, and return entire mixture to saucepan with rest of milk. Heat, but do not allow to boil. Stir with a wooden spatula until custard thickens slightly, and reaches 165° on a candy thermometer, about 10 minutes. The mixture is ready when it will coat the back of the spatula, and you can make a clean cut through it.

Mix gelatin with water and dissolve over hot water. Remove custard from heat and add dissolved gelatin and Grand Marnier. Pour into a bowl, and place the bowl in a larger bowl filled with shaved ice. Whip cream to soft-peak stage, and fold into cooled custard. Pour into four 1-cup molds, and refrigerate until set.

Strawberry Coulis

1 basket (about 10 ounces) ripe
  strawberries, washed and hulled
¼ cup plus 1 tablespoon sugar

Juice of ½ lemon
2 perfect strawberries, halved, for
  garnish

Place strawberries and sugar in food processor. Puree and strain. Add lemon juice. Ladle a little of this sauce onto each dessert plate. Unmold mousse on top of sauce, and garnish with half a strawberry.

SERVES 4
PREPARATION TIME: 20 minutes, plus cooling time
COOKING TIME: 20 minutes

Housed in a turn-of-the-century Oakland house, Bay Wolf was opened by Michael Wild and Larry Gold in 1974, and was one of the first restaurants to offer what has become known as California nouvelle cuisine. Its sunny, art-filled interior is a nice match for the innovative, constantly changing menu, planned and carried out each week by Wild and chef Carol Brendlinger.

AROMATIC CHICKEN SOUP
CREOLE SHRIMP STEAMED IN RUBY CHARD
CHOCOLATE FLAN WITH HAZELNUT PRALINE

AROMATIC CHICKEN SOUP

1 quart Chicken Stock (page 294)
1 tablespoon peeled and minced fresh
  gingerroot
1 tablespoon minced fresh lemongrass
1 cup cooked basmati (or Texmati) rice
1 cup diced smoked poussin (baby
  chicken)
2" piece lotus root, peeled and sliced
  thin
½ red bell pepper, seeded and finely
  diced

2 scallions, white bulb and part of green
  tops, sliced
1 tablespoon fresh cilantro (coriander)
  leaves, torn up, or to taste
1 tablespoon fresh basil leaves, shredded,
  or to taste
Salt
Pinch dried red chili flakes

Bring stock to a boil. Add ginger and lemongrass. Simmer for 15 minutes and strain. Return stock to pot and add rice. Bring to a boil and reduce heat to simmer. Add the smoked poussin, lotus root, bell pepper, and scallions. Season to taste with cilantro, basil, salt, and chili flakes, and simmer just long enough to heat through, about 1 minute. Serve immediately.

SERVES 6
PREPARATION TIME: 15 minutes
COOKING TIME: 16 minutes

CREOLE SHRIMP STEAMED IN RUBY CHARD

Sauce

6 tomatoes

2 pasilla chilies, or 1 teaspoon dried red
    chili flakes

2 tablespoons chopped fresh herbs in
    season (such as thyme, marjoram,
    tarragon, basil, etc.)

Juice of 1 lemon

Salt and freshly ground black pepper

Shrimp Packages

12 large ruby chard leaves (or spinach,
    Chinese cabbage, or Savoy cabbage)

1 bunch scallions (6 to 8), white bulbs
    and green tops

1 large clove garlic, peeled

1 teaspoon salt

½ bunch parsley, stems removed

1 stalk celery, sliced

½ red bell pepper, seeded and sliced

½ green bell pepper, seeded and sliced

2 pounds raw shrimp, peeled and
    deveined

½ teaspoon freshly ground black pepper

Sauce: Preheat oven to 450°. Place tomatoes and chilies in a roasting pan just large enough to hold them tightly in one layer. Roast until they start to char, about 45 minutes to 1 hour. Puree tomatoes and chilies through a food mill and discard seeds. (Alternatively, force through a sieve, or chop in a food processor and leave seeds in the sauce.) Add herbs, lemon juice, and salt and pepper to taste.

Shrimp Packages: Bring a large pot of water to a boil. Cut ribs out of chard leaves. Blanch leaves for 30 seconds, to make them pliable, and drain. Cut the scallions in half lengthwise. Separate out 12 to 16 long pieces for ties and drop them in boiling water for a few seconds to wilt them slightly.

Place garlic in the bowl of a food processor with salt. Process until chopped and add parsley. Chop fine. Add rest of scallions, celery, and red and green bell peppers. Chop coarsely, pulsing the machine on and off. Add shrimp and black pepper and process until minced. Fry a small ball of the mixture, taste, and adjust seasoning if necessary.

Divide filling into 12 portions. Wrap in the chard leaves, forming packages. Tie with the scallion strips, like a present. Place in a steamer and steam over rapidly boiling water for 10 to 15 minutes. (Alternatively, place in a baking dish, cover with oiled baking parchment, and bake at 350° for 15 minutes.) Reheat sauce if necessary and pour into a deep serving platter. Arrange packages on top of sauce.

SERVES 6
PREPARATION TIME: 45 minutes
COOKING TIME: 1¼ hours

CHOCOLATE FLAN WITH HAZELNUT PRALINE •

4 ounces bittersweet chocolate, coarsely
   chopped
6 large egg yolks
2 cups half and half
¾ cup plus 3 tablespoons sugar

⅛ teaspoon salt
½ teaspoon vanilla extract
2 tablespoons unsalted butter
½ cup (3 ounces) hazelnuts
½ teaspoon ground cinnamon

Combine chocolate, egg yolks, half and half, ¾ cup sugar, salt, and vanilla in top of double boiler, or in a steel or glass mixing bowl. Cook over simmering water, stirring gently with a wire whisk, until the chocolate has melted and the egg yolks have thickened, about 15 minutes. Pour into 6 individual ramekins, and chill.

Heat butter and sauté hazelnuts over low heat until golden brown, about 6 minutes. Add 3 tablespoons sugar and cinnamon, and toss until sugar has melted. Remove nuts from pan and cool. Chop coarsely. Sprinkle over flans just before serving.

SERVES 6
PREPARATION TIME: 10 minutes, plus chilling time
COOKING TIME: 15 minutes

Proprietor Doug "Bix" Beiderbeck has created a tribute to the Jazz Age that recalls the era of the great luxury ocean liners. A striking mural of a jazz club scene is the focal point of this sleek Jackson Square–area restaurant, which features a torch singer, a sax player, and a jazz pianist as background music for chef Cindy Pawlcyn's lively contemporary cuisine.

SCALLOPS WITH TOMATO AND WHITE WINE
PAN-FRIED CHICKEN CUTLETS WITH CAPERS
MOCHA POTS DE CRÈME

SCALLOPS WITH TOMATO AND WHITE WINE •

1 pound sea scallops
All-purpose flour for dredging
Salt and pepper
2 tablespoons virgin olive oil
4 to 6 tablespoons (½ to ¾ stick) butter, cut up
1 teaspoon minced garlic
4 medium ripe tomatoes, peeled, seeded, and sliced lengthwise

1 tablespoon fresh basil, finely shredded
1 tablespoon chopped fresh Italian parsley
½ cup white wine
1 to 2 teaspoons freshly squeezed lemon juice
Croutons (diagonal slices from a baguette, spread with olive oil and baked until golden brown)

Slice scallops and dust with flour. Season lightly with salt and pepper.

Heat olive oil in small sauté pan. When hot, add 2 tablespoons butter. Add scallops and sauté until just opaque but not fully cooked, about 1 minute. Pour off fat. Add garlic and cook for 30 seconds. Add tomatoes, basil, and parsley and toss. Deglaze with white wine and lemon juice. Rapidly whisk in 2 to 4 tablespoons butter bit by bit—sauce should emulsify. Season to taste with salt and pepper, and serve with croutons.

SERVES 6 TO 8
PREPARATION TIME: 15 minutes
COOKING TIME: 5 minutes

PAN-FRIED CHICKEN CUTLETS WITH CAPERS •

6 chicken breast halves, skinned and
    boned, about 6 ounces each
2 eggs
Salt and pepper
All-purpose flour for dredging
1¼ cups freshly grated Parmesan cheese
5 to 6 tablespoons chopped fresh
    tarragon
2 tablespoons chopped fresh chervil

½ to ¾ cup Clarified Butter (page 291)
1½ tablespoons chopped shallots
5 to 6 tablespoons chopped fresh parsley
5 to 6 tablespoons capers, drained
6 to 8 tablespoons (¾ to 1 stick) butter,
    softened
1 pound haricots verts or asparagus,
    cooked al dente, for garnish

Pound chicken to ¼" thickness between sheets of waxed paper. Beat eggs lightly and season with salt and pepper. Just before cooking, dust chicken breasts with flour and dip in egg. Combine Parmesan, tarragon, and chervil. Bread cutlets in this mixture.

Heat clarified butter and sauté cutlets until golden brown, about 1½ minutes per side. (Do 2 or 3 at a time if necessary; do not crowd the pan.) Remove to warm platter, and keep warm. Add shallots, parsley, and capers to pan. Whisk in butter, bit by bit, and season with salt and pepper to taste. Place cutlets on heated plates and pour sauce on top. Garnish with haricots verts or asparagus.

SERVES 6
PREPARATION TIME: 15 minutes
COOKING TIME: 4 minutes

MOCHA POTS DE CRÈME

3 cups heavy cream

3 tablespoons sugar

⅔ cup coffee beans

2" piece vanilla bean, split lengthwise

4 ounces semisweet chocolate, cut up
  (see Editor's Note below)

6 large egg yolks

2 teaspoons Cognac

Preheat oven to 350°. Put cream in a heavy saucepan with sugar, coffee beans, and vanilla bean. Bring to a simmer. Remove from heat and steep for 30 minutes.

Melt chocolate over a pan of hot water. Whisk eggs just long enough to mix them. Pour coffee mixture into eggs. Strain. Gradually whisk coffee-egg mixture into melted chocolate. Add Cognac and stir well.

Pour mixture into 6 or 8 *pots au crème* or custard cups, and place them in a shallow roasting pan. Add enough hot water to reach halfway up sides of cups. Cover loosely with a sheet of aluminum foil, and bake for 20 to 25 minutes. Serve at room temperature, or chilled.

SERVES 6 TO 8

PREPARATION TIME: 10 minutes, plus steeping and cooling time

COOKING TIME: about 25 minutes

EDITOR'S NOTE: Good-quality semisweet chocolate sold in bars or blocks will give much smoother results than chocolate chips.

Recently acquired and refurbished by Gianni Fassio, son of one of the original owners, the venerable fifty-five-year-old Blue Fox still has its Ionic columns, Florentine gold accents, and opulent crystal chandeliers. The food, however, is quite different: Chef Patrizio Sacchetto has chosen to re-create *La Cucina Nobile Italiana*, the aristocratic cuisine of sixteenth- and seventeenth-century Italy.

CREPES WITH RADICCHIO
NOISETTES OF LAMB WITH ARTICHOKES
IL RUSTICO DE PERA (PEAR DESSERT)

CREPES WITH RADICCHIO

Crepes

2 large eggs
¾ cup plus 3 tablespoons all-purpose flour
2 tablespoons butter, melted

Pinch salt
Scant 1 cup milk
2 to 3 tablespoons virgin olive oil

Filling

4 tablespoons (½ stick) butter
1 pound radicchio, leaves separated and cut into shreds
2 shallots, peeled and chopped
⅔ cup dry white wine

Salt and freshly ground black pepper to taste
White Sauce (recipe follows)
½ cup freshly grated Parmesan cheese

Crepes: In a bowl, mix together the eggs and flour. Add melted butter and salt. Gradually stir in milk.

Heat a little oil in an 8-inch nonstick skillet. Pour in just enough crepe batter to coat bottom of pan and cook quickly on both sides, about 1 minute. Repeat with remaining batter, overlapping crepes on a plate.

Filling: Preheat oven to 425°. Melt butter in a skillet and fry radicchio and shallots for about 15 minutes. Add white wine, season with salt and pepper, and cook for another 10 minutes.

Pour half the white sauce into the radicchio mixture and spoon a little of this mixture into the center of each crepe. Fold each crepe in four and place in a buttered ovenproof dish. Pour remaining white sauce on top and sprinkle with Parmesan. Bake filled crepes in preheated oven for 15 minutes.

White Sauce

4 tablespoons (½ stick) butter
½ cup all-purpose flour
4½ cups hot milk

Salt
White pepper

Melt butter in a small saucepan, add flour and stir for 3 minutes. Gradually pour in hot milk and cook for 10 minutes, stirring constantly. Season with salt and white pepper to taste.

SERVES 4 TO 6
PREPARATION TIME: 30 minutes
COOKING TIME: 50 minutes total

NOISETTES OF LAMB WITH ARTICHOKES

8 baby artichokes
Slice of lemon
14 ounces lamb filet or boneless lamb
 cut from rack
1 tablespoon capers (preferably dry-cured
 in salt)
Virgin olive oil for skillet
1 bunch scallions, white bulbs and part
 of green tops, chopped

2 ounces sliced prosciutto, with fat, cut
 into strips
1 cup Chicken Stock (page 294) or
 canned chicken broth
2 tablespoons chopped fresh parsley
Freshly ground black pepper
Salt

Wash artichokes and pull off tough outside leaves. Trim off tops and cut artichokes into quarters. If they have already developed spiny centers, cut out with a sharp knife. Set aside in a bowl of cold water with lemon slice.

Cut lamb into 1″-thick noisettes. Put capers to soak in cold water to wash off surplus salt (or brine, if using brine-cured capers).

Heat enough olive oil in a medium-sized skillet to just coat the bottom. Sauté lamb noisettes, turning to brown on both sides, about 3 minutes total.

Remove as they cook and keep warm. Add scallions and prosciutto to the pan. Fry briefly over high heat and then add pieces of artichoke. Stir-fry all together for 5 to 6 minutes. Add stock and drained capers, reduce heat, and simmer for 10 to 15 minutes more, or until the artichokes are cooked.

Return lamb noisettes to pan, add parsley, black pepper, and salt (if required). Mix meat with artichokes and serve at once with pan sauce.

SERVES 4
PREPARATION TIME: 30 minutes
COOKING TIME: 30 minutes

IL RUSTICO DE PERA

3 pounds pears
¾ cup sugar
⅓ cup freshly squeezed orange juice
1½ teaspoons ground cinnamon

¾ cup butter, melted
½ cup seedless raisins
5 cups dry 1"-square bread cubes, white
   or whole wheat
Marsala Sabayon (recipe follows)

Preheat oven to 400°. Butter eight 1-cup molds and set aside.

Peel and core pears, reserving 2 of them, and puree remainder in food processor with sugar and orange juice. Transfer puree to a mixing bowl. Stir in cinnamon, butter, and raisins. Cut 2 reserved pears into 1" pieces and add to bowl. Stir in bread cubes.

Pack mixture into molds and bake for 45 minutes. Unmold while warm. Serve warm with Marsala Sabayon on the side.

Marsala Sabayon

1 cup Marsala
5 large egg yolks

¾ cup sugar
½ cup heavy cream

Combine all ingredients in an unlined copper sabayon pan or in the top of a double boiler and whisk over medium heat (or over simmering water) until pale in color and very thick and fluffy, about 8 minutes.

SERVES 8
PREPARATION TIME: 30 minutes
COOKING TIME: 45 minutes total

Bua Thong Kitchen

Located on a tree-lined street in Burlingame and reminiscent of a simple, up-country Thai temple in its decor, Bua Thong is a small, family-run, authentic Thai restaurant. Bua Thong means "golden lotus," the nickname of the chef and co-owner, Preeya Charmornmarn, who learned her cooking skills first from her mother and later from chefs of several of the best-known restaurants in Bangkok.

> THAI BEEF SALAD
> GARLIC AND PEPPER PRAWNS
> THAI PUMPKIN CUSTARD

THAI BEEF SALAD •

1 pound tender cut of beef (such as strip steak), very well trimmed

2 tablespoons freshly squeezed lime juice

2 tablespoons Thai fish sauce (available in Thai grocery stores)

½ teaspoon sugar

1 stalk celery, thinly sliced

1 small yellow onion, peeled and thinly sliced

1 English hothouse cucumber, peeled and sliced ¼" thick

6 small tomato wedges

2 teaspoons minced fresh mint leaves

1 scallion, white bulb and part of green top, chopped

Loose-leaf lettuce

Grill beef until brown outside but still red and juicy inside (medium rare), about 4 minutes on each side. Slice across the grain into bite-sized pieces.

In a saucepan, combine lime juice, fish sauce, and sugar. Cook over medium heat for 1 minute. Remove from heat and add celery, onion, cucumber, tomato, mint, scallion, and beef. Mix well. Taste, and add more fish sauce or lime juice if desired. Serve on a bed of lettuce leaves.

SERVES 4 TO 6
PREPARATION TIME: 20 minutes
COOKING TIME: 10 minutes

GARLIC AND PEPPER PRAWNS •

5 cloves garlic, peeled
1 teaspoon finely minced cilantro
   (coriander) root (white part)
1 teaspoon ground white pepper
2 tablespoons vegetable oil
1 pound prawns (shrimp), 31 to 35
   count, shelled and deveined

1 tablespoon light soy sauce
1 teaspoon sugar
Shredded cabbage leaves
Chopped fresh cilantro (coriander) for
   garnish
Hot cooked rice

Using a mortar and pestle, pound garlic, cilantro root, and pepper into a paste. Heat oil in a skillet and add the garlic and pepper paste, prawns, soy sauce, and sugar. Stir-fry over medium-high heat until prawns are cooked, about 3 minutes. Do not overcook or prawns will toughen. Taste for seasoning and adjust if necessary. Spoon over shredded cabbage and garnish with cilantro. Serve with rice.

SERVES 4 TO 6
PREPARATION TIME: 25 minutes
COOKING TIME: 5 minutes

THAI PUMPKIN CUSTARD

1 Japanese pumpkin (Kabocha squash,
   available at Japanese markets. See
   Editor's Note below.)

8 large eggs
1 14-ounce can coconut milk
3 cups brown sugar, firmly packed

Remove skin and seeds from pumpkin. Slice flesh into ¾″ to 1″ matchsticks, to make 1 cup. (Save remainder for another use.)

Place eggs in bowl of an electric mixer and beat for 8 to 10 minutes, until pale and thick. Add coconut milk and brown sugar, and beat until well mixed. Strain through a strainer or dampened cheesecloth into a 9″-×-9″-×-2″ baking pan. Sprinkle the pumpkin evenly on top. Steam in a steamer for 45 minutes to 1 hour, or until a toothpick inserted in the center comes out clean. Check to make sure the water does not boil away during cooking. (A large wok with a bamboo ring and a cover makes an excellent steamer.) Cool, cover with plastic wrap, and refrigerate until serving time. Cut into squares and serve with tea or coffee.

SERVES 6 TO 8

PREPARATION TIME: 20 minutes, plus cooling time

COOKING TIME: 45 minutes to 1 hour

EDITOR'S NOTE: Kabocha squash has a green husk and a golden flesh, with a sweet flavor. In this recipe, the julienned squash sinks into the custard, which has a very good, caramel-like flavor.

The big windows in this handsome Marin restaurant offer expansive views of Richardson's Bay and Mount Tamalpais—a stunning natural setting for the American nouvelle cuisine on the innovative menu. Former co-chef Heidi Krahling, creator of these menus, has since left Butler's to become chef at Smith Ranch Homes.

TUNA TARTARE
SALAD OF FRESH SHIITAKE MUSHROOMS
GRILLED FLANK STEAK OR CHICKEN AND
  FRESH HORSERADISH-TOMATO RELISH
PEACH-BLUEBERRY UPSIDE DOWN CAKE

TUNA TARTARE •

1 small red bell pepper
1 cup diced (¼" square) raw, top-quality
  ahi tuna
⅓ cup diced celery
2 tablespoons diced red onion
2 tablespoons capers, rinsed in water,
  and drained
1 tablespoon chopped fresh chives
1 tablespoon minced fresh parsley
½ tablespoon minced fresh thyme

1 tablespoon minced fresh basil
1 teaspoon minced fresh marjoram
2 tablespoons pitted and chopped
  Kalamata olives
2 teaspoons freshly squeezed lemon juice
2 teaspoons virgin olive oil
Salt and pepper
4 large handfuls assorted lettuce leaves
Toasted baguette rounds

Cut bell pepper in quarters, and remove ribs and seeds. Broil until skin is charred and blistered, about 7 minutes. Steam in a paper bag for 10 minutes, then slip off skin. Cut flesh into dice.

Combine tuna, celery, onion, capers, seasonings, olives, and bell pepper in a bowl. Whisk together the lemon juice and olive oil. Add to bowl and toss mixture gently but thoroughly, seasoning to taste with salt and pepper.

Arrange a bed of lettuce leaves on each of 4 salad plates, and top with tuna mixture. Serve with toasted baguette rounds.

SERVES 4

PREPARATION TIME: 15 minutes

COOKING TIME: 17 minutes

SALAD OF FRESH SHIITAKE MUSHROOMS •

½ cup virgin olive oil

1 pound fresh shiitake mushrooms, 1" diameter, halved

3 tablespoons chopped fresh tarragon

1 medium shallot, peeled and minced

¼ cup toasted pine nuts

3 tablespoons freshly squeezed lemon juice

Salt and pepper

2 cups arugula leaves

In a stainless-steel sauté pan, heat ¼ cup of olive oil to almost smoking. Add half of mushrooms and sear quickly until lightly browned, about 2 minutes. Remove to a bowl. Repeat with remaining oil and mushrooms. Add tarragon, shallot, pine nuts, and lemon juice to warm mushrooms. Season to taste with salt and pepper, and toss well. Taste for seasoning, and add a little more olive oil if desired. Divide arugula among plates and top with mushroom salad.

SERVES 4

PREPARATION TIME: 15 minutes

COOKING TIME: 5 minutes

GRILLED FLANK STEAK OR CHICKEN AND FRESH HORSERADISH-TOMATO RELISH •

Flank steak or chicken for 4 persons, prepared for grilling

Olive oil for grill

Salt and pepper

⅓ cup rice wine vinegar

½ cup virgin olive oil

Scant 1 tablespoon whole-grain mustard

1 cup halved yellow cherry tomatoes

1 cup halved red cherry tomatoes

½ medium yellow onion, peeled and finely diced

½ red bell pepper, seeded and finely diced

2 tablespoons chopped fresh parsley

1½" long × 2" wide piece horseradish, peeled and grated, or to taste

Build an intense charcoal fire. When ready to cook, brush grill rack with olive oil, and grill flank steak or chicken to desired doneness, seasoning lightly with salt and pepper.

Meanwhile, place vinegar, oil, and mustard in a large bowl and whisk together. Add tomatoes, onion, bell pepper, parsley, salt and pepper, and grate horseradish to taste. Mix well, taste, and adjust seasoning as necessary. Serve with the grilled flank steak or chicken.

SERVES 4

PREPARATION TIME: 10 minutes

COOKING TIME: Will vary depending upon your fire and whether you are using steak or chicken.

EDITOR'S NOTE: The result will be different, but meat or chicken can be broiled if no grill is available.

PEACH-BLUEBERRY UPSIDE DOWN CAKE

3 peaches, peeled and thinly sliced
½ tablespoon vanilla extract
1 tablespoon freshly squeezed lemon juice

2 tablespoons sugar
Grated zest of 1 lemon
½ cup blueberries

Batter

1 cup cake flour
¾ cup sugar
1 teaspoon baking powder
4 tablespoons (½ stick) unsalted butter, cut up
½ teaspoon vanilla extract

½ cup heavy cream
3 large eggs, separated
Grated zest of 1 lemon

Vanilla Cream (recipe follows)

Preheat oven to 350°. Grease a shallow 6-cup gratin dish generously with butter. Arrange peach slices attractively in bottom of dish. Mix vanilla and lemon juice together. Sprinkle sugar, vanilla-lemon juice mixture, and lemon zest over peaches. Arrange blueberries around outside edge.

Batter: In a mixing bowl, combine flour, sugar, and baking powder. Add butter and cut in with a pastry blender or 2 knives until mixture resembles coarsely ground meal. In a small bowl, mix together vanilla, cream, egg yolks, and lemon zest, beating slightly to break down egg yolks. Add liquid mixture to dry ingredients, mixing until just blended. Beat egg whites to soft-peak stage and carefully fold into batter, working quickly so as not to deflate them. Spread over fruit in dish. Bake for 35 minutes, or until cake springs back to light finger pressure. Invert cake onto serving platter. The peaches should form an attractive pattern on top. Serve warm, with vanilla cream.

Vanilla Cream

½ cup heavy cream, lightly whipped   *½ teaspoon vanilla extract*

Mix ingredients together in a small bowl.

SERVES 6

PREPARATION TIME: 20 minutes

COOKING TIME: 35 minutes

Café Beaujolais is a small-town restaurant with a national reputation, thanks to the vision and hard work of owner/chef Margaret Fox. Located in a Victorian house in the coastal village of Mendocino, about 150 miles north of San Francisco, the restaurant is famous for its exceptional breakfasts as well as its savory lunches and dinners. Chef Fox and co-chef (and husband) Christopher Kump draw from many cuisines for culinary inspiration.

FRESH TOMATO AND MOZZARELLA SALAD
SAUTÉED HAZELNUT CHICKEN BREASTS, VIENNESE-STYLE
CLAFOUTIS

FRESH TOMATO AND MOZZARELLA SALAD •

3 to 4 fresh ripe tomatoes, sliced ¼"
thick, to yield 16 pieces
¾ pound fresh mozzarella cheese, sliced
into 12 pieces

Freshly ground black pepper
Kosher salt
Fruity virgin olive oil
1 tablespoon minced fresh basil leaves

Arrange tomato and mozzarella slices alternately on a large plate. Season with pepper and salt; then drizzle with olive oil. Sprinkle basil over the slices and serve immediately.

SERVES 4
PREPARATION TIME: 10 minutes
COOKING TIME: None

SAUTÉED HAZELNUT CHICKEN BREASTS, VIENNESE-STYLE •

4 skinless and boneless chicken breast
 halves, about 6 ounces each
3 tablespoons lemon juice
½ teaspoon kosher salt
½ teaspoon freshly ground black pepper
⅓ cup all-purpose flour
1 egg, lightly beaten with 1 teaspoon
 water

1 cup ground toasted hazelnuts
½ cup dry unflavored bread crumbs
2 tablespoons unsalted butter
2 tablespoons vegetable oil
Lemon wedges and/or cranberry relish
 for garnish

Separate each chicken breast half into 3 parts, using the following technique: Lay breast half on a cutting board, skinned side down, and peel the small filet with the white tendon running down it away from the larger breast muscle. Grasp the end of this tendon securely and pull it out, pinning the flesh to the cutting board with a knife held in your other hand. Discard tendon and set small filet aside. Divide the larger breast filet in half horizontally by turning it over (skinned side up) and, laying the palm of your hand gently on top of the breast, carefully slicing in half parallel to the board.

Marinate the chicken in lemon juice, salt, and pepper for 10 minutes. Remove to paper towels and pat dry.

Set up 3 small bowls in the following order next to your skillet: the first with flour; the second with beaten egg and water; and the third with ground hazelnuts and bread crumbs mixed together. Turn heat under pan to medium-high and add butter and oil. When foam from butter subsides, dredge a piece of chicken in flour to dust lightly, dip in beaten egg to coat, and then roll in nut–bread crumb mixture. Carefully place chicken in pan, and repeat coating process with remaining pieces, adding them to the pan as they are ready. Cook for about 2 minutes per side and monitor the heat so that the pieces turn golden brown and springy to the touch without blackening (they should sizzle as they touch the pan). Remove pieces to a warm platter as soon as they are done, and serve as soon as the last pieces are cooked. Garnish with lemon wedges and/or cranberry relish.

SERVES 4
PREPARATION TIME: 30 minutes, plus marination time
COOKING TIME: 10 minutes

CLAFOUTIS

1 large egg	*1⅓ cups pitted fresh cherries*
6 tablespoons sugar	*3 tablespoons butter, melted, cooled to*
3 tablespoons all-purpose flour	*lukewarm*
6 tablespoons heavy cream	*Confectioners' sugar for topping*

Preheat oven to 400°. Butter an 8″ pie pan.

In a bowl, whisk egg and sugar together until the mixture is pale and thick. Stir in flour and cream. Beat until completely smooth. Place cherries in a mixing bowl. Pour half the batter over the cherries and fold together gently. Spread the cherry mixture evenly over bottom of prepared pie pan. Bake for 15 minutes.

Meanwhile, beat butter into remaining batter, then pour over half-baked cherry batter. Return to oven and bake for another 15 minutes, or until golden brown. Cool for 10 minutes. Sprinkle with confectioners' sugar and serve warm.

SERVES 4

PREPARATION TIME: 15 minutes

COOKING TIME: 30 minutes

CHEF'S NOTE: Use sweet or sour cherries according to taste.

Chef/owner Stanley Eichelbaum and co-chef Peter DeMarais present an eclectic mixture of early California dishes brought up to date, and nouvelle California, in romantic Victorian surroundings. The Café Majestic's stately dining room has been restored to its 1902 splendor, complete with a beautiful old bar that came from a Paris bistro.

PEAR-PARSNIP SOUP
SEA BASS EN PAPILLOTE WITH TOMATO-
   BASIL SAUCE
LEMON MOUSSE WITH CASSIS SAUCE

GARLIC SOUP
RABBIT WITH POLENTA AND PECAN-
   PESTO SAUCE
ORANGE-RUM CRÈME CARAMEL

PEAR-PARSNIP SOUP

4 tablespoons (½ stick) butter
1 medium onion, peeled and sliced
1 leek, well washed and sliced,
   including part of green top
1 clove garlic, peeled and chopped
2 stalks celery, sliced
1 potato, peeled and sliced
4 medium parsnips, peeled and sliced
⅓ cup parsley stems (no leaves)
1 teaspoon fresh thyme, or ½ teaspoon
   dried

2 small bay leaves
2 whole cloves
½ teaspoon white peppercorns, crushed
1 teaspoon salt, plus extra
5 cups Chicken Stock (page 294) or
   canned chicken broth
2 firm pears, peeled, cored, and diced
¼ cup white wine
½ cup heavy cream
Freshly ground black pepper

Melt 2 tablespoons of butter in a heavy pot and simmer onion, leek, and garlic for 10 minutes, covered. Add celery, potato, parsnips, parsley stems, and seasonings. Cover with chicken stock. Bring to a boil. Reduce heat and simmer, uncovered, for 40 minutes. Discard cloves and bay leaves, and puree in batches in a food processor. Strain through a coarse sieve (optional) and return to rinsed pan.

Heat remaining 2 tablespoons of butter in a skillet and sauté diced pears for 5 minutes, stirring often. Add wine and continue cooking for another 5 minutes. Add pears to pureed soup. Stir in cream. Taste and add salt or pepper as necessary, and reheat without boiling.

SERVES 6 TO 8 (MAKES APPROXIMATELY 2 QUARTS)
PREPARATION TIME: 20 minutes
COOKING TIME: 1 hour

SEA BASS EN PAPILLOTE WITH TOMATO-BASIL SAUCE

3 teaspoons virgin olive oil

3 cups finely shredded Chinese cabbage

6 slices sea bass filet, ½" thick, 5 ounces each

6 medium tomatoes, peeled, seeded, and diced

1½ cups julienned fresh basil leaves

3 teaspoons chopped shallots

2 jalapeño chili peppers, seeded and chopped (or season to taste with cayenne pepper)

3 tablespoons lemon juice

2 tablespoons butter

Salt and pepper

Cut six 12"-×-16" sheets of baking parchment or aluminum foil and fold in half. Open each one out and grease one half lightly with some of the olive oil. Above crease, arrange ½ cup shredded cabbage. Top with a fish filet. Mix tomatoes with basil and sprinkle over fish. Season each with equal amounts of shallots, jalapeño chili (or cayenne pepper), and lemon juice. Drizzle with remaining olive oil and dot with butter. Salt and pepper to taste. Fold other half of baking parchment over fish. Crimp and fold the edges tightly together to make an airtight seal. (Packets can be prepared ahead to this point and refrigerated for several hours.)

Preheat oven to 375° and heat a baking sheet. Place packets on hot baking sheet and bake for 10 to 12 minutes. Place on dinner plates and slit open at the table to release the aromas.

SERVES 6
PREPARATION TIME: 35 minutes
COOKING TIME: 10 to 12 minutes

LEMON MOUSSE WITH CASSIS SAUCE

4 lemons

1 cup sugar

10 large eggs, separated

¼ pound (1 stick) unsalted butter, softened

½ cup heavy cream, whipped

¼ cup dark rum

Cassis Sauce

2 cups black currants (available in jars   1 cup water
or cans) or blueberries   ½ cup crème de cassis
½ cup sugar

Lemon Curd Base for Mousse: Pare zest (colored part only) from lemons and chop very fine. Squeeze juice from lemons and place juice and chopped zest in the top of a double boiler. Add sugar and egg yolks. Stir well with wire whisk. Stir in softened butter, a little at a time. Cook over gently boiling water until thickened, stirring constantly, about 20 minutes. Set aside to cool.

Mousse: Place 1½ cups of the lemon curd in a mixing bowl with the whipped cream and the rum. Whisk until blended. Beat the egg whites until they hold stiff peaks, and gently fold into the mixture. Spoon mousse into 6 ramekins or stemmed glasses and chill.

Cassis Sauce: Combine 1½ cups of the black currants with the sugar and water and simmer for 10 minutes. Add crème de cassis. Simmer for 15 minutes longer. Sauce should be syrupy. When done, add remaining black currants. Set aside to cool. Before serving, spoon sauce over mousse.

SERVES 6
PREPARATION TIME: 15 minutes, plus cooling time
COOKING TIME: 45 minutes

EDITOR'S NOTE: Any leftover lemon curd is excellent as a filling for tartlets or as a spread for toast. It will keep in the refrigerator, covered, for a week or more.

GARLIC SOUP

4 tablespoons (½ stick) butter   2 potatoes, peeled and sliced
1 medium onion, peeled and sliced   1 teaspoon chopped fresh thyme, or ½
16 cloves garlic (approximately 1 large   teaspoon dried
head), peeled   5 parsley stems (no leaves)
1 leek, well washed and sliced,   1 bay leaf
including part of green top   Salt
3 stalks celery, sliced   White pepper
4 to 5 cups Chicken Stock (page 294) or   ½ cup heavy cream
canned chicken broth
4 yellow crookneck squash (or zucchini),
sliced

Heat butter in soup pot and add onion, garlic, leek, and celery. Simmer over low heat, without browning, for 7 minutes. Cover with chicken stock. Add squash, potatoes, thyme, parsley stems, and bay leaf. Bring to a boil. Season with salt and pepper. Reduce heat and simmer for 30 minutes. Remove and discard bay leaf. Puree soup in a blender or food processor, in batches. Strain through a coarse sieve into a clean pot. (Leave unstrained for a thicker soup if preferred.) Stir in cream and reheat gently. Taste for seasoning.

SERVES 4 TO 6
PREPARATION TIME: 15 minutes
COOKING TIME: 40 minutes

RABBIT WITH POLENTA AND PECAN-PESTO SAUCE

1 frying rabbit, about 2¼ pounds
3 tablespoons butter
3 tablespoons vegetable oil
Salt and pepper

2 cloves garlic, peeled and chopped
2 tablespoons chopped fresh basil
½ cup dry white wine

Polenta

6 to 7 cups water
1 tablespoon salt

2 cups coarse yellow cornmeal

Pecan-Pesto Sauce

2 cups fresh basil leaves, lightly packed
½ cup toasted pecans, roughly chopped
2 cloves garlic, peeled and chopped

1 cup olive oil
½ cup heavy cream
Salt and pepper

Cut rabbit into 6 serving pieces by severing back and front legs, and cutting saddle in half, through the backbone. Discard end of spine, but cook rib portion as it adds flavor. (Do not serve; it has very little meat.) Reserve rabbit kidneys and liver for another use.

Preheat oven to 350°. Combine butter and oil in a heavy ovenproof sauté pan and heat to bubbling. Sauté rabbit pieces until golden brown, about 7 minutes. Discard cooking fat. Season rabbit with salt and pepper. Add garlic, basil, and white wine. Bring to a simmer, cover, and transfer to oven. Bake for 30 minutes. Make polenta and sauce while rabbit is in the oven.

Polenta: Bring water to a boil in a large pot and add salt. Add cornmeal in a steady stream, stirring constantly with a wooden spoon. Reduce heat and simmer, stirring frequently, for 20 minutes, or until polenta thickens and comes away from sides of pot. Keep warm.

Sauce: Place all sauce ingredients in a food processor and blend. Transfer to a saucepan and heat gently, but do not allow to boil. (If sauce should separate, return to food processor just before serving and pulse machine on and off to blend.)

To serve, spoon a bed of polenta onto each heated dinner plate. Top with either a hind leg, or a front leg and half of the meaty saddle. Spoon sauce over rabbit.

SERVES 4
PREPARATION TIME: 15 minutes
COOKING TIME: 1 hour

ORANGE-RUM CRÈME CARAMEL

Caramel

½ cup sugar	Grated zest of 1 orange
½ cup water	1 tablespoon dark rum

Custard

2 cups milk	½ cup sugar
4 large eggs	1 teaspoon vanilla extract

Caramel: Preheat oven to 350°. Place sugar in a thick-bottomed saucepan and add two thirds of the water. Boil over moderate heat, without stirring, until sugar turns a golden brown color, about 7 minutes. Combine remaining water, orange zest, and rum. Add to sugar and cook for 5 minutes more, stirring constantly. Pour caramel into the bottom of a 4-cup soufflé mold or four 1-cup ramekins, tilting dish to make an even layer. (Hold soufflé mold with a folded dishcloth; caramel is very hot.)

Custard: Scald milk (heat until bubbles form around edge), and set aside. Beat eggs and sugar together and add vanilla. Whisk egg mixture into hot milk. Strain into soufflé mold. Place mold in a baking pan and fill with enough hot water to reach halfway up sides of mold. Bake for 30 minutes. Allow to cool, and then refrigerate for at least 1 hour.

To serve, loosen edges of custard with a knife blade. Turn out onto deep plate, letting caramel—which will have liquefied—flow over unmolded custard.

SERVES 4
PREPARATION TIME: 10 minutes, plus chilling time
COOKING TIME: 40 minutes

This bright and cheerful downtown San Francisco restaurant, located in the Hotel Nikko, was first called Les Célébrités, because that's what every Western restaurant in every Hotel Nikko, owned by Japan Airlines, is named. However, shattering tradition, it is now called Café 222. The cuisine is mainly California nouvelle, with regional American and Asian influences here and there, and the elegant appointments include white linen tablecloths, Rosenthal china, and luxuriant greenery.

THAI PRAWN SALAD
PENNE WITH CHICKEN AND BELL PEPPERS
TART DORYN

THAI PRAWN SALAD

1 cup peanut oil
Juice of 1 lime
1 small hot chili pepper, seeded and diced
1 tablespoon chopped fresh cilantro (coriander)
12 prawns or large shrimp, 16 to 20 count, shelled and deveined

6 to 8 cups mixed baby lettuce leaves
Soy-Lime Dressing (recipe follows)
Tomato wedges for garnish
Chopped scallions for garnish
Fresh cilantro (coriander) leaves for garnish

Combine oil, lime juice, diced chili, and chopped cilantro and marinate prawns in this mixture for 30 minutes. Grill or sauté prawns until cooked, 2 to 3 minutes. Toss lettuce with just enough dressing to coat leaves and add prawns. Divide among 4 plates and garnish with tomato, scallions, and cilantro.

Soy-Lime Dressing

¼ cup soy sauce
½ teaspoon sugar
1 teaspoon Oriental sesame oil
1 cup peanut oil

½ cup rice wine vinegar
½ teaspoon minced hot chili
1 teaspoon lime juice

Whisk all ingredients together.

SERVES 4

PREPARATION TIME: 20 minutes, plus marination time

COOKING TIME: 2 to 3 minutes

PENNE WITH CHICKEN AND BELL PEPPERS

1 pound penne (short, tubular pasta)

2 tablespoons virgin olive oil

4 skinless and boneless chicken breast halves, about 6 ounces each, cubed

1 small red bell pepper, seeded, deribbed, and sliced

1 small yellow bell pepper, seeded, deribbed, and sliced

1 clove garlic, peeled and chopped

1 cup tomato sauce

1 tablespoon chopped black Kalamata olives

½ cup Chicken Stock (page 294) or canned chicken broth

½ tablespoon chopped fresh thyme

½ tablespoon chopped fresh rosemary

Salt and pepper (optional)

Chopped fresh parsley for garnish

Cook pasta in boiling, salted water until *al dente* and set aside.

Heat olive oil in a large sauté pan. Add cubed chicken, bell peppers, and garlic and sauté until tender, about 4 minutes. Add pasta, tomato sauce, olives, chicken stock, thyme, and rosemary. Heat together for 2 to 3 minutes, and taste for seasoning. Add salt and pepper if desired. Divide among 4 heated bowls and garnish with chopped parsley.

SERVES 4

PREPARATION TIME: 20 minutes

COOKING TIME: 20 minutes

TART DORYN

12 tablespoons (1½ sticks) butter

6 tablespoons sugar

½ teaspoon vanilla extract

1 small egg

1 egg yolk

1½ cups all-purpose flour

Lemon Custard

3 large eggs

½ cup plus 1 tablespoon sugar

3 tablespoons butter

3 tablespoons heavy cream

6 tablespoons freshly squeezed lemon juice

Cream butter, sugar, and vanilla. Add whole egg and egg yolk. Add flour and mix until incorporated, but do not overmix. Gather dough into a ball, enclose in plastic wrap, and refrigerate for 1 hour.

Preheat oven to 350°. On a lightly floured surface, roll out dough ⅛″ thick. Fit dough into a 9″ fluted tart pan with removable base, pushing rim of pastry slightly over edge to prevent shrinkage while baking. Place in oven. After 5 minutes, deflate any air bubbles that form on base with tip of a knife. Bake until golden brown, about 30 minutes. Let cool.

Lemon Custard: Combine all ingredients in the top of a double boiler. Stir over simmering water until thick, about 15 minutes. It should coat the back of a spoon. Custard will thicken further as it cools. When lukewarm, pour into pastry shell, and let cool.

SERVES 8

PREPARATION TIME: 30 minutes, plus chilling time

COOKING TIME: 30 minutes

A sunny storefront on the edge of North Beach in San Francisco, Caffé Freddy's has somewhat limited cooking facilities, but chef Paula Blosky (who was catering chef at Alice Waters's Café Fanny) manages to turn out honest, upscale, tasty food for breakfast and lunch.

> ## ONION SOUP
> ## ROAST CHICKEN BREAST WITH NEW
> ##   POTATOES, ASPARAGUS, SPINACH,
> ##   AND AIOLI
> ## NECTARINE-BLUEBERRY CRISP

ONION SOUP

¼ cup virgin olive oil
2 cups thinly sliced onions
2 tablespoons dry Spanish sherry
1½ quarts Chicken Stock (page 294) or
  canned chicken broth
1 sprig thyme, leaves only

¼ teaspoon hot dried red pepper flakes,
  or more to taste
Salt and pepper
4 oval croutons, spread with grated
  Gruyère cheese, and toasted

Heat olive oil and sauté sliced onions until browned but not burned, about 10 minutes. Deglaze pan with sherry. Add chicken stock, thyme, and pepper flakes. Bring to a boil, lower heat, and simmer for 45 minutes. Add salt and pepper to taste. Ladle into soup bowls and top with a crouton.

SERVES 4
PREPARATION TIME: 15 minutes
COOKING TIME: 55 minutes

ROAST CHICKEN BREAST WITH NEW POTATOES, ASPARAGUS, SPINACH, AND AIOLI

4 boneless and skinless chicken breast
  halves, about 6 ounces each
Salt and pepper
1 sprig fresh thyme, leaves only, chopped
3 cloves garlic, peeled, 1 clove minced

Juice of 1 lemon
8 new red potatoes, unpeeled
2 tablespoons virgin olive oil
1 sprig fresh rosemary, leaves only
24 spears asparagus

1 bunch spinach, well washed, leaves only   Aioli (recipe follows)

Rub chicken breasts with mixture of salt and pepper, thyme, minced garlic, and lemon juice. Marinate for 1 hour before roasting.

Preheat oven to 400°. Wash and dry potatoes. Place in a roasting pan with olive oil, salt and pepper, whole garlic cloves, and rosemary. Cover with aluminum foil and bake for 45 minutes.

Blanch asparagus and spinach separately in boiling salted water. (Spinach will require only 1 minute; asparagus should be cooked until *al dente.*) Drain, plunge into cold water, and drain again. If necessary, reheat in a steamer over boiling water or in a microwave oven before serving.

Roast chicken breasts at 400° for 10 to 15 minutes. Slice each breast half into about 5 pieces, fan out on a bed of spinach, and garnish with 2 potatoes and 6 spears of asparagus. Drizzle aioli over all.

Aioli

3 large egg yolks
2 cups virgin olive oil
Juice of 2 lemons

4 cloves garlic, peeled and finely
 chopped
Salt and pepper

Beat egg yolks and slowly whisk in olive oil. When thick, add lemon juice and chopped garlic. Season to taste with salt and pepper.

SERVES 4
PREPARATION TIME: 30 minutes, plus marination time
COOKING TIME: 45 minutes

NECTARINE-BLUEBERRY CRISP

1 cup all-purpose flour
½ cup brown sugar, firmly packed
¼ pound (1 stick) butter, cut up
½ cup chopped walnuts

6 to 8 ripe nectarines, pitted and sliced
2 cups blueberries
⅓ cup white sugar

Preheat oven to 350°. Blend flour, brown sugar, butter, and walnuts together.

In an 8″-×-10″ baking dish, combine sliced nectarines, blueberries, and white sugar. Sprinkle with topping mixture, covering fruit completely. Bake until brown on top, about 40 minutes.

SERVES 4
PREPARATION TIME: 10 minutes
COOKING TIME: 40 minutes

Attractive Art Deco surroundings and flashy neon signs complement the lively American nouvelle cuisine of this upscale, contemporary café. The menu is characterized by variety, and by the freshest of ingredients and intriguing combinations of tastes, textures, and colors.

> **GRILLED VEGETABLES WITH SUN-DRIED TOMATO AIOLI**
>
> **ANGEL HAIR PASTA WITH CRAB MEAT, HAZELNUTS, AND LEMON**
>
> **LEMON CAKE WITH CRÈME ANGLAISE AND BLUEBERRIES**

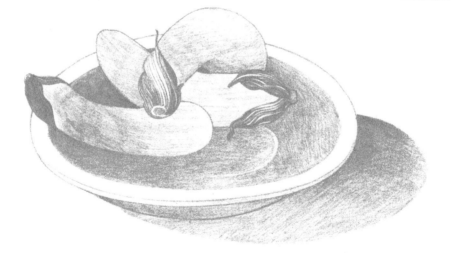

GRILLED VEGETABLES WITH SUN-DRIED TOMATO AIOLI

½ cup virgin olive oil

4 leeks, well-washed, split, white part only

2 Japanese eggplants, 6" to 8" long, unpeeled, halved lengthwise

8 baby carrots

2 red onions, peeled and quartered

2 small zucchini, cut lengthwise into ½" slices

Sun-Dried Tomato Aioli (recipe follows)

Lemon wedges and herb sprigs for garnish

Have a hardwood or charcoal fire very hot. Place oil on a plate. Dip vegetables lightly in oil and grill until outsides are lightly charred and insides are tender, about 25 minutes. Arrange a pool of aioli in center of each dinner plate and surround with grilled vegetables. Garnish with lemon wedges and herb sprigs.

Sun-Dried Tomato Aioli

4 egg yolks	8 oil-packed sun-dried tomatoes, drained
12 cloves garlic, peeled	2 cups virgin olive oil
1 teaspoon salt	¼ cup lemon juice

All ingredients should be at room temperature. Place egg yolks, garlic, salt, and sun-dried tomatoes in the bowl of a food processor. Using the steel blade, process for 2 minutes. Very slowly, with motor running, add olive oil, then the lemon juice.

SERVES 4
PREPARATION TIME: 20 minutes total
COOKING TIME: about 25 minutes

ANGEL HAIR PASTA WITH CRAB MEAT, HAZELNUTS, AND LEMON •

2 quarts water	¾ pound Dungeness crab meat, cooked
6 tablespoons (¾ stick) unsalted butter	Salt
6 tablespoons peeled and chopped roasted hazelnuts	¾ pound angel hair pasta
Grated zest of 2 lemons	16 chives, cut into ½" pieces, for garnish
¾ cup Chardonnay	Freshly ground black pepper

Bring water to a boil for pasta. Heat 4 tablespoons of the butter in a large skillet. When melted, add hazelnuts and cook gently for 1 minute. Add lemon zest and cook for 30 seconds. Add Chardonnay and boil until reduced by half, about 6 minutes. Slowly swirl in remaining 2 tablespoons butter. Add crab meat and heat through. Taste for seasoning.

While sauce is cooking, add a pinch of salt to pot of boiling water, then add pasta. Cook until al dente, about 4 minutes. Drain well, and toss with crab sauce. Divide among 4 heated plates. Garnish with chives, and offer freshly ground black pepper.

SERVES 4
PREPARATION TIME: 15 minutes
COOKING TIME: 15 minutes

LEMON CAKE WITH CRÈME ANGLAISE AND BLUEBERRIES

5⅓ tablespoons unsalted butter, melted
1 cup sugar
3 teaspoons lemon extract
2 large eggs
1½ cups all-purpose flour
1 teaspoon baking powder
1 teaspoon salt

½ cup milk
1½ tablespoons grated lemon zest
¼ cup lemon juice mixed with ½ cup
   sugar for top of cake
2 cups Crème Anglaise (page 297)
Fresh blueberries and mint leaves for
   garnish

Preheat oven to 350°. Butter and flour an 8″ loaf pan. In a large bowl, combine melted butter, sugar, and lemon extract and mix well. Beat eggs into mixture.

In a second bowl, sift together the flour, baking powder, and salt. Add flour mixture to batter alternately with milk. Fold in lemon zest. Pour into prepared loaf pan and bake for 1 hour, or until a skewer inserted near center of cake comes out clean. Cool in pan for 10 minutes. Remove from pan to a rack. Pour lemon juice–sugar mixture into cracks of cake. When completely cooled, wrap in foil and store for 24 hours before serving.

Cut eight ¾″-thick slices from cake and place on large dessert plates. Top each slice with ¼ cup crème anglaise and garnish with blueberries and mint leaves.

SERVES 8
PREPARATION TIME: 35 minutes
COOKING TIME: 1 hour

Housed in the old Germania Hall, an opulent theater that dates back to the thirties, the California Culinary Academy is one of the leading schools for chefs in this country, and also operates a popular restaurant. Diners sit in the auditorium, and can watch cooking operations taking place on the glassed-in stage.

SCALLOP SALAD
ESCALOPES OF TURKEY WITH MUSTARD SAUCE
CHOCOLATE DECADENCE CAKE

SCALLOP SALAD •

3 cups assorted baby greens
1 head radicchio, leaves separated and
chopped
Dijon Mustard Vinaigrette (recipe
follows)
¾ cup virgin olive oil

1 pound very fresh bay scallops
4 cloves garlic, peeled and minced
2 medium-sized ripe tomatoes, peeled,
seeded, and diced
Salt and pepper

Arrange mixed baby greens on 6 chilled salad plates. Distribute the chopped radicchio equally on top of the greens. Sprinkle approximately 2 tablespoons vinaigrette over each salad.

Heat olive oil in a skillet and sauté scallops until opaque, about 1 minute. Reduce heat and add garlic and tomatoes. Season to taste with salt and pepper. Heat through, about 1 minute. Place scallop mixture on top of radicchio.

Dijon Mustard Vinaigrette

¼ cup red wine vinegar
2 teaspoons Dijon mustard

1 cup virgin olive oil
Salt and pepper

Combine vinegar and mustard and slowly whisk in olive oil. Season to taste with salt and pepper.

SERVES 6

PREPARATION TIME: 10 minutes

COOKING TIME: 2 minutes

ESCALOPES OF TURKEY WITH MUSTARD SAUCE •

½ cup milk

1 cup all-purpose flour

Salt and pepper

2 pounds skinless and boneless turkey
 breast, cut into ¼" slices

2 to 3 tablespoons vegetable oil

½ cup dry white wine

2 shallots, peeled and finely chopped

2 cups crème fraîche

1 tablespoon Dijon mustard

Lightly cooked baby vegetables of choice
 for garnish

Pour milk in a pie pan. Combine flour, salt, and pepper in a separate pie pan. Just before cooking, submerge slices of turkey in milk, shake off excess, and dip in seasoned flour.

Heat vegetable oil in a large skillet. Sauté turkey scallops until golden brown, about 2 minutes per side. Do this in batches if necessary, adding a little more oil to the skillet if required. Remove from skillet and keep warm.

Add wine and shallots to skillet and reduce over high heat by two thirds, about 3 minutes. Add crème fraîche and cook until reduced by half, about 6 minutes. Reduce heat and stir in mustard. Taste for seasoning. Arrange escalopes on warmed plates, and spoon sauce alongside. Garnish plates with baby vegetables of choice.

SERVES 6

PREPARATION TIME: 10 minutes

COOKING TIME: 15 minutes

CHOCOLATE DECADENCE CAKE

1¼ cups sugar

½ cup water

5 ounces best-quality semisweet
 chocolate, chopped

7 ounces best-quality unsweetened
 chocolate, chopped

½ pound (2 sticks) unsalted butter, cut
 up

5 large eggs

Crème Anglaise (page 297) or whipped
 cream

Fresh raspberries for garnish

Preheat oven to 350°. Line the bottom of a 10″ cake pan with a circle of baking parchment that has been buttered on both sides.

Combine 1 cup of sugar and the water in a saucepan and bring to a boil. Add chopped chocolates to boiling mixture and dissolve, stirring gently. Remove from heat. Add butter bit by bit, stirring gently until melted. Beat remaining ¼ cup sugar with the eggs until mixture is pale and thick, and a slowly dissolving ribbon will form from a lifted beater. Fold chocolate mixture into beaten egg-and-sugar mixture. Pour batter into prepared pan. Place cake pan in a roasting pan and add enough boiling water to reach halfway up sides of cake pan. Bake until top of cake feels dry, about 35 minutes. Remove from oven and cool in the pan.

To unmold, warm the pan slightly on bottom and sides. Serve cake warm with crème anglaise and raspberries, or at room temperature with whipped cream and raspberries. Do not serve chilled!

SERVES 10

PREPARATION TIME: 30 minutes

COOKING TIME: 40 minutes total

Housed in the small, elegant hotel of the same name, Campton Place has earned critical acclaim since its opening in 1983. Large enough to promote a sense of occasion but small enough to be intimate, the restaurant's warm peach colors, soft lighting, custom furniture, abundant fresh flowers, and original artwork promote a feeling of comfort and relaxation. Executive chef Jan Birnbaum is dedicated to presenting American cuisine at its best, using native ingredients of the finest quality in imaginative combinations.

DUNGENESS CRAB ENCHILADAS
SPICY TOMATO SOUP WITH LIME-BASIL
    CRÈME FRAÎCHE
RABBIT ROULADES WITH GARLIC MASHED
    POTATOES
FIG AND CORNMEAL TART

DUNGENESS CRAB ENCHILADAS

2 tablespoons virgin olive oil

1 small red bell pepper, seeded, deribbed, and finely diced

1 small yellow bell pepper, seeded, deribbed, and finely diced

12 ounces Dungeness crab meat, picked over

1 poblano chili pepper, roasted, peeled, seeded, and diced

½ bunch scallions, thinly sliced on diagonal, including green tops

Salt and pepper

6 6" flour tortillas

4 tablespoons (½ stick) butter, softened

1 pound Sonoma jack cheese (garlic flavor preferred), grated

Tomatillo Sauce (recipe follows)

Heat oil in a large sauté pan. Sauté three quarters of the red and yellow bell peppers until softened, about 6 minutes, reserving the remainder for garnish. Off the heat, add crab meat, poblano pepper, and most of the scallions, reserving some for garnish. Season with salt and pepper. Spread out on a platter and refrigerate.

Butter tortillas and lay out on a work surface. Make a line of crab mixture down the center of each one. Sprinkle crab mixture with most of the grated cheese, reserving some for garnish. Roll tortillas. Recipe may be prepared to this point up to one day in advance.

Ladle 3 to 4 tablespoons of tomatillo sauce onto each hot plate. Place enchilada on top of sauce. Place plates under broiler until contents are heated through. Remove from broiler and sprinkle with cheese (you can return to broiler to melt cheese if you wish). Garnish with remaining bell peppers and scallions.

Tomatillo Sauce

8 tomatilloes
1 poblano chili pepper, roasted and
   seeded
⅛ bunch fresh cilantro (coriander)

2 tablespoons lime juice
10 spinach leaves
Salt and pepper

Place all ingredients in a blender or food processor and blend until smooth.

SERVES 6
PREPARATION TIME: 25 minutes
COOKING TIME: 8 minutes

SPICY TOMATO SOUP WITH LIME-BASIL CRÈME FRAÎCHE

1 whole head garlic
¼ cup virgin olive oil, plus a little extra
1 medium onion, peeled and diced
½ large bunch basil, stems only
2 bay leaves
2 jalapeño chili peppers, seeded and
   chopped
7 large, very ripe tomatoes, cut into
   eighths

1 quart Chicken Stock (page 294)
1 tablespoon salt
1 teaspoon freshly ground black pepper
½ teaspoon cayenne pepper
¼ teaspoon Tabasco sauce
¼ cup freshly squeezed lime juice
Lime-Basil Crème Fraîche (recipe
   follows)

Preheat oven to 350°. Cut head of garlic in half, toss with 1 tablespoon of the olive oil in a small baking dish, and roast until soft, about 40 minutes. Squeeze garlic pulp out of husks and reserve.

In a large saucepan, sauté onion in remaining 3 tablespoons olive oil. As onions become translucent, add basil stems, bay leaves, and roasted garlic pulp. Add jalapeños and tomatoes and cook until stewed, about 10 minutes. Add stock and simmer for 20 to 30 minutes. Pass soup through a sieve, pushing through as much of the solids as possible. Pass remaining solids through food mill, and add to soup. Season with salt, pepper, cayenne,

Tabasco, lime juice, and a little extra olive oil. Reheat soup gently and ladle into bowls. Garnish with a dollop of lime-basil crème fraîche.

Lime-Basil Crème Fraîche

½ large bunch basil, leaves only

2 tablespoons freshly squeezed lime juice

½ cup crème fraîche

Salt

Pick over basil leaves and place in a blender or food processor with lime juice. Puree until smooth. Add to crème fraîche. Season to taste with salt.

SERVES 6

PREPARATION TIME: 20 minutes

COOKING TIME: 70 to 80 minutes

RABBIT ROULADES WITH GARLIC MASHED POTATOES

1 teaspoon paprika

½ teaspoon dried oregano

1 teaspoon ground red sandalwood (optional)

1 teaspoon ground white pepper

1 tablespoon salt

1 medium red onion, peeled

1 large carrot, peeled

1 large yellow zucchini

1 large green zucchini

3 rabbit hindquarters (or substitute chicken breasts)

6 tablespoons whole-grain mustard

3 ounces aged dry provolone or asiago cheese, grated

Flour for dredging

¼ cup virgin olive oil

1 large yellow onion, peeled and diced

3 cloves garlic, peeled and chopped

1½ cups red wine (such as Cabernet Sauvignon)

1 quart Chicken Stock (page 294)

6 tablespoons tomato puree

Garlic Mashed Potatoes (recipe follows)

6 large handfuls assorted greens (spinach, watercress, baby mustard greens), sautéed in olive oil for 30 seconds

Mix paprika, oregano, sandalwood, pepper, and salt together to make seasoned salt. Cut onion, carrot, and zucchini into 2½″ julienne, discarding white centers of zucchini. (Use only zucchini julienne with colored skin.) Blanch carrot for 2 minutes in boiling salted water, and refresh in ice water. Drain well.

Bone out rabbit legs and pound into 6 cutlets, ¼″ to ½″ thick. Sprinkle with seasoned salt and brush with mustard. Lay julienned vegetables across width of each cutlet. Sprinkle with cheese and roll up into 2″ to 3″ roulades. Sprinkle with a little more seasoned salt and dust with flour.

Preheat oven to 350°. In a large roasting pan, heat olive oil and brown roulades on all sides, about 5 minutes. Remove and reserve. Add chopped onion to pan and brown lightly, about 4 minutes. Add garlic and cook for 1 minute. Deglaze pan with red wine, reduce by half, and add chicken stock and tomato puree. Bring to a boil.

Return roulades to pan, cover, and transfer roasting pan to oven. Bake until tender, about 20 minutes. Serve roulades with garlic mashed potatoes and a quick sauté of greens. Nap with strained and degreased sauce from roasting pan.

Garlic Mashed Potatoes

2½ pounds small red potatoes, peeled
4 tablespoons (½ stick) butter
1½ cups cream
1½ teaspoons salt

½ teaspoon ground white pepper
3 cloves garlic, peeled and finely
   chopped

Place potatoes in a pan and cover with cold water. Cook over medium heat until soft, about 15 minutes. Meanwhile, in a separate pot, combine butter, cream, salt, pepper, and garlic. Bring to a boil and simmer for 5 minutes. Strain. Add most of the hot liquid to the drained but hot potatoes. Blend with a potato masher until smooth, but do not overmix, as overworking potatoes will make them starchy. (Do not use a food processor!) For smoother results, pass through a food mill. Add remaining hot liquid if required to adjust consistency. Taste for seasoning.

SERVES 6
PREPARATION TIME: 40 minutes total
COOKING TIME: 35 minutes total

FIG AND CORNMEAL TART

Crust

1½ cups all-purpose flour
1 cup cornmeal
¾ cup sugar
¾ teaspoon salt
15 tablespoon (2 sticks minus 1
   tablespoon) unsalted butter, chilled,
   cut into ½" pieces

3 large egg yolks
1½ tablespoons honey
1½ tablespoons vanilla extract
1 tablespoon grated lemon peel

Filling

1½ cups red wine
½ cup water
½ cup plus 1 tablespoon sugar
Grated zest of ½ lemon
Grated zest of ¼ orange

1 teaspoon aniseseed
15 fresh figs
1 cup peeled and chopped toasted
   hazelnuts

Crust: Place flour, cornmeal, sugar, and salt in bowl of food processor. Process for 10 seconds to mix. Add butter and pulse until mixture resembles very coarse sand. Combine egg yolks, honey, vanilla, and lemon peel. Add to dry ingredients. Process until dough just begins to hold together. Remove from bowl and divide in half. Form into 2 disks, ¾″ thick. Enclose in plastic wrap and refrigerate for 20 minutes. Roll each disk into an 11″ circle. Fit one circle into a 10″ fluted tart pan with removable base and chill. Place the other disk on a baking sheet and chill.

Filling: Combine wine, water, ½ cup sugar, lemon zest, orange zest, and anise in a stainless-steel saucepan. Bring to a boil over medium heat. Reduce heat and simmer for 15 minutes. Strain, discarding solids. Place figs in a bowl and pour wine mixture over them. Cool to room temperature.

To make sauce, remove figs from liquid and reserve. Bring liquid to a boil. Add remaining 1 tablespoon sugar and continue to boil until sauce just coats the back of a spoon.

Preheat oven to 375°. Cut stems from figs and discard. Slice figs in half lengthwise. Sprinkle chopped hazelnuts over tart shell. Arrange figs to fill crust, cut side down. Cover tart with remaining circle of dough, lightly pressing around figs. Seal edges; remove excess dough. Prick top with a fork in a few places to let steam escape. Place a sheet of foil on bottom of oven to catch any drips, and place tart on center rack. Bake tart for 30 minutes, or until pastry is well browned. (Cover edges with a "doughnut" of aluminum foil if they start to darken too much.) Remove tart from oven and cool for 20 minutes before removing from pan. Cut into 10 portions, and serve with reduced fig liquid.

SERVES 10
PREPARATION TIME: 25 minutes, plus refrigerating and cooling time
COOKING TIME: 45 minutes

Big, noisy, and lots of fun, Chevys is a south-of-Market, south of the border–style restaurant with a difference: The food is all made from scratch, using only fresh ingredients, and the upscale menu includes such items as sizzling broiled quail. The décor is more cantina than hacienda—cases of beer are used as partitions between the bar and dining areas—but the ambience is wonderful.

CEVICHE WITH SCALLOPS
SEAFOOD ENCHILADA WITH SALSA VERDE
COCONUT EMPANADAS

CEVICHE WITH SCALLOPS •

1½ pounds fresh bay scallops
1 cup freshly squeezed lime juice
1 clove garlic, peeled and chopped
2 jalapeño chili peppers, seeded and chopped
Pinch dried oregano
Salt and pepper to taste
2 tablespoons virgin olive oil

1 tablespoon white wine
2 large tomatoes, peeled, seeded, and chopped
1 medium onion, peeled and chopped
¼ bunch cilantro (coriander), destemmed and chopped (about ⅛ cup)
Lime slices and cilantro (coriander) sprigs for garnish

Cut scallops into ½″ squares, cover with lime juice, and marinate in the refrigerator for 2½ hours.

In a food processor or blender, puree garlic, jalapeño peppers, oregano, salt and pepper, olive oil, and wine.

Drain scallops and place in a bowl. Add tomatoes, onion, cilantro, and pureed mixture. Toss together and chill. To serve, divide among glasses and garnish with lime slices and a cilantro sprig.

SERVES 6 TO 8
PREPARATION TIME: 15 minutes, plus marination and chilling time
COOKING TIME: None .

SEAFOOD ENCHILADA WITH SALSA VERDE

¼ cup virgin olive oil
2 cloves garlic, peeled and chopped
1 medium onion, peeled and chopped
2 stalks celery, chopped
2 jalapeño chili peppers, chopped
Pinch dried oregano
Pinch ground cumin
Pinch white pepper
½ pound mushrooms, sliced
1 tablespoon chopped fresh cilantro
   (coriander)

1½ pounds bay scallops
½ pound bay shrimp, shelled and
   deveined
1 tablespoon dry sherry
4 tablespoons (½ stick) butter
Scant ½ cup all-purpose flour
¾ pound Monterey Jack cheese, shredded
16 flour or corn tortillas
Salsa Verde (recipe follows)

Heat oil in a large skillet. Add garlic, onion, celery, jalapeño peppers, oregano, cumin, and white pepper, and sauté for 5 minutes. Add mushrooms and cook for 1 minute. Stir in cilantro and scallops and cook for another 2 minutes. Add shrimp and sherry, and continue to cook for another 2 minutes. Drain, saving all the juices.

In a heavy saucepan, melt butter and stir in flour. Cook slowly for 10 minutes, stirring. Add drained juices from skillet and stir well until smooth. Simmer slowly for 15 minutes.

Combine drained seafood mixture with enough of this sauce to moisten. Stir in a third of the shredded jack cheese and cool.

Preheat oven to 375°. Divide mixture among 16 tortillas. (If using corn tortillas, soften for 30 seconds on each side in hot oil first.) Roll up and place in a baking dish. Cover with salsa verde and sprinkle with remaining shredded cheese. Bake for 15 minutes.

Salsa Verde

2 cups Chicken Stock (page 294) or
    canned chicken broth
10 ounces tomatilloes, cleaned
2 jalapeño chili peppers
Pinch ground cumin

1 medium onion, peeled and sliced
2 tablespoons virgin olive oil
1 tablespoon chopped fresh cilantro
    (coriander)

Heat chicken stock, add tomatilloes and jalapeño peppers, and boil for 5 minutes. Partially drain liquid, and save. Add cumin and half the sliced onion to tomatillo mixture. Puree in food processor or blender until smooth.

In a separate saucepan, heat olive oil. Add cilantro and remaining sliced onion, and sauté for 5 minutes. Add tomatillo puree to saucepan and heat through. Add more chicken stock if necessary to make a sauce consistency. Do not overcook.

SERVES 8
PREPARATION TIME: 40 minutes total
COOKING TIME: 50 minutes total

COCONUT EMPANADAS

1½ cups all-purpose flour
3½ tablespoons sugar
1½ teaspoons baking powder
½ teaspoon salt
4 tablespoons (½ stick) butter or
    margarine, chilled

2 tablespoons lard or vegetable
    shortening, chilled
2½ to 3½ tablespoons cold water
Orange-Coconut Filling (recipe follows)
2 tablespoons milk

In a bowl, combine flour, 2 tablespoons of the sugar, baking powder, and salt. Cut in butter and lard with a pastry blender or 2 knives until mixture forms coarse crumbs. Sprinkle with water, 1 tablespoon at a time, stirring and tossing with a fork, until dough clings together. Shape dough into a 1"-thick disk. On a lightly floured surface, roll dough out ⅛" thick. Using a 3¼" round cutter, cut dough into circles. Gather trimmings into a ball, re-roll, and cut out additional circles. There should be 16.

Preheat oven to 375°. Grease a baking sheet lightly.

Place 1 teaspoon of orange-coconut filling on bottom half of each circle, leaving ½″ edge uncovered. Brush edges lightly with water. Fold top half of dough over filling and press edges together with a fork to seal. Arrange empanadas on baking sheet, 2″ apart. Brush tops lightly with milk and sprinkle with remaining 1½ tablespoons of sugar. Bake until lightly browned, 20 to 25 minutes. Remove from baking sheet and cool on a wire rack.

Orange-Coconut Filling

⅓ cup sugar

1 large egg

1 tablespoon orange juice

1½ teaspoons lime juice

½ teaspoon grated orange zest

Pinch salt

1 tablespoon butter or margarine

2 tablespoons flaked coconut

In the top of a double boiler, combine sugar, egg, orange juice, lime juice, orange zest, and salt. Whisk until blended and add butter. Cook mixture over simmering water, stirring frequently, until very thick, 10 to 12 minutes. Stir in coconut and transfer mixture to a bowl. Refrigerate, covered, until completely cool, about 30 minutes.

SERVES 8

PREPARATION TIME: 20 minutes total, plus chilling time

COOKING TIME: 30 to 37 minutes total

Owner/chef Alfred Schilling brings consummate artistry and skill to this nouvelle French restaurant on San Francisco's Union Street. Extremely well qualified in his native France, with numerous medals and awards to his credit, this chef is memorable for his contemporary combinations of textures, flavors, and colors.

ONION TART BONNE FEMME
FILET MIGNON MATHURIN
APRICOT CUSTARD WITH RASPBERRY COULIS

ONION TART BONNE FEMME

1 tablespoon virgin olive oil
1½ medium onions, peeled and thinly sliced in crescents
10 tablespoons heavy cream
10 tablespoons milk

2 large eggs
Salt and pepper
Pinch grated nutmeg
1 8" Pastry Shell, partially baked (page 298)
4 ounces imported Swiss cheese, grated

Preheat oven to 375°. Heat olive oil and sauté onions until transparent, about 5 minutes. Transfer to a bowl to cool.

Combine cream, milk, and eggs. Season to taste with salt, pepper, and nutmeg. Whisk until frothy. Spread onions in tart shell and cover with cheese. Pour in cream mixture. Bake for 18 minutes. Serve lukewarm or at room temperature, not straight from oven.

SERVES 4
PREPARATION TIME: 10 minutes
COOKING TIME: 23 minutes

FILET MIGNON MATHURIN •

¼ cup golden raisins
¼ cup plus 1 tablespoon white rum
1 tablespoon virgin olive oil
4 aged center-cut filet mignon steaks, 8 ounces each

1 shallot, peeled and minced
1 cup Veal Stock (page 294)
1 tablespoon green peppercorns in brine
Salt and pepper

Wash raisins, drain, cover with fresh water, and boil for 10 seconds. Drain, add ¼ cup rum, cover, and refrigerate overnight.

Preheat oven to 400°. Heat oil in an ovenproof skillet and sear steaks for 1 minute on each side. Transfer to oven and bake for 5 minutes. Remove steaks from pan and keep warm. Pour off any fat, add shallot, and stir for 10 seconds. Add remaining 1 tablespoon rum and flame. Add stock and bring to a boil. Let bubble for 5 minutes to reduce, then add raisins with their liquid and boil for 2 minutes. Squeeze peppercorns dry and add to sauce. Taste, and adjust seasoning with salt and pepper. Arrange steaks on warmed plates and nap with sauce.

SERVES 4

PREPARATION TIME: 10 minutes, plus marination overnight

COOKING TIME: 15 minutes

APRICOT CUSTARD WITH RASPBERRY COULIS •

8 ripe apricots, halved and pitted
4 large egg yolks
2 tablespoons sugar

2 tablespoons Grand Marnier
Raspberry Coulis (recipe follows)
Fresh mint leaves for garnish

Preheat broiler. Arrange apricot halves cut side up in a shallow baking dish. Combine egg yolks and sugar in the top of a double boiler and whip over simmering water for 3 minutes. Add Grand Marnier and continue whipping for 10 seconds. Fill cavities of apricots with the custard mixture and broil for 10 seconds.

Spoon raspberry coulis onto 4 dessert plates. Top with 4 apricot halves and garnish with mint leaves.

Raspberry Coulis

8-ounce basket raspberries
½ cup sugar

1 to 2 drops lemon juice

Combine raspberries and sugar in a food processor with lemon juice. Puree, then strain.

SERVES 4

PREPARATION TIME: 10 minutes

COOKING TIME: 3 minutes

Alice Waters opened a modest Berkeley neighborhood café in 1971, and by so doing was to play a key role in the American food revolution. Her originality, the uncompromising quality of the fresh ingredients used in her kitchen, and her genius for picking brilliant co-chefs (Jeremiah Tower, Joyce Goldstein, and Jean Pierre Moullé, to name but three) have helped to earn Chez Panisse an international reputation. Today, chef Paul Bertolli carries on the good work in an elegant, but simple setting.

TAPENADE TOAST
CHARCOAL-GRILLED SALMON VINAIGRETTE
BLOOD ORANGE AND STRAWBERRY COMPOTE

TAPENADE TOAST •

1 anchovy filet, packed in oil
1½ tablespoons capers, packed in brine,
  rinsed, and patted dry
½ cup pitted niçoise olives
½ cup pitted dry-cured black French
  olives with herbs
1 small strip orange zest, minced

¼ tablespoon lemon juice
¼ cup virgin olive oil
1 small clove garlic, peeled and finely
  chopped
Freshly ground black pepper
1 loaf crusty country-style bread

Coarsely chop anchovy and capers. Chop olives medium-fine, and add to anchovy and capers. Add orange zest, lemon juice, olive oil, garlic, and pepper; blend well. For a smoother paste, puree in a blender or food processor for a few seconds.

Cut bread into ½″ slices and grill until golden brown on both sides. Spread tapenade on each slice of toast and serve warm.

SERVES 6
PREPARATION TIME: 10 minutes
COOKING TIME: 2 minutes

CHARCOAL-GRILLED SALMON VINAIGRETTE •

2 pounds salmon filet (or any other very
  fresh fish), cut into 6 equal pieces
Salt and pepper
2 tablespoons virgin olive oil

3 large handfuls mixed garden lettuces
  (equal amounts of red leaf and oak
  leaf lettuce, rocket, and chervil make
  the best mixture), washed and dried
Red Wine Vinaigrette (recipe follows)

Prepare a medium-hot charcoal fire with aromatic hardwood. Season salmon filets with salt and pepper and brush with olive oil. Grill for 3 minutes. Turn, and grill for 3 minutes more, until firm. The salmon should be just rare on the inside and nicely grilled on the outside.

Arrange the lettuces on a platter, put salmon filets on top, and spoon the vinaigrette over them.

Red Wine Vinaigrette

3 shallots, peeled and finely diced
2 to 3 tablespoons red wine vinegar

Salt and pepper
Approximately ½ cup virgin olive oil

Macerate the shallots in the vinegar for 15 minutes. Add a little salt and pepper and whisk in olive oil to taste just before dressing the salad.

SERVES 6
PREPARATION TIME: 20 minutes, plus maceration time
COOKING TIME: 6 minutes

BLOOD ORANGE AND STRAWBERRY COMPOTE •

6 blood oranges, washed
2 cups hulled ripe strawberries, sliced
  lengthwise

Sugar to taste
Kirsch to taste

Remove all the skin and pith from 4 of the oranges, and remove sections by cupping orange in one hand and slicing between membranes. (Work over a bowl to catch juice, and let sections fall into bowl. Remove seeds.) Squeeze juice from the remaining 2 oranges and add to bowl. Add strawberries. Toss gently with sugar—the amount depends on the sweetness of the fruit—and kirsch to taste. Chill for 1 hour.

SERVES 6
PREPARATION TIME: 15 minutes, plus chilling time
COOKING TIME: None

A dedicated scholar in the field of Chinese culture, owner/chef Barbara Tropp presents a highly original cuisine based on carefully selected fresh American and Chinese ingredients. Her attractively presented food is spiced with a wide variety of Asian herbs and condiments, and is served in a classic Art Deco diner setting.

CHILI-ORANGE COLD NOODLES
ROASTED SZECHWAN PEPPER-SALT QUAIL
LIME-RUM ICE CREAM

CHILI-ORANGE COLD NOODLES

1 pound thin (¹⁄₁₆" wide) fresh or frozen egg noodles
1 pound bean sprouts
2 large carrots, peeled and finely shredded

²⁄₃ cup thin-cut green and white scallion rings
2 bunches fresh cilantro (coriander), stems and leaves, coarsely chopped

Dressing

¼ cup Chili-Orange Oil (recipe follows)
2 tablespoons strained residue from oil
¼ cup black soy sauce (see Chef's Notes below)
¼ cup distilled white vinegar

2 teaspoons kosher salt (see Chef's Notes below)
2 tablespoons sugar
Sprigs cilantro (coriander) and chopped roasted peanuts for garnish

Fluff noodles to separate strands. Cook in a generous amount of unsalted boiling water until *al dente*, about 2 minutes. Drain promptly, plunge into ice water to chill, then drain thoroughly.

Blanch bean sprouts in unsalted boiling water for 10 seconds, then drain and plunge into ice water to chill. Drain well just before using.

Combine dressing ingredients, then add to noodles and toss well with your fingers to coat and separate each strand. Scatter bean sprouts, carrots, scallions, and two-thirds of the chopped cilantro on top. Toss lightly to mix.

Taste and adjust seasoning if necessary with a dash more sugar to bring forth the heat.

To serve, heap in bowls of contrasting color to the ingredients, and garnish with the remaining chopped cilantro, several whole sprigs of cilantro, and a generous sprinkling of peanuts.

Chili-Orange Oil

Zest of 1 large or 2 small oranges, finely minced
¼ cup dried red chili flakes
2 tablespoons Chinese salted black beans

1 large clove garlic, peeled and smashed
1 cup corn or peanut oil
2 tablespoons Japanese sesame oil (see Chef's Notes below)

Combine all ingredients in a heavy 1-quart saucepan. Bring slowly to approximately 230° (use a candy thermometer, and do not exceed 250° or the orange peel will burn), and let bubble for 10 minutes. Remove pan from heat and let oil stand uncovered until cool. Scrape mixture into a clean jar and store at room temperature.

SERVES 4 TO 6
PREPARATION TIME: 30 minutes total, plus cooling time
COOKING TIME: 23 minutes total

CHEF'S NOTES: Black soy sauce is much more intensely flavored than regular soy sauce. Koon Chun and Superior brands are both fine.

Sesame oil in China and Japan is deep brown and aromatic, as it is made from toasted sesame seeds. Avoid brands packaged in plastic, as they are

almost always rancid, and many manufacturers apparently burn their seeds before pressing. Sesame oil manufactured in Japan seems to be fully reliable— Kadoya brand is favored at China Moon.

Coarse kosher salt is a mild backdrop for big flavors. If using sea salt or table salt, use only half as much. The taste, however, will not be as good. Diamond brand kosher salt has a truly mild, clean taste.

ROASTED SZECHWAN PEPPER-SALT QUAIL •

¼ cup Szechwan peppercorns
½ cup Diamond kosher salt
8 fresh whole quail
8 nickel-sized coins of fresh ginger, peeled
16 to 24 pieces of scallion, 2″ long, white bulbs and green tops

1 or 2 oranges, scrubbed clean
Japanese sesame oil or Chili-Orange Oil (see preceding recipe)
Fresh cilantro (coriander) sprigs for garnish

Combine peppercorns and salt in a dry, heavy skillet. Stir over moderate heat until salt turns off-white and the peppercorns smoke and become very fragrant, about 5 minutes. Do not let them scorch. Grind mixture fine in a food processor or mortar, then strain to remove peppercorn husks. Store in an airtight jar.

Trim the quail of their necks and feet, then flush the cavities clean with cold water, removing the kidneys lodged above the tail. Pat birds dry inside and out. Sprinkle the outside of each bird evenly with ½ teaspoon pepper-salt, then sprinkle ⅛ teaspoon pepper-salt inside the cavity.

Crush the ginger and scallions with the broad side of a heavy knife or cleaver to release the flavors, then stuff the cavity of each quail with the mixture.

To make the birds compact and pretty, cross the legs into the cavity, anchoring the "knees" in the spots where the kidneys were located. Cross the little wings over the back, which plumps up the breast.

Place the birds breast side up, not touching, on a platter. Dust evenly with a bit more pepper-salt, then grate orange peel lightly on top. Seal with plastic wrap and set aside for up to several hours at room temperature, or overnight in the refrigerator. Bring to room temperature before cooking.

Drain off any juices, then grill the quail over hot coals or mesquite, or roast in a hot oven, brushing lightly with sesame oil (or chili-orange oil) midway through to give them a glossy finish. Cook until the juices in the breast run clear when the breast is pierced to the bone with a skewer, about 10 minutes in a 450° oven. Do not overcook; the meat should be pink at the bone.

To serve, cut each bird in half through the breast and backbone and arrange the halves overlapping each other attractively. Garnish with sprigs of fresh cilantro and encourage eating with the fingers.

SERVES 4

PREPARATION TIME: 15 minutes, plus marination time

COOKING TIME: 10 minutes

CHEF'S NOTE: This pepper-salt seasoning is a fantastic ingredient for the creative cook. It is very potent, so a pinch goes a long way.

LIME-RUM ICE CREAM

10 to 12 plum limes with unblemished skins
2 cups sugar
1 quart half and half
2 pinches salt
1½ to 2 tablespoons dark rum

Wash limes well, then remove peel with a sharp vegetable peeler, leaving white pith behind. Peel as many as needed to yield 1⅛ cups strained juice.

Combine peel and sugar in the bowl of a food processor fitted with a steel blade. Process until peel is finely minced and sugar is slightly liquid, 4 to 5 minutes.

Add juice, and process to combine. Scrape mixture into a large mixing bowl and stir in half and half and salt. Add rum by the teaspoonful to taste, but do not add more than 2 tablespoons or the ice cream will not freeze well. Freeze in an ice cream machine according to manufacturer's instructions.

SERVES 8

PREPARATION TIME: 35 minutes, plus freezing time

COOKING TIME: None

Sensitive handling of seafood and pasta dishes highlight the cuisine at Circolo, an attractive nouvelle Italian restaurant in San Francisco's Crocker Galleria. A marble entry, rose-colored fabric on the walls, and soft lighting enhance the restaurant's appeal.

CALAMARI SALAD
AGNOLLOTTI WITH FRESH SAGE
GIOIA MIA *(Chocolate Tart in a Pecan Crust)*

GOAT CHEESE SALAD
LINGUINI WITH SEA SCALLOPS AND SUN-
   DRIED TOMATOES
APRICOT-GINGER ICE CREAM

CALAMARI SALAD •

1½ pounds calamari (squid), cleaned and sliced (see Editor's Note below)
1 red bell pepper, seeded, deribbed, and diced
¼ bunch cilantro (coriander), chopped
Juice of 2 lemons
¼ cup virgin olive oil

½ jalapeño chili pepper, seeded and minced
Salt
White pepper
6 large handfuls assorted greens (such as arugula, frisée, oak leaf lettuce, baby spinach leaves, radicchio, etc.)

Blanch calamari in boiling salted water for 5 to 10 seconds, drain, and plunge into ice water. Drain again and mix with bell pepper, cilantro, lemon juice, olive oil, and jalapeño. Season to taste with salt and white pepper. Refrigerate for at least 30 minutes. Serve on a bed of mixed greens

SERVES 6
PREPARATION TIME: 20 minutes, plus chilling time
COOKING TIME: 5 to 10 seconds

EDITOR'S NOTE: To clean calamari (squid), cut off the tentacles just above the eye. (These are edible, and can be used or not, as you prefer.) Squeeze out the beak, which looks like a large pea, and discard it. Holding the blade of a chef's knife at an almost flat angle, scrape along the body from the tail to the opening, while holding on to the tail end and pressing down to squeeze out the entrails. With the tip of the knife, spear the transparent quill that sticks out of the body. Pull the body away from the quill, and discard the quill. Slice the body into ½"-wide rings.

AGNOLLOTTI WITH FRESH SAGE

2 pounds Fresh Pasta (recipe follows) or use ready-prepared sheets of fresh pasta dough

2 cups Tomato Sauce (recipe follows) or use good-quality canned tomato sauce

2 tablespoons butter, plus ½ pound (2 sticks) butter, cut up

½ pound shiitake mushrooms, chopped

2 bunches spinach, about 1 pound each

½ pound ricotta cheese

½ cup grated Parmesan cheese, plus extra for garnish

Salt and pepper

1 egg

½ cup milk

2 to 3 tablespoons chopped fresh sage, plus whole sage leaves for garnish

The night before, prepare fresh pasta and tomato sauce.

Heat 2 tablespoons butter and sauté mushrooms for 5 or 6 minutes, until tender. Reserve. Wash spinach leaves in several changes of cold water, and destem. Blanch in boiling salted water for 1 minute. Drain, and plunge into cold water. Drain again, squeeze dry, and chop fine.

In a bowl, combine half the mushrooms, the chopped spinach, ricotta, and Parmesan. Season to taste with salt and pepper. Mix well, and refrigerate for at least 1 hour.

Cut prepared pasta into 2"-×-4" rectangles. Combine egg and milk to make egg wash. Place 1 teaspoon of filling on each rectangle of pasta, placing the filling to one side. Brush edges with egg wash, fold over, and press edges together to seal.

Bring a large pot of salted water to a boil. Reheat tomato sauce. Reheat remaining chopped shiitake mushrooms. Cook agnollotti in boiling water for 5 to 6 minutes, until *al dente*. Drain and arrange in a wheel shape on serving plates. Pour ¼ cup tomato sauce in center, and sprinkle with Parmesan. Sprinkle mushrooms around agnollotti. Melt cut-up butter and add chopped sage. Pour 1 or 2 tablespoons of sage butter over agnollotti. Dust with additional Parmesan, and garnish with fresh sage leaves.

Fresh Pasta

¾ pound all-purpose flour
¾ pound semolina
4 large eggs

¼ cup virgin olive oil
¼ cup water

Using an electric mixer or a food processor, combine flour and semolina and then add liquid ingredients. Mix until smooth. Remove, form into a ball, and wrap in plastic. Refrigerate overnight. The next day, run through a pasta machine according to manufacturer's instructions, forming thin sheets of dough.

Tomato Sauce

¼ pound (1 stick) butter
2 cups peeled and chopped ripe tomatoes or canned tomatoes (chopped) with juice

1 onion, peeled and halved
Salt and pepper

Melt butter in a heavy saucepan. Add remaining ingredients and simmer over low heat for 45 minutes, uncovered. Remove onion before using sauce.

SERVES 6
PREPARATION TIME: 1 hour total plus overnight rest for pasta, if home-made
COOKING TIME: 1 hour total

GIOIA MIA •

2 cups pecan halves
¼ cup brown sugar, firmly packed
Pinch ground cinnamon
2 tablespoons unsalted butter, softened

6 ounces best-quality semisweet or bittersweet chocolate, chopped
¾ cup heavy cream

Preheat oven to 325°. Grind pecans in a food processor with brown sugar and cinnamon. Add butter and process until incorporated. Press mixture into bottom and sides of an 8″ tart pan with removable base. Bake until firm, about 20 minutes.

Place cut-up chocolate in a bowl over simmering water. When completely melted, remove from heat and cool to lukewarm. Add cream and stir until mixture amalgamates. Cover with plastic wrap and refrigerate overnight to thicken.

Transfer chocolate filling to a pastry bag fitted with a large star tip. Pipe filling decoratively into crust. Chill in refrigerator.

S E R V E S 6 T O 8

P R E P A R A T I O N T I M E : 10 minutes, plus chilling overnight

C O O K I N G T I M E : 20 minutes

GOAT CHEESE SALAD

2 red bell peppers
2 yellow bell peppers
2 green bell peppers
½ cup olive oil
¼ cup lemon juice

Salt and pepper
18 ounces goat cheese
1 cup white homemade-type bread
   crumbs, dried in oven
½ cup pine nuts, toasted in dry skillet

Preheat oven to 375°. Place peppers on a foil-lined baking sheet and roast for 15 to 20 minutes, until the skins start to blister and the peppers are *al dente*. Transfer peppers to a paper bag and steam for 10 minutes, which helps to loosen the skins. Slip off skins, cut into quarters, and discard seeds. Combine olive oil, lemon juice, and salt and pepper to taste. Marinate the quartered peppers in this mixture for 30 minutes.

Preheat oven to 400°. Divide goat cheese into 6 equal portions and form into 3"-diameter patties. Roll in bread crumbs. Place on a foil-lined baking sheet and bake for 3 minutes, until warmed through but not melting. Divide different colored pieces of bell pepper among 6 plates. Add a goat cheese patty. Sprinkle with toasted pine nuts and the marinade from the peppers.

S E R V E S 6

P R E P A R A T I O N T I M E : 30 minutes, plus marination time

C O O K I N G T I M E : about 30 minutes

LINGUINI WITH SEA SCALLOPS AND SUN-DRIED TOMATOES •

6 tablespoons butter
¼ cup chopped fresh basil
1 pound sea scallops
Salt

White pepper
1 tablespoon chopped garlic
1 cup Tomato Sauce (see recipe, page 71)
2 cups heavy cream

6 ounces sun-dried tomatoes, oil-packed,
    sliced
3 ripe tomatoes, peeled, seeded, and
    chopped

1 pound Fresh Pasta (½ recipe, page 71),
    cut into ¼" noodles, or use ready-made
    fresh linguini
Grated Parmesan for garnish
Chopped fresh parsley for garnish

In a heavy skillet, heat butter and add basil. Sauté scallops in basil butter
for 1 minute, seasoning lightly with salt and pepper. Add garlic, tomato sauce,
cream, sun-dried tomatoes, and chopped fresh tomato. Cook until scallops
are firm, but not overcooked, about 3 minutes. At the same time, cook pasta
in boiling salted water until *al dente*, about 2 minutes for fresh pasta.

Spoon a thin layer of sauce onto heated plates, covering the center completely. Using tongs, place pasta on top. Spoon more sauce over pasta. Place
scallops around edge. Garnish with grated Parmesan and chopped parsley.

SERVES 6
PREPARATION TIME: 10 minutes, plus overnight rest for pasta, if using
    homemade
COOKING TIME: 6 minutes

APRICOT-GINGER ICE CREAM

½ pound dried apricots
1 cup water
¼ cup chopped crystallized ginger
    preserved in syrup
½ teaspoon almond extract

1 cup sugar
2 cups heavy cream
2 cups milk
⅛ teaspoon salt

Combine apricots with water and simmer, covered, until very soft—about
25 minutes. Transfer to the bowl of a food processor, add ginger, and puree
until very smooth. Add almond extract and blend to mix.

Combine sugar, 1 cup cream, milk, and salt, and bring to a simmer. Blend
with apricot puree, and chill for several hours. Strain, and freeze the chilled
mixture in an ice cream machine until half frozen. Whip remaining 1 cup
cream until peaks start to form, and blend with semifrozen mixture. Continue
freezing until ice cream is solid.

SERVES 6
PREPARATION TIME: 15 minutes, plus chilling and freezing time
COOKING TIME: 30 minutes

Dan Bowe and Jane Fehon, co-owners of this San Francisco–based catering company, specialize in catering and event coordination for large corporate and social events. Although their menus reflect the needs of their clients, their recipes are strongly influenced by the cuisines of southern Europe.

OVEN-DRIED TOMATOES AND HEARTS OF PALM SALAD
SALMON WITH AVOCADO CREAM SAUCE
BASMATI RICE
FRUIT AND LIGHT MASCARPONE

OVEN-DRIED TOMATOES AND HEARTS OF PALM SALAD

6 medium Roma or salad tomatoes
1 tablespoon virgin olive oil
½ teaspoon salt
¼ teaspoon freshly ground black pepper

1 12-ounce can hearts of palm, drained
8 slices prosciutto
Caper Vinaigrette (recipe follows)

Preheat oven to 425°. Cut tomatoes into quarters, or eighths if large. Place in a bowl and toss with olive oil. Sprinkle with salt and pepper. Spread on a baking sheet and bake for 20 minutes. Let cool.

Cut hearts of palm crosswise into disks. Lay 2 slices of prosciutto on each plate. Toss palm hearts and tomatoes with caper vinaigrette and spoon over prosciutto.

SERVES 4
PREPARATION TIME: 15 minutes
COOKING TIME: 20 minutes

CHEF'S NOTE: In a *home* oven, 35 minutes to dry the tomatoes is acceptable, but 2 hours at 250° is optimum if you have the time. It can even be done the night before. Cool and wrap before refrigeration.

Caper Vinaigrette

1 clove garlic, peeled and roughly
   chopped
1 tablespoon fresh Italian parsley leaves
2 tablespoons red wine vinegar
2 tablespoons balsamic vinegar

1 tablespoon Dijon mustard
½ cup virgin olive oil
1 tablespoon capers
½ teaspoon salt
¼ teaspoon freshly ground black pepper

Put garlic and parsley in the bowl of a food processor and chop fine. Add vinegars and mustard. With motor running, slowly add oil. Stir in capers and season with salt and pepper.

SALMON WITH AVOCADO CREAM SAUCE

4 salmon filets, about 6 ounces each
¼ cup soy sauce
¼ cup dry sherry

¼ cup virgin olive oil
1 tablespoon dried tarragon
Salt and pepper

Sauce

½ cup dry white wine
½ tablespoon finely chopped shallot
2 cups heavy cream

½ teaspoon salt
½ teaspoon white pepper
1 large avocado

Lay salmon filets in a flat dish. Combine soy sauce, sherry, olive oil, and tarragon and pour over salmon, turning to coat both sides. Cover and marinate in refrigerator for at least 30 minutes, turning once.

Preheat oven to 425°.

Sauce: Place wine and shallot in a heavy saucepan and reduce over medium-high heat by half, about 5 minutes. Add cream, salt, and pepper, and continue cooking at a low rolling boil, stirring occasionally, until reduced by half, about 10 minutes. Set aside to cool slightly. Peel, pit, and puree avocado and add to cooled sauce. For a smoother sauce, pass through a sieve. Place salmon filets on a rack in a small baking pan and season with salt and pepper. Bake for 8 to 10 minutes, depending on thickness of fish. Serve with sauce.

SERVES 4
PREPARATION TIME: 15 minutes, plus marination time
COOKING TIME: 25 minutes

BASMATI RICE ●

2 cups Chicken Stock (page 294) or
    canned chicken broth
1 cup basmati rice, rinsed and drained
Salt and pepper
½ cup young fresh peas (optional)

1 scallion, white bulb and part of green
    top, thinly sliced on diagonal
1 small red or green bell pepper, seeded,
    deribbed, and diced

Bring chicken stock to a boil and add rice. Reduce heat, cover, and simmer
for 15 to 20 minutes, or until liquid has evaporated. Season to taste with salt
and pepper and stir in peas, scallions, and bell pepper.

SERVES 4

PREPARATION TIME: 10 minutes

COOKING TIME: about 20 minutes

FRUIT AND LIGHT MASCARPONE ●

1 medium navel orange, peeled and
    sectioned (page 292)
½ ripe papaya, peeled, seeded, and diced
2 cups hulled ripe strawberries, halved if
    large
1 ripe kiwi fruit, peeled and diced
4 tablespoons amaretto liqueur

1 large egg white
1 tablespoon sugar
¼ pound mascarpone cheese, at room
    temperature
8 biscotti or other cookies of choice
    (page 156 or page 264)

Place fruit in a bowl and toss with amaretto. Marinate for up to 1 hour.

Whip egg white to medium-peak stage and beat in sugar. Fold a quarter of the egg white mixture into the mascarpone and stir until a smooth consistency is reached. Fold in remaining egg white mixture and refrigerate until serving time.

To serve, divide fruits among serving bowls and pour any accumulated juices on top. Top with a dollop of the lightened mascarpone and serve with cookies of choice.

SERVES 4

PREPARATION TIME: 20 minutes, plus marination time

COOKING TIME: None

When France's Moët and Chandon of champagne fame established themselves in the Napa Valley as Domaine Chandon, they also established a
restaurant with barrel-vaulted ceilings and glass walls to encompass the surrounding vineyards and beautiful winery gardens. Chef Phillipe Jeanty styles
his cuisine "to reflect California's openness to innovation, the readily available
fresh produce, and the great traditions of French cooking."

SMOKED DUCK BREAST SALAD
COUSCOUS WITH GRILLED LOBSTER, PRAWNS,
   AND SCALLOPS
WHISKEY ICE CREAM WITH FRESH PEACH
   MARMALADE

SMOKED DUCK BREAST SALAD

6 cups assorted greens and baby lettuces
   (frisée, arugula, red oak leaf, purple
   basil, etc.)
3 cups tiny green beans (haricots verts),
   cooked al dente and chilled
Walnut Vinaigrette (recipe follows)
2 smoked duck breast halves, skinned
   and boned (available at good
   delicatessens)

1 large ripe tomato, peeled, seeded, and
   chopped
12 walnut halves, roughly chopped
12 croutons (oval slices from baguette),
   spread with olive oil and toasted
18 quail eggs, poached (optional)
6 small sprigs fresh chervil for garnish
Walnut oil

Rinse and dry the greens, and place in a bowl. Add green beans and toss
gently with Walnut Vinaigrette. Arrange attractively on 6 plates.
   Carve duck breasts into thin slices and fan out over the dressed greens.
Dot with tomato and walnut pieces. Place 2 croutons on each plate, one on
each side. Arrange the quail eggs, if used, on and around the greens, using
3 per portion. Garnish with chervil sprigs and moisten duck slices with a
few drops of walnut oil.

Walnut Vinaigrette

2 shallots, peeled and finely chopped
Salt and pepper to taste
Juice of 1 lemon

Approximately ¼ cup virgin olive oil
Approximately 1 tablespoon walnut oil

Combine shallots, salt and pepper, and lemon juice. Whisk in olive oil—proportions should be approximately 4 parts oil to 1 part lemon juice—and add walnut oil to taste.

SERVES 6
PREPARATION TIME: 30 minutes
COOKING TIME: 5 minutes

COUSCOUS WITH GRILLED LOBSTER, PRAWNS, AND SCALLOPS

1 pound couscous (see Editor's Note below)
2 cups water
½ teaspoon salt
4 tablespoons (½ stick) unsalted butter, softened and cut up
1 leek, white bulb and part of green leaves, well washed and sliced into rings

¼ cup all-purpose flour for dredging
Vegetable oil for deep-frying
3 live Maine lobsters
6 large Hawaiian blue prawns or jumbo shrimp
6 large Maine or other sea scallops
½ cup sliced toasted almonds
¼ cup currants
Rouille Sauce (recipe follows)

Place the couscous in a large bowl and, while stirring, dribble in water and salt. Let stand for a few minutes until water is completely absorbed. Transfer to a steamer and steam for 15 minutes. Transfer to another container, add pieces of butter and, with your hands or a fork, "fluff up" until couscous is light and lump-free.

Toss the leek rings in flour and deep-fry in vegetable oil for about 1 minute. Do not allow to color. Drain on absorbent paper and set aside.

Drop lobsters in boiling water for 5 to 7 minutes. Pull out and cool in ice water. Shell the lobsters and set aside tails and claws. (Save bodies and shells for lobster cream or bisque, if desired.)

Split the prawns or shrimp and slice the scallops in half horizontally. Grill the prawns and scallops over hot coals for 3 minutes, turning once. Grill split lobster tails for 1 minute to reheat and absorb grill flavor. Divide the couscous among 6 plates. Distribute ½ lobster tail, a claw, 3 half prawns, and 2 scallop halves on each plate. Sprinkle with almonds, currants, and deep-fried leek rings. Place 1 teaspoon of rouille sauce on each prawn.

Rouille Sauce

1 small red bell pepper	1 tablespoon chopped garlic
1 cup mayonnaise	½ teaspoon cayenne pepper

Cut bell pepper into quarters and remove ribs and seeds. Place skin side up on a foil-lined pan and broil until skin is blackened and blistered, about 10 minutes. Fold up foil to enclose peppers and steam for 5 minutes. Peel off skins.

Place peppers in the bowl of a food processor or blender and puree. Add mayonnaise, garlic, and cayenne and process until well mixed.

SERVES 6
PREPARATION TIME: 30 minutes
COOKING TIME: 23 minutes total

EDITOR'S NOTE: If using quick-cooking couscous, a Moroccan form of pasta grain, follow the directions on the box. It requires only 5 minutes of cooking time.

WHISKEY ICE CREAM WITH FRESH PEACH MARMALADE

1 quart half and half
1 vanilla bean
1 cup sugar

15 large egg yolks
¾ to 1 cup bourbon whiskey

Peach Marmalade

3 medium peaches, peeled, sliced into
*   small pieces*
½ cup sugar
Juice of 1 lemon

¼ cup water
1 tablespoon unsalted butter
Blackberries for garnish
Mint sprigs for garnish

Place half and half in a saucepan. Split vanilla bean and scrape contents into pan, discarding the pod. Bring to a boil, being careful not to burn the liquid. Combine sugar with egg yolks and whisk until sugar dissolves. Pour approximately 1 cup of the hot half and half into the egg mixture, stirring constantly. Return entire mixture to the saucepan. Stirring constantly, cook over low-medium heat until it starts to thicken, 5 to 8 minutes. Strain into a bowl and set into a larger bowl full of chipped ice, stirring constantly to arrest the cooking. Add whiskey to taste, and process in an ice cream machine according to the manufacturer's instructions.

Peach Marmalade: In a saucepan, combine peaches, sugar, lemon, and water. Cook over medium heat until peaches are soft, about 8 minutes. Stir in butter to thicken, and remove from heat. Keep warm.

To serve, place 1 or 2 scoops of ice cream on each dessert plate. Surround with peach marmalade, and spoon a little of the sauce on top. Garnish liberally with blackberries and a sprig of mint.

SERVES 4 TO 6
PREPARATION TIME: 30 minutes, plus chilling time
COOKING TIME: about 15 minutes total

Named for the famed Renaissance sculptor, this elegantly decorated restaurant, located in the hotel of the same name near Union Square, is resplendent with Venetian glass, many mirrors, Fortuny fabric, and expanses of marble. Subtle northern Italian cuisine is the trademark here.

PUMPKIN TORTELLI
SADDLE OF VEAL WITH PANCETTA
CASSATA ALL'ITALIANA

PUMPKIN TORTELLI

*1 extra small pumpkin, or 1 cup plain
  canned pumpkin*
*½ ounce amaretti cookies (2 to 3
  imported crisp Italian macaroons),
  finely crushed (about 2 tablespoons)*
1¼ cups fresh white bread crumbs
1 large egg
*10 tablespoons freshly grated Parmesan
  cheese (preferably Italian)*

Salt
*Pinch grated nutmeg (preferably freshly
  grated)*
Fresh Egg Pasta (recipe follows)
*1 egg white and water, beaten together
  (optional)*
6 tablespoons butter, melted
2 tablespoons chopped fresh sage

Preheat oven to 400°. If using fresh pumpkin, place it on a baking sheet and bake for 1 hour, until tender. Remove from oven and reduce heat to 375°.

Divide pumpkin into quarters and remove seeds and filaments with a fork. Place pulp in a bowl, discarding skin. Mash with a fork, then strain into another bowl. Pass amaretti cookie crumbs through a sifter. Toast bread crumbs at 375° until golden brown, approximately 15 minutes.

Add amaretti crumbs and toasted bread crumbs to pumpkin pulp. Mix very well with a wooden spoon, then add egg, 4 tablespoons of the Parmesan, salt to taste, and nutmeg. Mix very well without stopping for about 10 minutes, then place bowl in refrigerator while making pasta.

Roll pasta ⅛″ thick as described below and cut into 2½″ circles. Place 1 tablespoon of filling in center of each circle and fold in half, using egg white and water to seal, if needed. Wrap around finger; join sides together, and pinch closed, resulting in a hat shape.

Fill a large pot with water, bring to a boil, and add salt. While waiting for the water to boil, prepare a warmed serving dish by coating with 2 tablespoons of the melted butter and the fresh sage. Add tortelli to boiling water quickly but gently, being careful not to break them. If the tortelli have been made an hour or two before, they will cook and rise to the surface in 1 minute. If already dried, cooking time may be 3 to 4 minutes. Remove the cooked tortelli with a strainer-skimmer and arrange in a layer in the prepared serving dish. Sprinkle with 2 more tablespoons of the butter and 3 tablespoons of Parmesan cheese. Then make a second layer of tortelli and cover with remaining butter and Parmesan. Serve hot.

Fresh Egg Pasta

3 extra large eggs
3 cups all-purpose flour

Pinch salt

Place flour on a work surface and shape into a mound. Form a well in the middle, add eggs and salt, and combine with a fork. Add more flour if necessary, but the mixture should not become stiff and dry. Knead thoroughly, turning and folding the dough until it is smooth and elastic, about 10 minutes. Pat into a flattened ball. Dust work surface lightly with flour. Roll ball of dough into a circle, constantly rotating one quarter turn so that the dough remains in a circle of even thickness. Keep rolling until it is ⅛″ thick.

SERVES 4 TO 6
PREPARATION TIME: 1 hour
COOKING TIME: 16 minutes, plus 1 hour for fresh pumpkin

EDITOR'S NOTE: In some areas it is possible to buy fresh egg pasta in sheets, which saves time.

SADDLE OF VEAL WITH PANCETTA

1 boneless saddle of veal (double loin),
    about 1¾ pounds
Salt and pepper
3 tablespoons Clarified Butter (page
    291), or half regular butter and half
    virgin olive oil

½ cup vodka
3 ounces pancetta, sliced ⅛" thick,
    julienned
1 cup heavy cream, not ultra-pasteurized
¾ cup Veal Stock (page 294)

Preheat oven to 475°. Tie veal securely with kitchen string and season lightly with salt and pepper. Heat butter in a heavy, ovenproof skillet and brown veal very well on all sides, about 8 minutes. Transfer skillet to oven and roast for 10 minutes, turning once. Remove veal and keep warm.

    Strain pan juices and reserve. Place pan back over heat and deglaze with vodka. Add reserved pan juices and reduce by half, about 5 minutes. Add pancetta, cream, and veal stock. Cook over high heat, stirring, until thickened, about 5 minutes. Correct for seasoning. Carve veal into ¾"-thick slices. Place on warmed plates and spoon sauce on top.

SERVES 4

PREPARATION TIME: 20 minutes

COOKING TIME: 28 minutes

CASSATA ALL'ITALIANA

5 tablespoons sugar
5 tablespoons water
2 large egg whites
¾ cup heavy cream, whipped
⅓ cup diced mixed candied fruit
⅓ cup toasted hazelnut halves
1 tablespoon peeled blanched pistachios

¼ cup raisins, soaked for 20 minutes in
    2 tablespoons dry Marsala
1 basket strawberries, washed and
    hulled, plus 6 perfect strawberries,
    sliced, for garnish
6 fresh mint leaves for garnish

Cook sugar and water together until mixture reaches soft-ball stage, 245° on a candy thermometer. In the bowl of an electric mixer, beat egg whites until stiff. Pour hot sugar syrup slowly around edge of bowl, beating constantly until incorporated; then continue beating until meringue is cool. (Feel bottom of stainless-steel mixer bowl to check.) Remove bowl from stand and fold in whipped cream, candied fruit, toasted hazelnuts, pistachios, and raisins. Pour into an 8" loaf pan and freeze for at least 3 hours.

Puree hulled strawberries and pass through a sieve. Pour this sauce on serving plates, place a slice of cassata on top, and garnish with a sliced strawberry and a mint leaf.

SERVES 6

PREPARATION TIME: 35 minutes, plus freezing time

COOKING TIME: None

Located in San Francisco's Opera Plaza, this elegant restaurant is renowned for both its inspired northern Italian cuisine and the ever-changing modern art collection that graces its walls. Both traditional and innovative new interpretations of classic Italian dishes are offered; dining here is a feast for the senses.

> **PENNE WITH CHICKEN, GARLIC, AND SUN-DRIED TOMATOES**
> **VEAL BAULETTO**
> **CHILLED ZABAGLIONE**

PENNE WITH CHICKEN, GARLIC, AND SUN-DRIED TOMATOES

1 cup chkn broth

Salt
8 ounces penne (short, tubular pasta)
2 tablespoons virgin olive oil
12 cloves garlic, peeled and chopped
2 large skinless and boneless chicken breasts, about 6 ounces each
3 cups Chicken Stock (page 294) or canned chicken broth

¼ cup chopped fresh parsley
8 oil-packed sun-dried tomatoes, diced
6 scallions, white bulbs and half of green tops, chopped
Freshly ground black pepper
4 tablespoons (½ stick) butter, softened
2

Fill a large pot with water and bring to a boil. Add salt, then penne. Cook until *al dente* or just tender to the bite. (Start testing after 10 minutes.)

While pasta is cooking, heat olive oil in a sauté pan. Sauté garlic for 3 to 5 minutes, until golden. Do not allow to burn. Add chicken and sauté for 2 minutes. Remove chicken from pan, cut into 1″ cubes, and reserve.

Pour chicken stock into pan and add parsley, tomatoes, scallions, salt, and pepper to taste. Bring to a boil and reduce for 5 to 10 minutes. Return chicken to pan and whisk in butter a bit at a time to thicken sauce, which should be quite soupy. Toss penne in sauce and serve on heated plates.

SERVES 4
PREPARATION TIME: 15 minutes
COOKING TIME: 15 to 20 minutes

VEAL BAULETTO

8 large veal scallops, pounded flat, about
    2 ounces each
4 thin slices prosciutto, approximately
    same size as pounded veal
4 slices Monterey Jack cheese,
    approximately same size as prosciutto
Salt and pepper
Flour for dredging
3 tablespoons virgin olive oil

2 shallots, peeled and chopped
1 pound mushrooms, sliced
½ cup white wine
1 cup Chicken Stock (page 294) or
    canned chicken broth
2 tablespoons chopped fresh parsley
4 tablespoons (½ stick) butter, softened
Fresh vegetables of choice for garnish

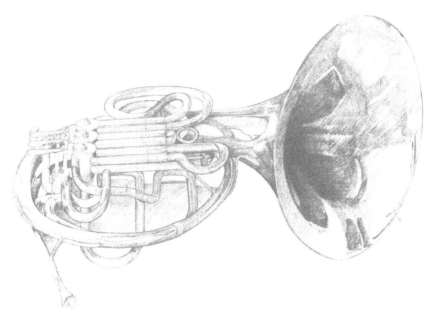

Place 4 of the veal slices on a work surface and top each with a slice of prosciutto and a slice of cheese. Cover with remaining veal slices. Put between 2 sheets of plastic wrap and pound gently until flattened. Season lightly with salt and pepper and dredge with flour.

Heat oil in a large skillet and sauté stuffed veal for 1 minute on each side. Remove and keep warm. Pour off any excess oil from pan and add shallots and mushrooms. Sauté for 3 or 4 minutes, then add wine, stock, and parsley. Bring to a boil and reduce for 5 minutes. Whisk in butter and spoon sauce over veal. Garnish with vegetables of choice.

SERVES 4
PREPARATION TIME: 20 minutes
COOKING TIME: about 15 minutes

CHILLED ZABAGLIONE •

7 large egg yolks
¾ cup sugar
1 cup Marsala wine
½ teaspoon vanilla extract

1 teaspoon freshly squeezed lemon juice
1 cup heavy cream
Fresh berries of choice for garnish

Combine egg yolks, sugar, and Marsala in the top of a double boiler over simmering water. Beat constantly with a wire whisk, scraping the sides and bottom, until the mixture forms soft mounds. Remove from heat and continue beating until cool. When cooled to room temperature, add vanilla and lemon juice. Place the container in a larger bowl filled with cracked ice, and continue beating until the mixture is thoroughly chilled. Beat the cream in a separate, chilled bowl until stiff. Fold into ice-cold zabaglione mixture. Pour into tall glasses and garnish with berries.

SERVES 4
PREPARATION TIME: 20 minutes
COOKING TIME: 10 minutes

A legend in its own time, Ernie's is one of the few San Francisco restaurants that has remained in the same family since its founding in 1934 by the grandfather of the present-day proprietors, Roland and Victor Gotti. Housed in a fine Victorian building, which was erected the year after the great earthquake and fire of 1906, it has splendid stained glass, champagne silk-covered walls, a coffered ceiling, and authentic period furniture. Executive chef Marcel Cathala's classical French training is evident in the elegant, well-executed cuisine.

TORTELLINI WITH MORELS AND PARMESAN
FILET OF BEEF MARCHAND DE VIN WITH
PARISIAN POTATOES
BENEDICTINE-ORANGE SABAYON

TORTELLINI WITH MORELS AND PARMESAN

¾ pound ready prepared fresh cheese-
  filled tortellini
Salt
Olive oil
1 large ripe tomato
1 teaspoon each chopped fresh chervil,
  tarragon, and chives, combined

4 fresh morels or shiitake mushrooms
2 tablespoons butter
1 cup crème fraîche
Pepper
¼ cup freshly grated imported Parmesan
  cheese

Drop tortellini into boiling water with salt and a splash of olive oil added. (This prevents the tortellini from sticking together.) Cook until tender, about 12 minutes. Drain and place under cold running water to stop the cooking.

Plunge tomato in boiling water for 15 seconds. Slip off skin and cut out core. Cut flesh into small cubes, discarding seeds, and sprinkle with mixed herbs. Clean mushrooms thoroughly and cut into julienne. Heat butter and sauté julienned mushrooms lightly, about 2 minutes.

Place crème fraîche in a saucepan and bring to a simmer. Reheat the tortellini in the crème fraîche. Salt and pepper lightly, and sprinkle with Parmesan.

To serve, divide tortellini and sauce among 4 warmed plates. Garnish with herbed tomato and sautéed mushrooms.

SERVES 4

PREPARATION TIME: 20 minutes

COOKING TIME: 20 minutes

FILET OF BEEF MARCHAND DE VIN WITH PARISIAN POTATOES

2-pound whole filet of beef, completely trimmed of fat or membrane

1 tablespoon butter, softened
Salt and pepper

Sauce

1 tablespoon finely chopped shallot

½ clove garlic, peeled and finely chopped

8 black peppercorns, crushed

Pinch dried thyme

1 small bay leaf

2 fresh white mushrooms, 1" diameter, sliced

1 cup good red burgundy

1 cup Brown Sauce (page 296)

4 tablespoons (½ stick) unsalted butter, cut up

6 ounces boneless beef marrow, sliced and poached in boiling salted water for 1 or 2 minutes

2 tablespoons chopped fresh parsley

Vegetable garnish: Parisian Potatoes (recipe follows) and buttered string beans

Preheat oven to 450°. Rub meat with butter and season with salt and pepper. Place on a rack in a shallow roasting pan and roast for 30 to 45 minutes. (A meat thermometer should register 110° to 115° for rare meat; 120° to 125° for medium.)

Sauce: Combine shallot, garlic, peppercorns, thyme, bay leaf, mushrooms, and burgundy in a saucepan and boil until reduced to a quarter of the original quantity, about 15 minutes. Add brown sauce, and boil gently for 15 minutes. When beef is cooked, remove from roasting pan and keep warm. Discard all fat from roasting pan and add sauce. Bring to a boil and stir in butter, little by little. Strain sauce through a fine sieve. Add poached marrow slices to strained sauce.

Place beef on a warmed platter and pour sauce over it. Place a few nice slices of marrow on top of meat. Sprinkle chopped parsley over roast. Garnish with Parisian potatoes and lightly cooked buttered string beans.

Parisian Potatoes

24 balls cut from all-purpose potatoes
    with a large melon baller
2 tablespoons Clarified Butter (page 291)

Kosher salt
1 tablespoon chopped fresh parsley

Place potatoes in a nonstick skillet. Cover with boiling water. Bring water back to a boil, and then drain. Add clarified butter to pan and heat until bubbling. Return drained potatoes to pan and season lightly with salt. Cover and cook slowly until tender, shaking pan from time to time to brown potatoes evenly on all sides, about 25 minutes. Dust with parsley before serving.

SERVES 4
PREPARATION TIME: 40 minutes total
COOKING TIME: 45 minutes total

BENEDICTINE-ORANGE SABAYON

1 cup freshly squeezed orange juice
Zest of ½ orange, finely grated
8 large egg yolks

½ cup sugar
¼ cup Benedictine
· 1 cup heavy cream

Place orange juice in a saucepan and reduce over low heat to 2 tablespoons, about 20 minutes. Add orange zest.

Combine egg yolks, sugar, and orange reduction in a round, flat-bottomed metal bowl. Place bowl over simmering water and whisk until mixture is very thick, about 15 minutes. Remove from heat and place bowl in a large container of shaved ice. Whisk until the mixture is cold, about 10 minutes, and add Benedictine. Whip cream to soft peaks and fold into egg yolk mixture. Spoon into stemmed glasses.

SERVES 6
PREPARATION TIME: 10 minutes
COOKING TIME: 45 minutes

Located on a suburban stretch of the Alameda de las Pulgas (Avenue of the Fleas) in Menlo Park, the food at the Flea Street Café is fresh, organic in the best sense, and as uncomplicated as the surroundings. Owner/chef Jesse Cool brings a great deal of integrity and originality to her heathful dishes, which rely on fresh herbs and artful combinations for full-bodied flavor.

STEAMED ARTICHOKES WITH POTATO-GARLIC PUREE
ROAST CHICKEN WITH GOAT CHEESE AND LEMON-GARLIC JALAPEÑO SAUCE
TANGERINE CUSTARD MERINGUE

STEAMED ARTICHOKES WITH POTATO-GARLIC PUREE

4 artichokes (organically grown if possible)
6 cloves garlic, peeled and smashed

1 lemon, quartered
2 tablespoons virgin olive oil
4 sprigs fresh dill

Potato-Garlic Puree

3 medium red potatoes
2 tablespoons chopped fresh chives, plus whole chives for garnish
½ cup dairy sour cream
2 cloves garlic, peeled and finely chopped

2 tablespoons virgin olive oil
3 to 6 tablespoons milk
Salt and pepper

Lemon wedges and olives for garnish

Trim artichokes by cutting off top 2″ and snipping off points of leaves. Place in the top of a steamer. Half fill bottom of steamer with water and add garlic, lemon, olive oil, and dill. Bring to a boil, assemble steamer, and cover. Steam artichokes until leaves pull away easily, 25 to 40 minutes, depending on size. Cool, slice in half, and remove inedible center leaves and feathery choke. Or, open leaves gently and pull out center and choke, forming an edible container for the puree.

Potato-Garlic Puree: Steam or boil potatoes until tender, 20 to 30 minutes. Cool slightly and slip off skins. Put potatoes, chopped chives, sour cream, garlic, olive oil, and 3 tablespoons milk in a food processor or blender. Puree, adding more milk as necessary to create a smooth, almost thin, mayonnaiselike consistency. Be *very careful* not to puree too fast or with too little liquid, or the mixture will become gummy. Season with salt and pepper, or add more olive oil or garlic if desired for a more intense sauce. Serve puree alongside, or fill cavities of whole artichokes. Garnish with lemon wedges, olives, and whole chives.

SERVES 4
PREPARATION TIME: 15 minutes
COOKING TIME: 40 minutes

ROAST CHICKEN WITH GOAT CHEESE AND LEMON-GARLIC JALAPEÑO SAUCE

2 chickens, about 3½ pounds each
  (corn-fed and free-range if possible)
Salt and pepper
½ pound fresh white goat cheese
2 tablespoons chopped fresh chives
1 tablespoon grated red onion
1 tablespoon calendula or geranium
  petals (unsprayed)

1 large egg
Lemon-Garlic Jalapeño Sauce (recipe
  follows)
2 tablespoons lightly toasted pumpkin
  seeds for garnish (optional)
2 tablespoons finely chopped red bell
  pepper for garnish (optional)

Preheat oven to 400°. Cut chickens in half, discarding backbone. Salt and pepper lightly. Place skin side up in a shallow baking pan and roast for approximately 30 minutes, until a meat thermometer registers 120° when inserted in thigh. Birds should be slightly underdone. Remove and set aside to cool.

In a bowl, combine goat cheese, chives, red onion, flower petals, and egg. Remove breast bone and thigh bones from chicken halves. Carefully lift skin and insert stuffing. Pull skin tight and pat to spread stuffing evenly.

Approximately 25 minutes before serving, preheat oven to 375°. Return stuffed chickens to baking pan, skin side up. Roast until warmed through, about 15 minutes. Place one chicken half on each plate and pour ½ cup lemon-garlic jalapeño sauce over each. Garnish with toasted pumpkin seeds and chopped red bell pepper.

Lemon-Garlic Jalapeño Sauce

¼ pound (1 stick) butter

⅔ cup chopped onions

1 or 2 jalapeño chili peppers, seeded and
  sliced

3 cloves garlic, peeled and chopped

Zest and juice of 1 lemon

3 tablespoons tequila

½ cup unbleached all-purpose white
  flour

3 to 4 cups Chicken Stock (page 294)
  or canned chicken broth

2 to 3 tablespoons balsamic vinegar

Salt and pepper

Pinch cayenne (optional)

Heat butter until foaming and sauté onions, peppers, and garlic until onions
are softened, about 5 minutes. Stir in lemon zest and juice. Deglaze pan
with tequila. Stir in flour and cook over low heat for 2 or 3 minutes. Gradually
whisk in 2 cups chicken stock, adding remainder if necessary to thin sauce
to desired consistency. Stir in balsamic vinegar and add salt and pepper to
taste. Taste sauce and adjust seasoning, adding cayenne if a spicier sauce is
desired.

SERVES 4

PREPARATION TIME: 25 minutes total

COOKING TIME: 45 minutes total

TANGERINE CUSTARD MERINGUE

1½ cups sugar

⅓ cup plus 1 tablespoon cornstarch

¼ teaspoon salt

3 cups milk

5 egg yolks

4 tablespoons (½ stick) unsalted butter,
  softened

½ cup fresh tangerine juice

1 tablespoon grated tangerine zest

Meringue

½ cup egg whites (from 5 to 6 eggs)

¼ cup sugar

¼ teaspoon cream of tartar

In a heavy saucepan, combine sugar, cornstarch, salt, and milk. Cook over
medium heat, stirring, until thick, about 5 minutes. Reduce heat to very
low, cover pan, and cook for 10 minutes more, stirring occasionally.

In a bowl, whisk egg yolks lightly. Remove milk mixture from heat and
whisk a few tablespoons of it into the egg yolks. Slowly whisk ½ cup of the
hot milk mixture into the yolks, then whisk yolks into remaining milk mix-

ture. Cook for 5 minutes more over low heat, stirring often. Remove from heat and stir in butter, tangerine juice, and zest. Pour into 6 custard cups and cool.

Meringue: Preheat oven to 350°. Beat egg whites until they just start to hold their shape, then slowly add sugar and cream of tartar. Beat at high speed until soft peaks form. Transfer to a pastry bag fitted with a large star tube and pipe decoratively over custards to cover tops completely, or simply spoon meringue on top. Bake for 15 to 20 minutes, until golden brown.

SERVES 6

PREPARATION TIME: 15 minutes

COOKING TIME: 35 to 40 minutes

CHEF'S NOTE: For a beautiful pink custard, use blood oranges instead of tangerines. For a different flavor, use lemons or limes.

Fleur de Lys

One of the city's most romantic dining spots since proprietor Maurice Rouas opened it in 1970, Fleur de Lys was designed by the late Michael Taylor, who created the feeling of an immense garden tent with 700 yards of locally hand-printed fabric gathered onto the walls and ceiling. In 1986, Rouas invited the renowned Hubert Keller to be his new partner and chef. Keller, who trained under such legendary figures as Paul Haeberlin, Gaston Lenôtre, Roger Vergé, and Paul Bocuse, is a master of his *métier*. His cuisine reflects both his classical background and his innovative style.

WARM BAY SCALLOPS AND FRENCH GREEN BEAN SALAD
VEAL MEDALLION SAUTÉ WITH WATERCRESS AND SPINACH SAUCE
WARM BOSC PEAR AND PECAN CREAM TART

CHILLED TOMATO AND RED BELL PEPPER SOUP
GRILLED SWORDFISH WITH ASPARAGUS SALAD
CRÈME BRÛLÉE AND CARAMELIZED APPLES

WARM BAY SCALLOPS AND FRENCH GREEN BEAN SALAD

10 ounces French green beans (haricots verts)
1 head Belgian endive
1 head radicchio
1 small head leafy green lettuce
½ pound very fresh bay scallops
Salt and freshly ground black pepper
1 teaspoon curry powder
Vinaigrette with Almonds (recipe follows)
1 tablespoon virgin olive oil
Croutons (recipe follows)

Trim beans. Blanch in boiling water for 3 to 4 minutes, then drain and plunge into cold water and drain again. This maximizes flavor and color, and makes them tender yet crisp. Separate, wash, and dry leaves of endive, radicchio, and lettuce. Season scallops with salt, pepper, and curry.

Transfer prepared vinaigrette to salad bowl. Reheat the green beans by plunging them briefly into boiling water. Heat 1 tablespoon of olive oil in a skillet. Sauté the seasoned scallops briefly, 1 minute or less, add the green beans, and pour into the bowl containing the vinaigrette. Toss gently and check the seasoning.

Divide the green bean and scallop salad attractively among 4 plates, and garnish with endive, radicchio, and lettuce. Decorate with croutons and serve immediately.

Vinaigrette with Almonds

1 tablespoon sherry or champagne vinegar	1 tablespoon chopped shallot
½ teaspoon Dijon mustard	1 ripe tomato, peeled, seeded, and diced
Salt and pepper	2 tablespoons finely chopped chives
3 tablespoons virgin olive oil	1 tablespoon sliced lightly toasted
1 small clove garlic, peeled and chopped	almonds

In a bowl, whisk together the vinegar, mustard, salt, and pepper. Then whisk in the olive oil, garlic, and shallot until smooth. Add the diced tomato, chives, and sliced almonds. (Dressing can be made ahead to this point, but do not let it stand for longer than 1 hour or the garlic will become too strong.)

Croutons

8 thin slices French bread (baguette)	¼ cup heavy cream, whipped
Olive oil	Salt
1 teaspoon drained prepared white horseradish	

Preheat oven to 375°. Smear both sides of bread lightly with olive oil. Place on a baking sheet and toast in the oven until crisp and golden, about 10 minutes, turning once after 5 minutes. (This can be done ahead of time.) Shortly before serving, combine horseradish with whipped cream and season to taste with salt. Spread this mixture onto the croutons.

SERVES 4
PREPARATION TIME: 30 minutes total
COOKING TIME: 15 minutes total

VEAL MEDALLION SAUTÉ WITH WATERCRESS AND SPINACH SAUCE

1 bunch watercress
1 quart salted water
8 large spinach leaves
3 tablespoons butter
1 tablespoon chopped shallot
2 tablespoons dry white wine
2 tablespoons Veal Glaze (page 294)
   (optional)

¾ cup heavy cream
Salt and pepper
3 tablespoons peeled, seeded, and cubed
   tomato
4 loin medallions of veal, about 6
   ounces each

Wash the watercress and trim off the leaves, discarding stems. Bring salted water to a boil. Add watercress leaves and blanch for 4 minutes. Drain in a strainer under cold running water and then squeeze all the moisture from the leaves with your hands.

Destem the spinach leaves. Carefully wash leaves to remove all sand and grit. Heat ½ tablespoon of the butter in a sauté pan and add spinach. Cook for about 3 minutes, stirring occasionally, until leaves are wilted but still bright green. Drain in a colander.

In a small heavy saucepan, heat another ½ tablespoon of butter. Add chopped shallot and cook, stirring, until they become a light golden color, about 3 minutes. Add white wine to deglaze pan, and reduce until mixture is almost dry. Add veal glaze if used (it adds a rich flavor and silky sheen to the sauce) and pour in the cream. Bring to a boil, then lower heat and simmer for 8 minutes. Stir in cooked watercress leaves. Puree mixture in a food processor or blender to obtain a light and tasty watercress sauce. Taste for seasoning and add salt and pepper as required. Just before serving, stir in the tomato cubes and spinach leaves.

Trim veal of any fat or membrane. Sprinkle medallions on both sides with salt and pepper. Melt the remaining 2 tablespoons of butter in a heavy skillet. When the butter sizzles, add veal and brown on both sides, about 8 minutes total. (Veal should be pink and juicy but not rare.) When the meat is cooked, cover the center of each warmed dinner plate with watercress sauce. Top with the veal medallions.

SERVES 4
PREPARATION TIME: 30 minutes
COOKING TIME: 20 minutes

WARM BOSC PEAR AND PECAN CREAM TART

7 ounces puff pastry dough (see Editor's
   Note below)
6 tablespoons (¾ stick) unsalted butter
3 tablespoons sugar
¼ cup (1½ ounces) ground pecans

1 large egg
2 or 3 Bosc pears
2 tablespoons honey
Crème Fraîche (page 297) or Caramel
   Sauce (page 7)

Preheat oven to 375°. On a lightly floured surface, roll dough to ⅛″ thickness. Cut out four 5½″ circles and place on a baking sheet. Refrigerate while preparing filling, as cold dough will puff better.

Place 3 tablespoons of the butter in the bowl of a food processor. Process until butter is white and smooth. Add sugar and process for another 20 seconds. Add ground pecans and blend well. Incorporate egg and continue processing until mixture is homogenized.

Peel and core pears and slice into thin wedges. Spread the creamy pecan mixture on top of the pastry circles to within ½″ of edge. Arrange the pear slices on top in overlapping, concentric circles. Dot with remaining 3 tablespoons of butter and drizzle with honey. Bake for 20 to 25 minutes. Serve immediately, with crème fraîche or caramel sauce.

SERVES 4
PREPARATION TIME: 20 minutes
COOKING TIME: 20 to 25 minutes

EDITOR'S NOTE: If you do not wish to make your own puff pastry, use 1 sheet or ½ package of frozen puff dough.

CHILLED TOMATO AND RED BELL PEPPER SOUP

4 red bell peppers, roasted, peeled,
  seeded, and chopped (page 291)
2 tablespoons virgin olive oil
1 medium onion, peeled and chopped
2 cloves garlic, peeled and chopped
3 tomatoes, peeled, seeded, and chopped
Pinch dried thyme
8 fresh basil leaves
1 teaspoon sugar

Salt and freshly ground black pepper
6 cups Chicken Stock (page 294) or
  canned chicken broth
1 tablespoon sherry or champagne
  vinegar
¾ cup half and half
20 watercress leaves, or 4 pinches dried
  chervil
4 teaspoons Beluga or golden caviar

In a medium saucepan, heat olive oil. Add chopped onion and simmer, stirring, until translucent, about 3 minutes. Add garlic, tomatoes, bell peppers, thyme, basil, sugar, salt, and pepper. Cook slowly for 5 minutes. Add chicken stock and bring to a boil. Reduce heat and simmer for 20 minutes. Transfer to a blender or food processor, in batches if necessary, and puree until completely smooth. Strain into a mixing bowl, cool, and refrigerate.

Just before serving, stir in the vinegar and half and half (use more if the soup is too thick), and taste for seasoning. Add salt and pepper as required. Ladle the soup into shallow, rimmed soup plates, and sprinkle with watercress leaves or chervil. Place 1 teaspoon of caviar in the center of each serving.

SERVES 4
PREPARATION TIME: 25 minutes, plus chilling time
COOKING TIME: 45 minutes

GRILLED SWORDFISH WITH ASPARAGUS SALAD

4 swordfish steaks, about 5 ounces each
Lemon Vinaigrette (recipe follows)
24 asparagus tips
1 small head radicchio
1 small head leafy green lettuce

1 head Belgian endive
Creoja Sauce (recipe follows)
Croutons (recipe follows)
Tapenade (recipe follows)
1 ripe tomato, peeled, seeded, and diced,
  for garnish

Place swordfish steaks on a plate and spread with 2 tablespoons vinaigrette to coat evenly on both sides. Leave to marinate for at least 20 minutes.

Poach or steam asparagus until just tender, about 7 minutes (try one to make sure; this depends on size). Drain, refresh in cold water, drain again, and marinate in a little of the vinaigrette.

Separate leaves of radicchio, green lettuce, and endive. Wash and dry, and place in a mixing bowl. Toss with remaining vinaigrette.

Heat barbecue grill (or broiler) until very hot. Grill or broil swordfish steaks for no longer than 2 to 3 minutes per side. (Swordfish tends to be dry if overcooked, so serve it on the medium to medium rare side.)

Place the salad leaves on the center of each plate. Arrange the asparagus tips attractively to one side. Top salad with a swordfish steak and spoon creoja sauce halfway over each one. Decorate with croutons spread with tapenade and a tablespoon of diced tomato.

Lemon Vinaigrette

Juice of 1 lemon
5 tablespoons virgin olive oil
Salt and pepper
1 clove garlic, peeled and chopped

1 branch fresh thyme
1 branch fresh cilantro (coriander)
1 bay leaf

Whisk together the lemon juice and olive oil. Add salt and pepper. Add remaining ingredients and combine well. Remove bay leaf before using.

Creoja Sauce

1 tablespoon finely chopped red onion
1 tablespoon finely chopped celery
1 tablespoon finely chopped carrot
1 tablespoon finely chopped green bell pepper
2 tablespoons finely chopped peeled, seeded tomato
1 tablespoon finely chopped fresh chives

1 tablespoon finely chopped fresh cilantro (coriander)
1 tablespoon finely chopped fresh parsley
Salt and pepper
½ cup hazelnut oil (available in specialty food stores)
3 tablespoons sherry or champagne vinegar

In a bowl, combine the red onion, celery, carrot, green bell pepper, tomato, chives, cilantro, and parsley. Season with salt and pepper and mix lightly. In a separate bowl, beat together the oil and vinegar. Pour over vegetables. Stir to mix and set aside at room temperature for 1 hour before serving.

Croutons

8 thin slices French bread (baguette)   Virgin olive oil

Preheat oven to 375°. Smear bread lightly with olive oil on both sides. Place on a baking sheet and toast in the oven until crisp and golden, about 5 minutes per side.

Tapenade

8 ounces dry, oil-cured black olives
  (French or Italian, not ripe
  California variety), pitted
1 2-ounce can anchovy filets, drained
1 teaspoon capers

1 teaspoon brandy
Black pepper
½ clove garlic, peeled
1½ tablespoons virgin olive oil
2 ounces canned tuna, drained

Combine all ingredients in a food processor and process until well blended. A delicious cocktail spread, it will keep, covered and refrigerated, for at least a week.

SERVES 4

PREPARATION TIME: 45 minutes total, plus marination and standing time

COOKING TIME: 10 minutes total

CRÈME BRÛLÉE AND CARAMELIZED APPLES

1 small orange
1 small lemon
1½ cups heavy cream
5 large egg yolks
3 tablespoons white sugar

1½ tablespoons butter
1 large Golden Delicious apple, peeled
  and cut into 20 wedges
2 tablespoons light brown sugar, tightly
  packed

Remove zest from orange and lemon with a vegetable peeler and place in a saucepan with the cream. Bring to a boil. In a mixing bowl, beat egg yolks with sugar. Continue beating while pouring in hot cream. Set aside to cool.

Preheat oven to 275°. Grease 4 crème brûlée molds or small porcelain ramekins lightly with butter. Strain egg-cream mixture into them, and place dishes in a roasting pan. Add enough hot water to reach halfway up sides of dishes, and cover lightly with a sheet of aluminum foil. Bake for 40 minutes, and then cool.

Meanwhile, in a large sauté pan, heat butter and cook apple slices over high heat until they start to color, about 7 minutes.

When the baked custards are cold, transfer molds to a baking sheet. Top each one with 5 slices of apple, and sprinkle brown sugar over all.

Preheat broiler to very hot. Broil custards until sugar melts and turns to a crisp golden caramel, which it will do almost immediately. Serve warm or at room temperature.

SERVES 4

PREPARATION TIME: 15 minutes, plus cooling time

COOKING TIME: 45 minutes

This sleek, trend-setting chrome and neon diner offers updated diner-style food. Chef Cindy Pawlcyn's assorted appetizer plates cater to the new American penchant for "grazing," a practice that is now popular in restaurants across the country, and there's plenty of traditional, albeit modernized diner fare for the nostalgia minded.

BAKED BUFFALO MOZZARELLA
MARINATED SKIRT STEAK WITH TOMATO
   AIOLI
ROOT BEER FLOAT

BAKED BUFFALO MOZZARELLA •

12 to 16 slices mozzarella cheese, ¼" to ⅓" thick (use the small fresh Italian import)
Virgin olive oil
Freshly ground white pepper
Croutons (12 to 16 slices baguette, cut on bias, ¼" thick)
Butter for croutons

Pesto Sauce (recipe follows)
2 to 3 red bell peppers, roasted, peeled, seeded, and sliced (page 291), for garnish
2 to 3 yellow bell peppers, roasted, peeled, seeded, and sliced (page 291), for garnish

Cover mozzarella cheese slices with olive oil, sprinkle with pepper, and marinate for at least 1 hour or overnight.

Preheat oven to 375°. Spread croutons with butter, place on a baking sheet, and toast in the oven. When light golden, place a slice of mozzarella on each crouton. Bake until cheese just begins to melt, about 5 minutes. Transfer to a serving platter. Drizzle each toast with pesto sauce and garnish with strips of red and yellow bell pepper.

Pesto Sauce

2 cups fresh basil leaves
4 to 5 cloves garlic, peeled
Salt

White pepper
¼ cup freshly grated Parmesan cheese
¾ cup virgin olive oil

Place basil, garlic, salt, pepper, and Parmesan in a food processor or blender. Process until blended, then with the motor running, add the olive oil in a thin stream.

SERVES 6 TO 8

PREPARATION TIME: 10 minutes, not including roasting peppers or marination

COOKING TIME: 10 minutes

MARINATED SKIRT STEAK WITH TOMATO AIOLI

1½″ piece gingerroot, peeled and grated
¼ cup chopped garlic
Pinch white pepper
6 tablespoons maple syrup
6 tablespoons double-concentrated black soy sauce

6 tablespoons olive oil
6 tablespoons rice vinegar
1½ tablespoons Oriental sesame oil
2 pounds skirt or flank steak
Tomato Aioli (recipe follows)
French fries

Combine gingerroot, garlic, pepper, maple syrup, soy sauce, olive oil, vinegar, and sesame oil and mix well. Pour over steak and marinate overnight in the refrigerator.

Grill steak for 5 minutes on each side for medium rare, and slice across the grain. Transfer to plates and serve with tomato aioli and french fries.

Tomato Aioli

2 ounces sun-dried tomatoes in oil
¼ cup peeled, seeded, and chopped tomato
1 head garlic, separated into cloves, peeled and chopped

2½ tablespoons virgin olive oil
2 cups mayonnaise
Salt and pepper

Combine sun-dried and fresh tomatoes, garlic, and oil, and cook over medium heat until garlic is soft, about 10 minutes. Blend until smooth and mix into mayonnaise. Season to taste with salt and pepper.

SERVES 6

PREPARATION TIME: 25 minutes total, plus marination time

COOKING TIME: 10 minutes total

ROOT BEER FLOAT •

1 quart best-quality vanilla ice cream   *6 bottles root beer*

Place 3 scoops ice cream in each of six 10-ounce glasses. Add root beer to brim.

SERVES 6

PREPARATION TIME: 2 minutes

COOKING TIME: None

Housed within the elegant Stanford Court Hotel on top of Nob Hill, but with its own entrance and separate identity, Fournou's Ovens is on two levels: The original one, graced with antique furniture and filigree ironwork, contains huge brick ovens faced with blue and white Portuguese tiles. The newer level is a long, light-filled, glass-walled room with faux bamboo upholstered chairs and luxuriant greenery. The American cuisine is in the capable hands of Executive Chef Lawrence Vito and pastry chef Joann Vazquez.

**GRILLED MARINATED SHIITAKE MUSHROOMS
WITH RED ONION JAM
GRILLED PRAWNS WITH FRESH TOMATO,
LEMON, AND BASIL SAUCE
ORANGE-PECAN CAKE**

GRILLED MARINATED SHIITAKE MUSHROOMS WITH RED ONION JAM

½ cup balsamic vinegar
1½ cups virgin olive oil
4 sprigs fresh thyme
4 cloves garlic, peeled and quartered
½ teaspoon salt
½ teaspoon black pepper

24 fresh shiitake mushrooms
Red Onion Jam (recipe follows)
1 bunch chives, chopped, for garnish
*2 ounces smoked ham, thinly sliced and
    julienned, for garnish*

Combine vinegar, oil, thyme, garlic, salt, and pepper in a nonreactive bowl. Allow to steep for 4 hours.

Trim stems from mushroom caps, reserving them for stock. Stir marinade with a whisk, add mushroom caps, and marinate for 10 seconds, remove, and drain. Grill over hot coals, or approximately 2″ from an electric or gas broiler, for 30 seconds per side.

Arrange 6 mushrooms in a circle on each plate. Garnish center area with a dollop of onion jam, and sprinkle generously with chives and ham.

Red Onion Jam

2 tablespoons unsalted butter

1½ pounds red onions, peeled and thinly
    sliced

1 cup red wine

6 tablespoons red wine vinegar

2 tablespoons grenadine

1 tablespoon sugar

1 teaspoon salt

¼ teaspoon black pepper

Melt butter in a sauté pan over medium heat. Add onions and sauté gently until transparent, about 10 minutes. Add remaining ingredients and reduce to a jellylike consistency, about 30 minutes. Refrigerate.

SERVES 4

PREPARATION TIME: 20 minutes total, plus steeping time

COOKING TIME: 40 minutes total

GRILLED PRAWNS WITH FRESH TOMATO, LEMON, AND BASIL SAUCE •

2½ pounds fresh prawns, with heads, or
    1¾ pounds headless "tiger" prawns,
    3½" to 4" long

½ cup virgin olive oil

2 tablespoons finely chopped garlic

¼ cups finely chopped shallots

½ cup white wine

Juice of 2 lemons, strained

2 large, ripe tomatoes, peeled, seeded,
    and chopped

10 large fresh basil leaves

4 tablespoons (½ stick) butter, cut into
    small pieces

Salt and pepper

Hot cooked rice tossed with chopped
    fresh parsley

Build an intense charcoal fire in a grill. Shell and devein prawns, leaving heads and tails attached. Lay prawns flat on a plate, and cover with all but one tablespoon olive oil, coating well.

Heat a 7″ sauté pan over medium heat. Add remaining 1 tablespoon olive oil to coat bottom of pan. Add garlic and shallots. Sauté for 5 seconds, and add white wine and lemon juice. Reduce volume to a quarter of original, about 5 minutes. Turn heat up to high and add tomato. Sauté for about 30 seconds, or until a quarter of the juice has evaporated. Stack basil leaves and roll up like a cigar, then cut into fine julienne. Stir butter into pan and add basil. Season to taste with salt and pepper.

Season prawns on both sides with salt and pepper. Grill for approximately 20 seconds per side on a covered grill, turning with tongs. Remove with tongs, place on dinner plates, and divide the sauce equally among the portions, spooning it directly over the prawns. Flank prawns with rice.

SERVES 4

PREPARATION TIME: 20 minutes

COOKING TIME: 6 minutes

EDITOR'S NOTE: The result will be different, but the prawns can be broiled if no grill is available.

ORANGE-PECAN CAKE

¼ pound (1 stick) unsalted butter
1 cup sugar
1 tablespoon finely minced orange zest
¼ teaspoon vanilla extract
1 large egg
1 cup sliced pecans

1⅓ cups cake flour
4 teaspoons baking powder
¼ teaspoon salt
1 cup milk
Sliced ripe peaches marinated in Grand Marnier for 1 hour

Adjust oven rack to middle level and preheat oven to 375°. Butter and flour a 9″ springform pan.

Cream together butter, sugar, orange zest, and vanilla extract until smooth and light in color. Add egg and mix until blended. Scrape down sides of bowl.

Place ¾ cup of pecans on a baking sheet and toast lightly in oven, about 6 minutes. Allow to cool completely. Place in the bowl of a food processor with the flour, and process until pecans are ground to powder. Add baking powder and salt. Pulse a few times to blend. Add half the flour mixture to the butter, then remaining flour and milk. With a spatula, mix until smooth.

Spoon batter into prepared cake pan. Sprinkle remaining sliced raw pecans on top of cake. Bake until center springs back, about 45 minutes. Unmold and cool on a rack. When cool, slice, and serve with marinated peaches.

SERVES 8

PREPARATION TIME: 15 minutes

COOKING TIME: 50 minutes

Berkeley's Fourth Street Grill has a relaxed, friendly, neighborhood feeling, with varnished wood tables, wood-framed windows, lots of contemporary and folk art on the walls, and plenty of flowers. Chef Curt Koessel spends a lot of time tracking down fresh local ingredients (some come from the showcase urban market garden right across the street), and his internatonal presentations are both satisfying and original.

BUTTERNUT SQUASH SOUP WITH APPLES AND FRESH THYME

SWORDFISH WITH LIME, TEQUILA, AND ROASTED GARLIC

STEVE'S CHOCOLATE-WALNUT TORTE

BUTTERNUT SQUASH SOUP WITH APPLES AND FRESH THYME

2 tablespoons virgin olive oil

2 cups peeled and coarsely chopped butternut squash or pumpkin

1 cup peeled and chopped tart green apples (such as Granny Smith)

1 onion, peeled and chopped

1 teaspoon chopped garlic

2 teaspoons chopped fresh thyme (reserve thyme flowers if available), plus extra for garnish (optional)

3 cups Chicken Stock (page 294) or canned chicken broth

3 tablespoons unsalted butter, softened

Heat olive oil in a large pan and gently sauté squash, apple, onion, garlic, and thyme until softened, about 20 minutes. Add chicken stock and simmer for another 10 minutes. Puree the soup in batches in a blender or food processor, and strain through a fine sieve. Place soup in a double boiler over simmering water and reheat as necessary. Whisk in butter.

Ladle soup into warmed bowls and garnish with thyme flowers, or a little chopped fresh thyme.

SERVES 4

PREPARATION TIME: 25 minutes

COOKING TIME: 30 minutes

EDITOR'S NOTE: This fragrant soup has a delicate texture. For a heartier soup, omit straining the puree.

SWORDFISH WITH LIME, TEQUILA, AND ROASTED GARLIC

2 heads garlic
¼ cup water
Branch fresh rosemary
¼ pound (1 stick) unsalted butter, softened
4 swordfish steaks, 6 ounces each
Salt
Cornmeal seasoned with black pepper for dredging
¼ cup virgin olive oil

4 tomatilloes, husked, washed, and thinly sliced into wedges
½ cup tequila
½ cup Chicken Stock (page 294) or canned chicken broth
Juice of 1 or 2 limes
Pepper (optional)
Cilantro (coriander) sprigs and lime wedges for garnish

Preheat oven to 350°. Place garlic, root end down, in an ovenproof pan with the water and rosemary. Cover with foil and bake for 45 minutes. Remove foil and bake 5 minutes more to toast rosemary. Strip leaves from stalk and chop them fine. When cool, separate garlic cloves and squeeze out pulp. Mix garlic pulp with soft butter and chopped rosemary. Set aside for sauce. (This step can be done ahead.)

Season swordfish steaks with salt and dredge lightly in cornmeal. In a large sauté pan, heat olive oil, add fish and brown, about 4 minutes. Turn fish over and continue cooking another 4 or 5 minutes over low heat, or until cooked through.

Place fish on a warmed serving platter. Remove oil from sauté pan, add sliced tomatilloes, and brown slightly, about 2 minutes. Deglaze pan with tequila, then add chicken stock and lime juice. Stir in ¼ cup of garlic butter mixture (reserve the remainder for another use). Taste for seasoning, adding more lime juice, salt or pepper if required. Spoon sauce over fish and garnish with cilantro sprigs and lime wedges.

SERVES 4

PREPARATION TIME: 20 minutes

COOKING TIME: about 1 hour

STEVE'S CHOCOLATE-WALNUT TORTE

4 large eggs, separated

½ cup sugar

2 tablespoons brandy

2 ounces semisweet chocolate, grated (see Editor's Note below)

2½ cups ground walnuts (see Editor's Note below)

⅛ teaspoon cream of tartar

Chocolate Glaze

10 ounces semisweet chocolate, cut up

1 ounce unsweetened chocolate, cut up

½ cup water

2 tablespoons corn syrup

6 tablespoons (¾ stick) unsalted butter

Preheat oven to 350°. Butter and flour a 9″ springform pan. Whisk egg yolks and sugar together until pale and thick. Add brandy. Fold in grated chocolate and ground walnuts. Beat egg whites with cream of tartar until stiff but not dry. Fold egg whites into chocolate mixture and pour batter into pan. Bake for 40 minutes. Let cake stand in pan for 1 minute, then loosen edges with a knife blade before releasing rim. Unmold onto a rack and cool.

Glaze: Combine all ingredients in top of a double boiler and melt over simmering water, stirring until smooth.

Place cake on a rack set over a plate and pour chocolate glaze over top and sides of cake. Refrigerate for at least 10 minutes to set glaze. Serve at room temperature.

SERVES 10 TO 12

PREPARATION TIME: 20 minutes, plus chilling time

COOKING TIME: 40 minutes

EDITOR'S NOTE: The chocolate for the cake should be grated by hand, or with a hand-cranked nut mill, as this results in little flakes that melt into the batter. A food processor makes tiny granules, which do not melt as well. If grinding the walnuts in a food processor (and here, too, a nut mill is preferable as it will make a fluffy powder that results in a lighter cake), be sure to pulse the machine on and off repeatedly to prevent forming a heavy paste.

Executive chef Kelly Mills creates imaginative, light, and healthful food, using the best fresh ingredients California has to offer. Under his aegis, the luxuriously gilded French Room has become a national leader in "spa" cuisine.

SALAD OF MIXED GREENS WITH PAPAYA AND MACADAMIA NUTS •

GRILLED PAILLARD OF CHICKEN WITH RED BELL PEPPER COULIS

CREAM BISCUITS WITH POACHED FRESH FRUIT AND RASPBERRY SAUCE

SALAD OF MIXED GREENS WITH PAPAYA AND MACADAMIA NUTS •

½ ripe papaya, peeled and seeded
¼ cup water
2 tablespoons sherry vinegar
1 to 2 teaspoons lemon juice
2 tablespoons hazelnut oil

Dash Worcestershire sauce
Salt and pepper to taste
4 cups mixed greens (watercress, arugula, radicchio, endive, etc.)

Garnish

8 red or yellow cherry tomatoes
2 tablespoons finely chopped toasted macadamia nuts

½ pound Dungeness crab meat (optional)

In a blender or food processor, combine papaya, water, vinegar, lemon juice, oil, and Worcestershire sauce. Blend until very smooth and season with salt and pepper. Refrigerate dressing until serving time.

Toss greens with dressing and divide among 4 plates. Garnish with tomatoes, nuts, and crab (if used).

SERVES 4
PREPARATION TIME: 15 minutes
COOKING TIME: None

GRILLED PAILLARD OF CHICKEN WITH RED BELL PEPPER COULIS

4 skinless and boneless chicken breast halves, 4 ounces each, pounded flat
1 clove garlic, unpeeled, halved
1 tablespoon virgin olive oil
Salt and pepper
1 sprig fresh rosemary, chopped

2 large russet potatoes, peeled
Pinch saffron threads
2 quarts Chicken Stock (page 294) or canned chicken broth, boiling
1 cup Red Bell Pepper Coulis (recipe follows)

Rub chicken with split clove of garlic and olive oil. Season with salt, pepper, and rosemary, and set aside.

Using a mandoline, a Japanese vegetable shredder, or a food processor fitted with a shredding disk, shred the potatoes as fine as angel hair pasta. Dissolve the saffron in the boiling chicken stock and cook the potatoes until just tender, about 5 minutes. Drain and season lightly with salt. Grill the chicken on both sides until just cooked, about 5 minutes altogether. Transfer to heated plates and garnish with potato threads and red bell pepper coulis.

Red Bell Pepper Coulis

1 tablespoon olive oil
¼ cup diced onion
1 cup seeded and coarsely diced red bell pepper
1 tablespoon sherry vinegar

2 tablespoons red wine
1 cup consommé
Salt and pepper
2 tablespoons heavy cream (optional)

Heat a heavy saucepan until very hot, then add oil. Add onions and peppers. Sauté until caramelized and a little burnt for a roasted flavor, about 15 minutes. Add vinegar, then red wine, and reduce by half, about 5 minutes. Add consommé and simmer for 15 minutes. Puree in a food processor and strain to eliminate skins. Season to taste with salt and pepper. For a richer sauce, add the cream.

SERVES 4
PREPARATION TIME: 25 minutes total
COOKING TIME: 40 minutes total

CREAM BISCUITS WITH POACHED FRESH FRUIT AND RASPBERRY SAUCE

2 pears
2 peaches (optional)
3 cups water
1 cup sugar
½ cup white wine
2" piece vanilla bean
1 basket raspberries

½ cup heavy cream
4 Cream Biscuits (recipe follows)
1 cup strawberries, hulled and sliced
1 basket blueberries for garnish
4 sprigs mint for garnish
Confectioners' sugar

Peel, halve, and core/pit pears and peaches, if used. Combine 2 cups water, ½ cup sugar, wine, and vanilla bean in a saucepan and poach pears and peaches separately until tender, 5 to 10 minutes. Drain and cool immediately to arrest cooking.

Combine remaining ½ cup sugar and 1 cup water in a separate saucepan and boil for 5 minutes. Reduce heat, add raspberries, and simmer for 3 minutes. Cool, puree in a blender or food processor, and strain out seeds.

Whip cream and place in a pastry bag fitted with a large star tip. Pour raspberry puree onto 4 dessert plates. Slice biscuits in half and place lower half on top of puree. Pipe cream decoratively onto biscuits. Lay a pear half and a peach half over cream. Arrange strawberry slices around side. Garnish with blueberries and mint sprigs. Dust top of biscuits with confectioners' sugar and place over fruit filling at an angle.

Cream Biscuits

1 cup all-purpose flour
1½ teaspoons baking powder
¼ teaspoon salt

2 tablespoons sugar
2 tablespoons unsalted butter
½ cup heavy cream

Preheat oven to 400°. In a bowl, stir together the flour, baking powder, salt, and sugar. Cut in butter, leaving the mixture very coarse, with lumps about the size of a peanut. Mix in heavy cream, but do not overwork dough. Roll out on a lightly floured surface, ½ inch thick, and cut into four 3½″ rounds. Place on a baking sheet and bake for 15 minutes until flaky and golden. Cool on a rack.

SERVES 4
PREPARATION TIME: 30 minutes total
COOKING TIME: about 40 minutes total

EDITOR'S NOTE: The simple syrup used for poaching the fruit may be saved and used for poaching other fruits. It will keep in the refrigerator, tightly covered, for several days.

A onetime military warehouse transformed into a big, lively restaurant with soaring ceilings and correspondingly expansive views of the San Francisco Bay, which laps just outside, Greens' highly innovative vegetarian menu appeals enormously even to nonvegetarians. Chef Annie Somerville's sure touch with the freshest of organic produce has become a byword around the city.

> **SUMMER BEANS AND CHERRY TOMATOES WITH LEMON AND TARRAGON**
> **LINGUINI WITH ROASTED PEPPERS, BASIL, PINE NUTS, AND NIÇOISE OLIVES**
> **WARM BERRY GRATIN**

SUMMER BEANS AND CHERRY TOMATOES WITH LEMON AND TARRAGON •

1 quart water
Salt
1½ pounds assorted fresh summer beans (such as young Blue Lake green beans, Romano, and yellow wax beans)
1½ cups sweet, ripe cherry tomatoes (preferably red and yellow pear tomatoes or sweet 100s) stems removed

1 large handful rocket, washed and spun dry
Lemon-Tarragon Vinaigrette (recipe follows)
Additional lemon juice and zest, as needed
Freshly ground black pepper

Bring water to a boil and salt lightly. Remove stem end of beans, leaving tail. Blanch beans for about 1 minute, until tender yet still crisp. Blanch different varieties of beans separately, as cooking times will vary slightly. Drain beans, plunge into cold water, and drain again. Cut cherry tomatoes in half if large, leave whole if small. Toss rocket in vinaigrette and arrange on a serving platter. Toss beans and cherry tomatoes in vinaigrette to coat, seasoning with additional lemon juice and lemon zest if salad needs more acidity. Sprinkle generously with freshly ground black pepper.

Lemon-Tarragon Vinaigrette

2 tablespoons freshly squeezed lemon
 juice
Grated zest of 1 lemon
1 tablespoon champagne vinegar
1 small shallot, peeled and minced

1 tablespoon coarsely chopped fresh
 tarragon
½ cup virgin olive oil
Salt and pepper

Whisk together lemon juice, lemon zest, vinegar, shallot, and tarragon. Slowly whisk in olive oil and season to taste with salt and pepper.

SERVES 4

PREPARATION TIME: 20 minutes total

COOKING TIME: 3 to 4 minutes

LINGUINI WITH ROASTED PEPPERS, BASIL, PINE NUTS, AND NIÇOISE OLIVES

1 large yellow bell pepper, roasted,
 peeled, and seeded (page 291)
1 large red bell pepper, roasted, peeled,
 and seeded (page 291)
½ cup virgin olive oil
Balsamic vinegar
3 cloves garlic, peeled and minced

Salt and pepper
¼ cup pine nuts
⅓ cup Niçoise olives, Ligurian olives,
 or other small black olives with pits
1 small bunch fresh basil
1 pound fresh egg linguini
½ pound freshly grated Parmesan cheese

Slice roasted and peeled bell peppers into ¼"-wide strips. Place in a dish with a little of the olive oil. Sprinkle lightly with balsamic vinegar, a little of the garlic, salt, and pepper. Marinate for at least 20 minutes, or overnight if more convenient.

Preheat oven to 375°. Place pine nuts on a baking sheet and toast until they turn golden, about 5 minutes. Pit and coarsely chop the olives. Strip basil leaves from stems and chop, or bundle together and slice into thin ribbons.

Cook linguini in boiling salted water until *al dente*, 1 to 1½ minutes if the pasta is freshly made. Do not overcook. Drain pasta and combine with bell peppers, remaining olive oil, remaining minced garlic, toasted pine nuts, and chopped olives. Season to taste with salt, pepper, and a little balsamic vinegar. Divide among warmed plates and sprinkle with Parmesan.

SERVES 4

PREPARATION TIME: 10 minutes, not including marination time

COOKING TIME: 5 minutes

WARM BERRY GRATIN •

1 basket blueberries

1 basket blackberries

1 basket raspberries

¾ cup crème fraîche

Framboise or kirsch

2 tablespoons brown sugar

Preheat broiler. Wash blueberries and drain. Sort through blackberries and raspberries, but do not wash. Ladle 2 tablespoons crème fraiche into each of 4 gratin dishes and arrange ⅓ cup of each of the berries on top. Sprinkle each gratin with a very small amount of framboise or kirsch, then sprinkle with 1½ teaspoons brown sugar. Place gratins under broiler for 2 to 3 minutes, until berries begin to bubble and release their juices. Serve immediately.

SERVES 4

PREPARATION TIME: 10 minutes

COOKING TIME: 2 to 3 minutes

CHEF'S NOTE: Berries are one of the best things summer has to offer. Use any berries that are available as long as they are ripe and sweet.

This sophisticated, Hong Kong–style restaurant, decorated with handsome Chinese antiques and teak furnishings, is located in the sleek Embarcadero #4 complex, and has fine harbor views. Their award-winning chefs specialize in dim sum and elegant Chinese banquets.

ROAST DUCK SALAD
GOLDEN SHRIMP PUFFS
MARINATED PAN-FRIED PORK CHOPS
CRISPY BANANA ROLLS

ROAST DUCK SALAD ●

1 duck, roasted and cooled
4 red bell peppers, halved, seeded, and
   deribbed
4 cups very fresh bean sprouts

Vegetable oil
4 eggs, lightly beaten
Sesame Dressing (recipe follows)

Remove meat from bones and julienne the duck meat. Cut bell peppers into julienne. Trim bean sprouts and blanch in boiling water for a few seconds. Cool under cold running water and drain well.

   Heat a skillet and grease with a little oil. Pour in eggs and make a thin egg pancake. Roll the pancake and cut into julienne. Combine duck meat, bell peppers, bean sprouts, and julienned egg and toss well. Place on a platter. Drizzle with dressing.

Sesame Dressing

½ cup white vinegar
½ cup sesame paste
2 tablespoons sugar
3 teaspoons salt

2 tablespoons Oriental sesame oil
¼ cup soy sauce
½ cup tomato ketchup
½ cup water

Combine all ingredients and place in a saucepan. Bring to a boil, remove from heat, and cool.

SERVES 4
PREPARATION TIME: 15 minutes (precooked duck)
COOKING TIME: 4 minutes total

GOLDEN SHRIMP PUFFS •

10 ounces raw peeled and deveined
   shrimp
½ teaspoon salt
1 large egg
½ teaspoon juice from fresh gingerroot
   (puree in food processor)

1 tablespoon rice wine or dry sherry
1 tablespoon cornstarch
1 cup fine, dry bread crumbs
1½ quarts vegetable oil

Place shrimp in a food processor and grind to a paste. Add salt, egg, ginger juice, rice wine or sherry, and cornstarch; mix well. Form paste into 12 balls. Roll in bread crumbs.

Heat oil to 375° (see Editor's Note, page 130), and deep-fry puffs until golden brown, 1 to 2 minutes.

SERVES 4
PREPARATION TIME: 5 minutes
COOKING TIME: 1 to 2 minutes

MARINATED PAN-FRIED PORK CHOPS •

4 boneless pork chops, 3 ounces each
2 tablespoons curry powder
2 tablespoons minced garlic
2 teaspoons Chinese five-spice powder
¼ cup soy sauce
3 teaspoons salt

½ teaspoon white pepper
2 tablespoons sugar
2 tablespoons rice wine or dry sherry
4 large egg yolks
6 tablespoons potato starch
½ cup vegetable oil

Quarter the pork chops and place in a bowl. Combine curry powder, garlic, five-spice powder, soy sauce, salt, pepper, sugar, and rice wine or sherry. Pour over pork and mix well. Let stand for 30 minutes. Add egg yolks and mix well. Add potato starch and mix again.

Heat oil in a skillet. Fry pork over medium heat until golden brown on both sides, about 5 minutes per side.

SERVES 4
PREPARATION TIME: 10 minutes, plus marination time
COOKING TIME: 10 minutes

CRISPY BANANA ROLLS •

2 bananas
8 spring roll wrappers

1 egg, beaten, for sealing packages
1 quart vegetable oil

Cut bananas in half, then split the halves lengthwise. Place a piece of banana on a spring roll wrapper and fold up ends, then roll up as for a spring roll, sealing the flaps with beaten egg.

Heat oil to 375° (see Editor's Note, page 130), and fry banana rolls until golden brown, about 2 minutes.

SERVES 4
PREPARATION TIME: 5 minutes
COOKING TIME: 2 minutes

An offshoot of the original Harry's Bar in Florence, this restaurant offers contemporary Italian food in streamlined surroundings, with the accent on wood paneling and crisp white napery.

INSALATA ALL'ARANCIA *(Salad with Oranges and Fennel)*

PENNE ALLA PUTTANESCA *(Pasta with Olives, Capers, and Tomato Sauce)*

POLLO AL PEPERONI *(Chicken with Red and Yellow Bell Peppers)*

FRESH FRUIT OF CHOICE

INSALATA ALL'ARANCIA •

2 oranges, peeled and sectioned (page 292)
1 head fennel, trimmed and thinly sliced
1 pound seedless green grapes
2 bunches watercress, large stalks removed

2 tablespoons freshly squeezed lemon juice
¼ cup virgin olive oil
Salt and pepper

Place orange sections, sliced fennel, grapes, and watercress in a bowl. Whisk lemon juice and olive oil together, and season to taste with salt and pepper. Pour over salad and toss gently but thoroughly.

SERVES 4
PREPARATION TIME: 10 minutes
COOKING TIME: None

PENNE ALLA PUTTANESCA

6 tablespoons virgin olive oil
2 teaspoons finely chopped fresh oregano
40 oil-cured black Italian olives, pitted
¼ cup capers, drained
¼ teaspoon hot chili pepper flakes

2½ cups Tomato Sauce (recipe follows)
1 pound penne (short, nib-shaped, tubular pasta)
Freshly grated Parmesan cheese

In a skillet, heat oil until sizzling. Add oregano, olives, capers, and hot pepper flakes. Cook for 1½ to 2 minutes over medium heat, then add tomato sauce. Heat until tomato sauce bubbles.

In a separate pot of boiling salted water, cook pasta until *al dente*, about 10 minutes. Drain, and put in a warmed serving bowl. Add sauce, and mix well. Serve with grated Parmesan cheese on the side.

Tomato Sauce

2 pounds fresh Roma tomatoes
½ cup virgin olive oil
1 teaspoon finely chopped garlic
½ cup coarsely chopped onion

1 piece prosciutto, 3 to 4 ounces
5 large basil leaves, coarsely chopped
Salt and pepper to taste

Cut tomatoes in half lengthwise, place in a heavy saucepan, and cook over low-medium heat, covered, for 20 minutes.

Heat half the olive oil in a separate skillet. Sauté garlic, onion, and prosciutto until onion is transparent, about 5 minutes. Add this mixture to tomatoes and simmer, uncovered, for 30 minutes. Remove and discard the prosciutto. Puree tomato mixture in a food processor, and return to pan. Add remaining olive oil, basil, salt, and pepper. Simmer, uncovered, for 15 minutes more.

SERVES 4
PREPARATION TIME: 20 minutes total
COOKING TIME: 1 hour total

CHEF'S NOTE: If using canned Roma tomatoes, use 2 cups tomatoes with their juice. Omit the first 20-minute cooking period.

POLLO AL PEPERONI

2 chickens, 2½ pounds each
1 red bell pepper, halved, seeded, and deribbed
1 yellow bell pepper, halved, seeded, and deribbed
1 cup virgin olive oil
4 cloves garlic, peeled and finely chopped

1½ 16-ounce cans Roma tomatoes, chopped, juice reserved
1 cup Chicken Stock (page 294) or canned chicken broth
3 tablespoons finely chopped fresh oregano
Salt and pepper

Preheat oven to 400°. Cut chickens into quarters. Cut bell peppers into strips.

Pour olive oil into a large roasting pan or ovenproof sauté pan and heat on top of stove. When oil is hot, sear chicken parts over high heat for about 2 minutes on each side, or until browned. Add bell peppers, garlic, chopped tomatoes, chicken stock, oregano, and salt and pepper to taste. Cover loosely with aluminum foil, set in preheated oven, and bake for 10 minutes. Uncover, add juice from tomatoes, and bake for another 20 minutes, until most of the juices have evaporated.

SERVES 4

PREPARATION TIME: 10 minutes

COOKING TIME: 35 minutes

Patricia Unterman serves some of the freshest seafood to be had in San Francisco—or possibly anywhere—in great contemporary style: simple, straightforward, and perfectly prepared. A true bistro atmosphere prevails at this restaurant, with its polished brass accents, coat hooks along the walls, and a blackboard-and-chalk menu describing the day's catch, sauce options, and wine suggestions.

WARM GOAT CHEESE WITH PECANS AND GREENS
HALIBUT IN PARCHMENT WITH GINGER MUSHROOMS
APRICOT CRISP

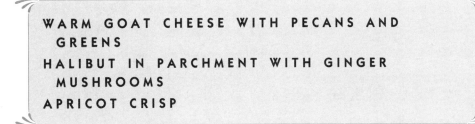

WARM GOAT CHEESE WITH PECANS AND GREENS •

2 cloves garlic, peeled
1 sprig fresh rosemary
1 cup virgin olive oil
6 to 8 ounce log fresh white goat cheese, about 2½" diameter
½ cup coarsely chopped pecans

4 generous handfuls mixed greens (frisée, curly green leaf lettuce, red leaf lettuce, arugula, watercress, mâche, endive)
Sherry-Shallot Vinaigrette (recipe follows)

Marinate garlic and rosemary in olive oil overnight. Slice goat cheese into ½"-thick rounds and marinate in the oil for 1 hour, or overnight if more convenient.

Preheat oven to 350°. Place chopped pecans on a baking sheet and toast about 5 minutes, until they start to smell aromatic. Watch carefully to be sure they do not burn. Lift goat cheese from marinade and coat each slice with toasted nuts. Place on a baking sheet.

Wash and dry salad greens, combine them in a bowl, and toss with just enough sherry-shallot vinaigrette to coat each leaf without any dressing remaining in the bottom of the bowl. Divide salad greens among 4 plates. Warm the goat cheese slices under the broiler or in a toaster oven until the cheese just starts to melt, 1 minute or less. Be careful not to burn the nuts! Place the warm goat cheese on top of the salad and serve immediately.

Sherry-Shallot Vinaigrette

¼ cup minced shallots
¼ cup sherry vinegar (preferably La Bodega)

¼ teaspoon salt
Freshly ground black pepper
¾ cup virgin olive oil

In a bowl, stir together the shallots, vinegar, salt, and pepper. Whisk in the olive oil and taste for salt. Adjust seasoning if necessary.

SERVES 4
PREPARATION TIME: 15 minutes, plus marination overnight
COOKING TIME: 5 or 6 minutes

HALIBUT IN PARCHMENT WITH GINGER MUSHROOMS

4 filets of halibut (or Atlantic cod or other medium-grained white-fleshed fish)
Soy-Ginger Marinade (recipe follows)
6 tablespoons Clarified Butter (page 291)
½ pound fresh shiitake mushrooms, thinly sliced
1 pound regular white mushrooms, thinly sliced
2 tablespoons peeled and minced fresh gingerroot

2 tablespoons minced garlic
Salt
½ tablespoon seeded and minced serrano or jalapeño chili pepper
6 scallions, green tops only (save white bulbs for another use), cut into thin threads on the diagonal, plus extra sliced tops for garnish
4 tablespoons (½ stick) butter
Hot cooked rice (preferably aromatic basmati)

Marinate fish in soy-ginger marinade for 10 minutes. Heat clarified butter in a large sauté pan. Add mushrooms and toss until all the butter is absorbed. Add ginger and garlic and cook over medium-high heat until mushrooms are cooked through, about 2 minutes. Add salt and minced chili to taste. Cook for a moment longer and set aside.

Fold four 12″-×-16″ sheets of baking parchment or aluminum foil in half, making a triangle. Open each one out and place a marinated fish filet above the crease. (Discard marinade.) Top with one quarter of mushrooms and one quarter of sliced scallion tops. Dot with butter, then close packet by bringing top half over and crimping and folding edges together to make a tight seal. Packets can be prepared in advance to this point and refrigerated for a few hours.

Preheat oven to 375° and preheat a baking sheet. Place packets on hot baking sheet and bake for 6 to 8 minutes, depending on thickness of fish. Place a packet on each plate and cut open. Sprinkle with more scallions and serve with rice.

Soy-Ginger Marinade

¼ cup soy sauce

¼ cup water

¾ cup lemon juice

½ teaspoon minced garlic

1 tablespoon peeled minced fresh gingerroot

Combine all ingredients.

SERVES 4

PREPARATION TIME: 30 minutes, plus marination time

COOKING TIME: about 10 minutes

APRICOT CRISP

4 cups pitted apricot halves

Juice of 1 lemon

¼ to ½ cup white sugar, or none at all, depending on tartness of fruit

1 cup all-purpose flour

¼ pound (1 stick) cold unsalted butter, cut into pieces

1 cup brown sugar, firmly packed

Pinch salt

1 teaspoon ground cinnamon

Softly whipped cream, crème fraîche, or vanilla ice cream

Preheat oven to 375°. Toss fruit in lemon juice and white sugar to taste. Pile into a 9″ pie pan.

Put flour, butter, brown sugar, salt, and cinnamon in a bowl. Rub together with fingertips until mixture resembles coarse meal. The butter should not be totally incorporated. Sprinkle on top of fruit and bake for 45 minutes, until fruit bubbles up at corners and top is brown. Serve with whipped cream, crème fraîche, or vanilla ice cream.

SERVES 4

PREPARATION TIME: 10 minutes

COOKING TIME: 45 minutes

Proprietor Alice Wong brings a touch of authentic Hong Kong opulence to this popular Peninsula restaurant, which boasts silk tapestries and hand-carved screens, and which is one of several Flower Lounge restaurants owned by her Hong Kong–based family. Chef Philip Lo produces subtly-spiced, authentic Cantonese food, and a number of fine northern Chinese dishes as well.

TENDER SQUAB MARINATED IN BEER
BRAISED TOFU DUMPLINGS STUFFED WITH
 SHRIMP AND CRAB
PRAWNS WITH WALNUTS
TARO WITH TAPIOCA

TENDER SQUAB MARINATED IN BEER •

1 squab (baby pigeon), about 1 pound
2 whole star anise
3 bay leaves
2 ounces (a 5"-by-1" piece) gingerroot, peeled and sliced
2 scallions, white bulbs and green tops, cut up

2 teaspoons salt
1 cup white wine
2 bottles Tsingtao beer
½ cup liquid fish sauce (available in Chinese markets)

Place squab, star anise, bay leaves, gingerroot, scallions, salt, and wine in a small saucepan with barely enough water to cover the squab. Bring liquid to a boil. Reduce heat to medium and boil for 15 minutes. Drain squab and chill in cold water. Drain again.

In a separate bowl, combine beer and fish sauce. Add squab and marinate, covered, overnight. Chop into small pieces, bones and all, and serve cold.

SERVES 4
PREPARATION TIME: 10 minutes, plus marination time
COOKING TIME: 15 minutes

BRAISED TOFU DUMPLINGS STUFFED WITH SHRIMP AND CRAB

¼ *pound raw fresh shrimp meat*
1 *16-ounce package soft tofu, diced*
1 *ounce fresh crab meat*
3 *teaspoons cornstarch*
½ *teaspoon salt*
Dash pepper
Dash Oriental sesame oil

1 *sprig fresh cilantro (coriander), chopped*
10 *large egg whites*
5 *heads Shanghai (miniature) bok choy*
Oil and salt for frying bok choy
2 *tablespoons vegetable oil*

Sauce

1 *cup Chicken Stock (page 294) or canned chicken broth*
¼ *teaspoon salt*

¼ *teaspoon sugar*
½ *teaspoon oyster sauce*
¾ *teaspoon cornstarch*

Mince shrimp meat. Combine tofu, crab meat, cornstarch, salt, pepper, sesame oil, cilantro, and egg whites with shrimp meat and mix well. Fill 12

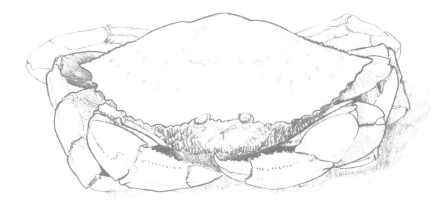

to 16 Chinese tablespoons or regular soup spoons with this paste. Place in top of steamer over simmering water and steam for 5 minutes. Remove dumplings from spoons with a knife tip.

Cut bok choy in quarters lengthwise. Pan-fry with a dash of oil and salt, about 3 minutes. Drain.

Heat the 2 tablespoons oil in a wide pan. Carefully place tofu dumplings in pan, and fry them until golden brown, about 1 minute. Remove from pan and arrange on a warmed platter in 3 rows, placing bok choy in between.

Sauce: Combine chicken stock, salt, sugar, and oyster sauce in a pan and bring to a boil. Mix cornstarch with a little cold water and add to chicken stock. Boil for a few seconds, stirring, until sauce clears and thickens. Pour over tofu dumplings.

SERVES 4
PREPARATION TIME: 25 minutes
COOKING TIME: 15 minutes

PRAWNS WITH WALNUTS

¾ pound fresh prawns (shrimp) in the shell (approximately 32)
1 egg yolk
Salt
Dash pepper
1 cup cornstarch

3 cups vegetable oil
½ cup mayonnaise
½ teaspoon sugar
3 teaspoons water
5 ounces sweet walnuts (glazed walnuts, available in Chinese markets)

Shell, devein, and rinse prawns. Pat dry with paper towels. Combine egg yolk, ¼ teaspoon salt, and pepper. Mix with cornstarch. Dip prawns in this batter.

Heat oil in a deep skillet to 350°. Add prawns one by one, a few at a time, and deep fry for 3 minutes. Remove with a strainer and drain on paper towels. Pour oil out of pan. Add mayonnaise, ¼ teaspoon salt, sugar, and water. Stir well. Add prawns and stir-fry for a few seconds. Place prawns in center of platter and surround with sweet walnuts.

SERVES 4
PREPARATION TIME: 20 minutes
COOKING TIME: 15 minutes

EDITOR'S NOTE: If you do not have a deep-fat frying thermometer, check temperature of oil by throwing in a 1″ cube of bread. Bread should turn golden brown in approximately 60 seconds.

TARO WITH TAPIOCA

¼ cup (1½ ounces) small pearl tapioca
   (not the quick-cooking variety)
2½ cups water
½ pound taro root, peeled .

½ cup milk
6 tablespoons coconut milk
¾ cup sugar

Soak tapioca overnight in 1 cup water. Steam taro until very soft, about 30 minutes, and slice. Blend taro with milk and coconut milk to form a paste. Drain tapioca, place in a saucepan, and add ½ cup fresh water. Bring to a boil and then simmer until soft and transparent, about 5 minutes. (Let stand for a few minutes after cooking; it will become more jellylike.)

In a separate nonstick pan, combine sugar with 1 cup water and bring to a boil. Add taro paste and tapioca and bring to a boil again, stirring. Taste, and add more sugar if necessary. Serve this soothing dessert warm, in little bowls.

SERVES 4
PREPARATION TIME: 15 minutes, plus soaking overnight
COOKING TIME: about 35 minutes

An upscale, sophisticated Italian restaurant, Il Fornaio serves authentic Italian food in sleek surroundings. Pizza and focaccia are baked in an oak-wood-fired brick oven; rabbit, poultry, and lamb are spit-roasted over an open fire, and the pasta is made on the premises. Although unusual for an Italian restaurant in San Francisco, Il Fornaio has also become famous for its exceptional breakfasts, so a sample breakfast menu is given here in addition to the dinner menu.

TIZIANO *(Champagne Cocktail)*
MANZO SALMISTRATO *(Polenta with Corned Beef Hash)*
BACCA DI SOTTOBOSCO ALLA CREMA FRESCA
  (Berries with Crème Fraîche)

CAPELLINI AL POMODORO NATURALE *(Pasta with Fresh Tomato)*
GALLETTO AL FORNO *(Baby Chicken Baked in Terracotta)*
TIRAMISÚ *(Layered Rum Cream Dessert)*

TIZIANO •

2 cups champagne (preferably Carpene Malvolti)

1 cup freshly squeezed grape juice
4 grapes

Combine liquids, stir, pour into champagne flutes, and garnish with a grape.
SERVES 4
PREPARATION TIME: 5 minutes
COOKING TIME: None

MANZO SALMISTRATO

Polenta

8 tablespoons (1 stick) butter
6¼ cups water
2 teaspoons sea salt

2¼ cups polenta
4 ounces Parmesan cheese, grated
2 ounces Italian Gorgonzola cheese

Corned Beef Hash

12 ounces cooked corned beef, cut into
½" cubes
12 ounces cooked potatoes, fork tender,
cut into ½" cubes

1 sprig rosemary, minced
6 tablespoons Clarified Butter (page
291)

Garnish

2 ounces Italian Gorgonzola
2 ounces mascarpone

8 large eggs
Chopped parsley

Polenta: Grease a glass loaf pan with 2 tablespoons of butter, and set aside. In a deep pot, preferably of tin-lined copper, heat water to a boil. Add salt. Swirl to create a whirlpool effect and drizzle in polenta; continue to swirl. Stir polenta until it pulls away from sides of pan, about 40 minutes. Remove from heat, add cheeses and remaining 6 tablespoons butter. Mix well and pour into prepared loaf pan. Smooth top with a spatula and set aside to cool. Chill in refrigerator.

Corned Beef Hash: Combine corned beef, potatoes, and rosemary. Heat 4 tablespoons of butter and fry beef-potato mixture until crusty golden. Cut four 4½-ounce slices of chilled polenta, and fry in remaining 2 tablespoons of butter until crusty and golden brown.

Garnish: Whip together the Gorgonzola and mascarpone. Poach eggs, remove with slotted spoon, and drain. Place corned beef mixture in center of plates. Arrange polenta slices and eggs alternately on each side. Garnish polenta with cheese mixture and parsley.

SERVES 4
PREPARATION TIME: 20 minutes
COOKING TIME: 1 hour

BACCA DI SOTTOBOSCO ALLA CREMA FRESCA •

1½ pints assorted seasonal berries
4 tablespoons crème fraîche

4 mint leaves

Wash and dry berries. Arrange in bowls; place a tablespoon of crème fraîche on top of each serving. Garnish with mint leaf.

SERVES 4
PREPARATION TIME: 5 minutes
COOKING TIME: None

CAPELLINI AL POMODORO NATURALE •

Salt
6 tablespoons virgin olive oil
3 cups chopped Roma tomatoes,
  unpeeled
20 fresh basil leaves, shredded

1 teaspoon chopped garlic
12 ounces capellini
Sea salt
Freshly ground black pepper

Bring a large pot of water to a boil; add a pinch of salt and touch of olive oil.

Place sauté pan on burner and let it get very hot. Add olive oil and immediately add chopped tomatoes and all accumulated liquid. Reduce for 1 to 2 minutes—there should be plenty of liquid left. Add basil and garlic and set aside.

Add pasta to boiling water and stir so that the strands do not stick together. Boil for 1½ minutes. (Pasta will be not quite *al dente* but will finish cooking with tomatoes.) Return tomato mixture to a simmer and stir in drained pasta—the starch from the pasta will help to thicken the sauce. Pasta will take on a rosy hue, and sauce should cling to it, not pool up in bottom of pan. Quickly season to taste with salt and pepper and serve at once.

SERVES 4
PREPARATION TIME: 10 minutes
COOKING TIME: 4 to 5 minutes

GALLETTO AL FORNO

4 poussins (baby chickens), 14 to 16
  ounces each, or Cornish game hens,
  24 ounces or smaller
Salt and pepper

2 lemons, halved
4 sprigs rosemary
8 cloves garlic, peeled
2 tablespoons virgin olive oil

4 thin slices pancetta
½ cup white wine
4 tablespoons (½ stick) butter, melted

Lemon wedges and cherry tomatoes for garnish
Seasonal vegetables (optional)

Preheat oven to 475°. Soak in water for 10 minutes the top and bottom of an unglazed clay pot that is large enough to hold chickens in one layer. Wash chickens and trim off wings. Season inside with salt and pepper. Stuff cavity of each bird with ½ lemon, 1 sprig rosemary, and 2 cloves garlic. Rub skin with olive oil, and sprinkle with salt and pepper. Drape a slice of pancetta over each chicken. Place in drained clay pot and drizzle with wine and butter. Cover pot and bake for 30 to 40 minutes, depending on size of birds.

Remove chickens from pot and place on warmed plates. Garnish with lemon wedges and cherry tomatoes. Serve seasonal vegetables, if desired.

SERVES 4
PREPARATION TIME: 15 minutes
COOKING TIME: 30 to 40 minutes

TIRAMISÚ

Genoise Layers

6 large eggs
¾ cup sugar
½ teaspoon vanilla extract

1 cup all-purpose flour
3 tablespoons unsalted butter, melted
  and cooled to lukewarm

Zabaglione

4 large egg yolks
¼ cup sugar

3 tablespoons Marsala

Mascarpone Cream

¼ pound mascarpone
¾ cup heavy cream
6 tablespoons confectioners' sugar, sifted

1 large egg yolk
½ teaspoon vanilla extract

Soaking Liquid

½ cup espresso coffee, cooled

½ cup dark rum

Garnish

2 to 3 tablespoons unsweetened cocoa
  powder

Preheat oven to 350°. Generously butter and flour three 9″ layer cake pans.

Genoise: In the top of a 2- to 3-quart glass or stainless-steel double boiler, mix eggs, sugar, and vanilla. Set over barely simmering water until just lukewarm, stirring occasionally, 5 to 10 minutes. Pour into the bowl of an electric mixer. Beat at high speed until tripled in volume, scraping sides of bowl several times, about 10 minutes. Remove bowl from stand. Sift ¼ cup of flour over egg mixture and fold in with a rubber spatula until smooth. Repeat 3 times with remaining flour. Pour butter around edge of bowl; fold in gently until thoroughly combined, but do not deflate batter. Divide batter equally among the 3 prepared pans. Smooth tops gently with a rubber spatula. Bake until springy to the touch and edges begin to pull away from sides of pans, 10 to 15 minutes. Loosen edges and invert layers onto racks to cool. Each layer should be about ½″ thick.

Zabaglione: In top of a 2- to 3-quart glass or stainless-steel double boiler, off the heat, beat egg yolks and sugar with a hand-held electric mixer or whisk until mixture is lemon-colored and creamy, about 5 minutes. Set over barely simmering water. Add Marsala and continue beating until egg mixture increases in volume and holds soft peaks, about 6 minutes. Remove from heat and set aside. There should be about 2 cups.

Mascarpone Cream: In a small bowl, beat cheese until smooth and set aside. In a large bowl, beat cream until it holds soft peaks. Stir in cheese, confectioners' sugar, egg yolk, and vanilla. There should be about 2½ cups.

To Assemble: Place a genoise layer in a flat-bottomed shallow casserole or bowl, 9″ or a little more in diameter. Mix espresso and rum together; brush a third of mixture evenly over cake. Spread with a third of the mascarpone cream, then spread with a third of the zabaglione. Repeat with remaining genoise layers, soaking liquid, mascarpone cream, and zabaglione to make 3 layers, ending with zabaglione. Sift cocoa powder evenly on top of dessert. Cover lightly and refrigerate for at least 4 hours to blend flavors.

Dessert can be stored, refrigerated, for up to 3 days. To serve, cut into wedges or spoon onto dessert plates.

SERVES 12 TO 14

PREPARATION TIME: 45 minutes, plus chilling time

COOKING TIME: 15 to 20 minutes

CHEF'S NOTE: Bakery-made sponge layer cakes can be used in place of genoise layers. Instant espresso can be used in place of freshly made espresso.

A businessman's restaurant since 1864, long before the Financial District became the Financial District, Jack's is an immensely popular San Francisco institution. Owner Jack Redinger very sensibly retains the restaurant's minimalist Gold Rush decor: high ceilings, white walls, coathooks along the walls, and wooden chairs, but the comprehensive French/Continental menu keeps pace with the times.

> **CELERY VICTOR**
> **CHICKEN MASCOTTE**
> **FRIED CREAM WITH RUM**

CELERY VICTOR

Pinch salt
2 tablespoons freshly squeezed lemon
  juice
4 celery hearts, trimmed

Bibb or butter lettuce leaves
French Dressing (recipe follows)
8 anchovy filets for garnish

Bring a pot of water to a boil. Add salt and lemon juice. Add celery hearts and simmer until tender, about 30 minutes. Drain, press gently to remove excess water, and cool. Arrange a bed of lettuce leaves on each plate. Place a celery heart on top of the lettuce, and drizzle with French dressing. Garnish with anchovies.

French Dressing

⅓ cup wine vinegar
⅔ cup virgin olive oil

⅛ teaspoon dry mustard
Salt and pepper

Whisk vinegar, oil, and mustard together and season to taste with salt and pepper.

SERVES 4
PREPARATION TIME: 10 minutes, plus cooling time
COOKING TIME: 30 minutes

CHICKEN MASCOTTE

4 tablespoons (½ stick) butter
2 chickens, about 2¾ pounds each,
   disjointed
12 mushrooms, cut into wedges
4 artichoke hearts, cut into wedges

2 shallots, peeled and chopped
Salt and pepper
½ cup Spanish sherry
1½ cups Chicken Stock (page 294) or
   canned chicken broth

Melt butter in a skillet and sauté chicken pieces until golden on all sides, about 10 minutes. Remove and set aside.

Pour off all but 2 tablespoons of fat from skillet and add mushrooms, artichokes, and shallots. Sauté until golden, about 3 minutes. Return chicken to skillet. Season to taste with salt and pepper. Add sherry and stock and bring to a boil. Reduce heat and simimer until chicken is tender, about 20 minutes.

SERVES 4
PREPARATION TIME: 15 minutes
COOKING TIME: 35 minutes

FRIED CREAM WITH RUM •

3 large eggs
6 large egg yolks
1¼ cups all-purpose flour
1¼ cups sugar
¼ teaspoon salt

1 quart milk
¼ pound (1 stick) unsalted butter, cut
   up
1 tablespoon vanilla extract

Coating

Vegetable oil for deep-frying
2 large eggs
2 tablespoons water

1 cup fine bread crumbs
2 to 4 tablespoons sugar
½ cup dark rum, warmed

Butter an 8"-×-12" rectangular dish and set aside. Combine eggs and egg yolks and beat lightly. Whisk in flour, sugar, and salt, and mix thoroughly. Bring milk to a boil. Reduce heat and add egg mixture, stirring constantly. Add butter and continue stirring until butter is melted and mixture is very thick, about 7 minutes. Remove from heat and stir in vanilla. Pour into buttered dish (the mixture should be about ¾" deep), cool, and then chill in refrigerator until firm.

Coating: Heat oil in a deep frying pan to a depth of 2″. (It should reach 350° on a deep-fat frying thermometer, or a 1″ cube of bread should turn golden brown in 60 seconds.) Beat eggs lightly with the water. Cut chilled cream into 2½″ squares. Dip in egg mixture and then in crumbs and fry until golden, about 2 minutes. Immediately place on dessert plates and sprinkle with sugar. Pour heated rum on top of each portion and light with a match.

SERVES 8
PREPARATION TIME: 15 minutes, plus chilling time
COOKING TIME: 15 minutes

EDITOR'S NOTE: Any extra unfried custard will keep in the refrigerator for 3 days.

Jean Pierre Moullé, a native of Bordeaux, first distinguished himself in the Bay Area as chef of Chez Panisse and Pierre at the Meridien. Today, he and his wife, Denise Lurton-Moullé, a member of one of Bordeaux's most active wine-growing families, run a novel program for interested visitors that combines wine appreciation with cooking lessons. Guests stay in an eighteenth-century château and explore the regional cuisine in depth.

MUSSELS BAKED WITH CREAM
FILET OF BEEF IN HERB AND MUSTARD BUTTER
FLOATING ISLANDS WITH RASPBERRIES

MUSSELS BAKED WITH CREAM

6 dozen mussels in the shell
1 tablespoon butter
4 shallots, peeled and chopped
1 clove garlic, peeled and chopped
1 bouquet garni (sprig thyme, sprig parsley, and a bay leaf)
1 cup dry white wine

¼ cup Pineau de Charente (see Editor's Note below)
3 large egg yolks
1 cup heavy cream
Pinch curry powder
Lemon juice
2 tablespoons chopped fresh parsley

Rinse mussels well in cold water and scrub to remove any "beards." Heat butter in a shallow pan and add shallots, garlic, and bouquet garni. Cook over low heat for 5 minutes to soften. Pour in wine and bring to a boil. Add the mussels. Cover pan and steam mussels until they open, about 2 minutes. Discard any that do not open.

Remove the top shell from each mussel and arrange the lower shell with the mussel in a baking dish large enough to hold them in one layer.

Strain the cooking juices and reduce by one third over high heat, about 5 minutes. Add the Pineau.

Preheat oven to 375°. In a bowl, mix egg yolks, cream, curry powder, and lemon juice to taste. Add this mixture to the reduced juices and cook, stirring constantly, until the sauce thickens, about 7 minutes. Taste for seasoning, and add more lemon juice if required.

Bake mussels in preheated oven for 5 minutes. Pour sauce over mussels and sprinkle with parsley. Serve immediately.

SERVES 4
PREPARATION TIME: 25 minutes
COOKING TIME: 25 minutes

EDITOR'S NOTE: Pineau de Charente is a sweet fortified wine made in the Charente region of France. When the wine is made, Cognac is added to arrest fermentation of the grapes, so it has a relatively high alcohol content. It is usually served chilled as an apéritif before meals. If unavailable, add a dash of Cognac and 3 tablespoons regular dry white wine

FILET OF BEEF IN HERB AND MUSTARD BUTTER

6 tablespoons (¾ stick) unsalted butter, softened
1 teaspoon chopped fresh tarragon
1 teaspoon chopped fresh chives
1 teaspoon chopped fresh parsley, plus extra for garnish
1 teaspoon chopped fresh chervil
2 tablespoons Dijon mustard
Juice of ½ lemon

Black pepper
4 slices filet of beef, approximately 8 ounces each
Salt
¼ cup water
8 ounces wild mushrooms (cepes, morels, chanterelles, etc.), sliced
2 shallots, peeled and chopped

In a bowl, mix 3 tablespoons of butter with herbs, mustard, and lemon juice. Season with black pepper. Spread in the bottom of a serving platter.

Heat 2 tablespoons of butter in a heavy sauté pan until foaming. Sear meat quickly on both sides, about 4 minutes altogether and season with salt and pepper. If butter gets too dark, discard and replace with fresh butter. Turn off heat and let meat rest on top of the herb butter for 10 minutes.

Remove meat from pan and drain off fat. Add water to pan and reduce liquid to a glaze over high heat, about 2 minutes. When ready to serve, spoon this glaze over the meat.

In a separate pan, heat remaining tablespoon of butter and sauté mushrooms quickly, about 5 minutes. Add shallots and cook for 1 minute. Season with salt and pepper and garnish with chopped parsley. Arrange around beef and serve immediately.

SERVES 4
PREPARATION TIME: 30 minutes
COOKING TIME: about 12 minutes

FLOATING ISLANDS WITH RASPBERRIES •

1 cup milk
½ vanilla bean
3 large eggs, separated
3 tablespoons sugar

Pinch salt
1 basket fresh raspberries for garnish
Mint leaves for garnish

Place milk and vanilla bean in a saucepan and slowly bring to a boil. Beat egg whites until stiff. Using 2 spoons, shape meringue into large "eggs" and place in simmering milk. Poach until firm, about 1 minute per side. Drain and reserve.

Strain the milk. Whisk egg yolks, sugar, and salt in a bowl until light and thick. Pour the hot milk into the yolk mixture, whisking constantly, and return entire mixture to saucepan. Cook over medium heat, stirring constantly with a wooden spoon. The custard or crème anglaise is cooked when it coats the spoon (or reaches 165° on a candy thermometer), about 10 minutes. Strain into a bowl, cover, and refrigerate until needed.

To serve, pour custard onto dessert plates, top with poached meringues, and garnish with fresh raspberries and mint leaves.

SERVES 4

PREPARATION TIME: 10 minutes, plus chilling time

COOKING TIME: 15 minutes

EDITOR'S NOTE: This classic dessert is known as *Oeufs à la Neige* or Snow Eggs in France. Some chefs like to beat 1 tablespoon sugar into the egg whites; it is up to individual taste.

Restaurant design elements such as high ceilings, stepped arches, open beams, subtle "grapey" colors, and French windows that open onto a dining terrace with superb views of well-tended vines form the suitable backdrop for co-owner/chef John Ash's innovative food. His cuisine is a showcase for Sonoma's very best produce: cheese, free-range poultry, and milk-fed lamb, while nearby Bodega Bay is the source for fresh seafood.

ROASTED EGGPLANT SOUP
WARM SALAD OF WINTER GREENS WITH PANCETTA
GRILLED POLENTA WITH SONOMA JACK CHEESE
POACHED WINTER PEARS WITH GINGER CRÈME ANGLAISE

ROASTED EGGPLANT SOUP

3 medium eggplant, about 1 pound each
⅓ cup virgin olive oil, plus extra for baking sheet
2 medium onions, peeled and thinly sliced
⅓ cup minced shallots (or scallions)
2 cups thinly sliced, seeded red bell pepper
3 tablespoons minced garlic
2 quarts Chicken Stock (page 294) or canned chicken broth

3 cups peeled, seeded, and diced tomatoes (fresh or canned)
½ teaspoon chopped fresh thyme
2 tablespoons chopped fresh basil
½ teaspoon fennel seeds
½ teaspoon dried red pepper flakes
Salt and pepper
Crème fraîche or dairy sour cream for garnish

Preheat oven to 450°. Slice unpeeled eggplant into rounds and lay on oiled baking sheet. Heat ⅓ cup oil in a heavy sauté pan or skillet. Sauté onions, shallots, bell pepper, and garlic until soft but not brown, about 6 minutes. Spread on top of eggplant rounds and roast for 15 to 20 minutes, or until

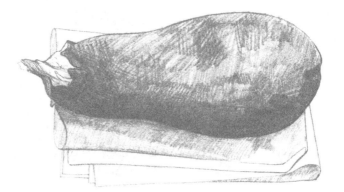

eggplant is soft. Watch carefully so that topping does not burn—it should be toasty brown.

Puree eggplant mixture in a food processor with stock, tomato, and seasonings. Gently reheat and correct seasoning. Ladle into soup bowls and garnish with a dollop of crème fraîche or sour cream.

SERVES 6 TO 8
PREPARATION TIME: 30 minutes
COOKING TIME: about 25 minutes

WARM SALAD OF WINTER GREENS WITH PANCETTA ●

6 cups winter greens (such as
  combination of mustard, kale, endive,
  spinach, and radicchio)
6 thin slices pancetta
6 tablespoons walnut oil

4 tablespoons raspberry vinegar
2 tablespoons honey
2 tablespoons lightly toasted pine nuts,
  for garnish
Chrysanthemum petals for garnish
  (optional)

Wash greens thoroughly and tear into serving-sized pieces.

Sauté pancetta in a nonstick skillet until lightly cooked, about 3 minutes, drain, and keep warm.

In a large skillet, heat walnut oil, vinegar, and honey. Add greens and stir for a few seconds, until slightly wilted; do not overcook.

Serve on warmed plates garnished with pancetta, pine nuts, and chrysanthemum petals, if used.

SERVES 6
PREPARATION TIME: 10 minutes
COOKING TIME: 5 minutes

GRILLED POLENTA WITH SONOMA JACK CHEESE

*1 quart Chicken Stock (page 294) or
canned chicken broth*
Salt
2 teaspoons ground white pepper
1 teaspoon minced fresh thyme
1 cup polenta or yellow cornmeal
8 tablespoons (1 stick) butter
½ cup minced mushrooms
*½ cup minced scallions (white bulbs and
part of green tops)*

Freshly ground black pepper
½ cup dry white wine
1 tablespoon minced fresh parsley
½ pound sliced Sonoma jack cheese
*⅓ pound fresh shiitake mushrooms,
grilled or sautéed in butter, for
garnish*
*1 ounce sun-dried tomatoes packed in
oil, drained and slivered, for garnish*

In a large saucepan, bring stock, salt to taste, white pepper, and thyme to a boil. Slowly beat in polenta or cornmeal with a whisk to avoid lumps. Reduce heat to low and stir to prevent sticking. Cook slowly for 10 minutes.

In a separate skillet, heat 2 tablespoons of butter. Sauté minced mushrooms and scallions until just starting to brown, about 5 minutes. Season with a little salt and pepper, add wine, and reduce until most of the wine cooks away. Add to polenta mixture with remaining 6 tablespoons of butter and the parsley.

Butter a large shallow dish or baking sheet. Spread polenta mixture in the dish to a depth of ½" and smooth top. Cool, cover with plastic wrap, and refrigerate. Can be made 1 or 2 days ahead of time.

Cut polenta into 4" diamonds. Grill until surface is lightly toasted. Turn, cover with a slice of jack cheese and grill until cheese is just starting to melt. Serve warm, garnished with grilled shiitake mushrooms and slivers of sun-dried tomatoes.

SERVES 6
PREPARATION TIME: 15 minutes, plus chilling time
COOKING TIME: 30 minutes

CHEF'S NOTE: Diamonds of polenta may be sautéed in Clarified Butter (page 291) instead of toasted on grill.

POACHED WINTER PEARS WITH GINGER CRÈME ANGLAISE

6 firm winter pears
2½ cups white wine
1 cup sugar

1 3" piece lemon zest
1 small vanilla bean, split (optional)
3 ounces mascarpone

Ginger Crème Anglaise

¼ cup peeled and chopped gingerroot
½ cup sugar
¼ cup water
2 cups half and half

1 vanilla bean, or ½ teaspoon vanilla
    extract
5 large egg yolks

Peel pears, leaving stems on, and core from underneath. In a saucepan just large enough to hold pears upright, combine wine, sugar, lemon zest, and vanilla bean if used. Bring to a boil and simmer for 5 minutes. Add pears and poach for 10 minutes, or until cooked through. (A toothpick should pierce them easily.) Allow pears to cool in the poaching liquid. Drain (saving liquid to poach other fruits), and stuff cored cavity with mascarpone.

Ginger Crème Anglaise: In a heavy-bottomed saucepan, place chopped ginger, 2 tablespoons of sugar, and the water. Simmer until syrup becomes very thick, about 10 minutes, but do not allow it to turn color and caramelize. Add half and half and vanilla bean or extract and bring to a boil. Remove from heat and let stand for 30 to 60 minutes.

Beat egg yolks with remaining sugar. Reheat cream mixture to simmering point, and whisk into egg yolk mixture. Return entire mixture to pan and cook, stirring constantly, until thickened, or until it reaches 182° on a candy thermometer. Fill a large bowl with shaved ice and set a second bowl within it. Strain the custard into this bowl and cool, stirring occasionally.

To serve, pour a pool of crème anglaise onto each dessert plate. Top with a poached stuffed pear.

SERVES 6
PREPARATION TIME: 20 minutes, plus cooling time
COOKING TIME: 30 minutes

Organized in the manner of a Bordeaux château, Jordan is a fully integrated vineyard and winery complex located in Sonoma's Alexander Valley. The winery does not operate a restaurant, but guest quarters and a private dining room are maintained for the exclusive use of invited guests who are directly involved with the marketing of Jordan's estate-bottled wines. The menus, which are designed to complement these wines, emphasize the freshest local ingredients.

TUNA TARTARE
GRILLED DUCK BREAST WITH BAGNAT
ORANGE SORBET WITH BASIL CREAM

TUNA TARTARE •

1¼ pounds very fresh ahi tuna
1 tablespoon chopped fresh chives
1 tablespoon chopped fresh cilantro
  (coriander)
1 tablespoon chopped fresh dill

Vinaigrette (recipe follows)
6 medium-sized radicchio or butter
  lettuce leaves
1 hard-boiled egg, pressed through a
  sieve

Cut tuna into ¼″ dice. Combine with chives, cilantro, and dill. Toss with vinaigrette and chill until just before serving. Place a lettuce leaf on each serving plate. Top with a ball of tuna tartare, and sprinkle with egg.

Vinaigrette

3 tablespoons freshly squeezed lemon
  juice

9 tablespoons virgin olive oil
Salt and pepper

SERVES 6
PREPARATION TIME: 10 minutes, plus chilling time
COOKING TIME: None

GRILLED DUCK BREAST WITH BAGNAT

6 boneless duck breast halves
Salt and pepper
1 bunch Italian flat leaf parsley,
  destemmed and coarsely chopped by
  hand (about 1 cup, chopped)
2 cloves garlic, peeled and finely minced
3 to 4 anchovy filets, drained and
  minced

2 to 3 tablespoons oil-packed sun-dried
  tomatoes, diced, or 3 tablespoons
  diced pimiento
3 tablespoons balsamic vinegar
Approximately ¾ cup virgin olive oil
Roast potatoes and baby vegetables of
  choice

Prepare an intense charcoal fire. Slash the skin of the duck breasts with 3 or 4 shallow, slanting cuts, season with salt and pepper to taste, and set aside.

In a stainless-steel bowl, combine parsley, garlic, anchovies, sun-dried tomatoes, and balsamic vinegar. Stir in olive oil until the sauce is flavorful but not runny. Season with salt and pepper to taste. (To ensure a rich green color, add the balsamic vinegar not more than 30 minutes before serving.)

Place duck on grill, skin side down, and grill for 8 minutes. Turn over and grill for an additional 8 minutes, or until medium rare. Remove to a warm platter and let stand for 5 minutes before slicing. Slice on the diagonal, and fan out each duck breast on a serving plate. Spoon the room temperature sauce over the hot duck breasts. Garnish with roast potatoes and baby vegetables.

SERVES 6
PREPARATION TIME: 15 minutes
COOKING TIME: 16 to 20 minutes

EDITOR'S NOTE: The result will be different, but the duck breasts can be broiled if no grill is available.

CHEF'S NOTE: Bagnat—a Piedmontese version of salsa verde—is quick and simple to prepare. It is great for meat and fish, as well as for poultry. It will keep for a week in a sealed jar in the refrigerator, but is usually consumed long before then. Don't let the thought of anchovies deter those who don't normally eat them. The flavor they impart, though not dominant, is essential to the success of this sauce.

ORANGE SORBET WITH BASIL CREAM •

8 to 10 sprigs fresh basil (approximately ½ cup, lightly packed)
2 cups heavy cream
2 tablespoons sugar

½ teaspoon cornstarch, dissolved in 1 tablespoon water
Freshly squeezed lemon juice
12 scoops Orange Sorbet (recipe follows)

Cut up stems and leaves of basil, reserving best leaves for garnish. Place cream, sugar, and chopped basil in a saucepan and bring slowly to a boil. Reduce heat and stir in cornstarch mixture. Simmer for a few seconds to thicken slightly. Turn off heat and cover pan. Leave to infuse for 30 minutes, then strain and stir in lemon juice to taste. Refrigerate before serving.

To serve, place 2 scoops of orange sorbet in each of 6 flat, rimmed soup plates (or stemmed glasses) and surround with basil cream. Decorate with reserved basil leaves.

Orange Sorbet

1 quart freshly squeezed orange juice   Sugar to taste

Sweeten orange juice to taste with sugar and freeze in a sorbetière or ice cream machine according to manufacturer's instructions.

SERVES 6
PREPARATION TIME: 10 minutes, plus freezing time
COOKING TIME: 5 minutes, plus infusion time

CHEF'S NOTE: This is a very clean, simple sorbet with concentrated fruit flavor.

American-born chef Ken Hom has been described by Craig Claiborne as "one of the world's greatest authorities on Chinese cooking." His celebrated television series, "Ken Hom's Chinese Cookery," was one of the most successful television cooking shows every produced by the British Broadcasting Corporation (BBC-TV), and was shown in the United States on more than 200 public television stations. Chef Hom speaks several languages and travels throughout the world to conduct cooking demonstrations.

RICE PAPER SHRIMP ROLLS

FIVE-SPICE ROAST SQUAB WITH RICE WINE—
    BUTTER SAUCE

GREEN SALAD WITH SESAME AND WALNUT
    OIL DRESSING

CHINESE PEAR APPLE WARM COMPOTE WITH
    CANDIED GINGER À LA MODE

RICE PAPER SHRIMP ROLLS

Kosher salt
½ pound fresh shrimp, peeled and
    deveined
Pepper
1 tablespoon olive oil
2 tablespoons fresh tarragon leaves
2 tablespoons chopped scallions (white
    bulbs and part of green tops)

2 tablespoons oil-packed sun-dried
    tomatoes
2 cups water
1 2-ounce package bean thread noodles
1 1-pound package edible rice paper
    rounds (available in Oriental grocery
    stores)
2 cups peanut oil

Fill a large bowl with cold water, add 1 tablespoon kosher salt, and gently wash the shrimp in the salt water. Drain and repeat the process. Then rinse the shrimp under cold running water, drain, and blot dry with paper towels.

Combine shrimp with salt and pepper to taste, olive oil, tarragon, scallions, and sun-dried tomatoes. Mix well, cover with plastic wrap, and refrigerate for about 1 hour.

Bring water to a boil, add bean thread noodles, and simmer for 5 minutes. Drain and cool. Chop into 1″ lengths and set aside.

Fill a large bowl with warm water. Dip a rice paper round in the water to soften for a few seconds. Remove and drain on a clean linen towel.

Place 1 shrimp (with a little of the marinade) and about 1 teaspoon bean thread noodles on the edge of the rice paper. Roll the edge over the shrimp and noodles. Fold up both ends, and continue to roll paper. The roll should be compact, like a short, thick cigar, about 3″ long. Set on a plate and repeat the process until all the shrimp mixture is used up—you should have 15 to 16 rolls.

Heat peanut oil in a wok or deep-fryer until moderately hot, about 350° on a deep-fat frying thermometer. Deep-fry the spring rolls a few at a time until crisp, about 5 minutes. They have a tendency to stick to one another, so slide them in one by one, and do only a few at a time. Drain spring rolls on paper towels as they are cooked, and keep warm. Serve at once.

SERVES 4 TO 6

PREPARATION TIME: 45 minutes, plus chilling time

COOKING TIME: 15 minutes

EDITOR'S NOTE: If you do not have a deep-fat frying thermometer, drop a 1″ bread cube into the hot fat and count slowly to 60; if the bread browns in 1 minute, it is at about the right temperature.

FIVE-SPICE ROAST SQUAB WITH RICE WINE–BUTTER SAUCE

6 squab (baby pigeons), 12 to 14 ounces each

1 tablespoon Oriental sesame oil

1 tablespoon Chinese five-spice powder

2 teaspoons kosher salt

1 teaspoon Szechwan peppercorns, roasted (at 400° for 5 minutes) and finely ground

2 tablespoons minced orange zest

½ cup Chicken Stock (page 294) or salt-free canned chicken broth

½ cup rice wine or dry sherry

2 tablespoons butter, cold, cut into small pieces

2 tablespoons finely chopped scallions (white bulbs and green tops)

Cooked rice and snow peas (optional)

Butterfly the squab by cutting out the backbone and spreading them flat with the palm of your hand. To keep the squab in shape while roasting, make 2 little slits through the skin on either side near the tail, and insert the ends of the leg bones in them. Rub birds with sesame oil. Combine five-spice powder, salt, ground peppercorns, and orange zest. Rub squabs with this mixture. Place in a shallow roasting pan skin side up, and leave at room temperature for 1 hour.

Preheat oven to 400°. Roast squabs for 30 minutes without turning, basting once or twice with pan juices. Remove squab from roasting pan and skim off any fat. Place pan over medium heat and deglaze with chicken stock and rice wine or sherry, scraping up brown bits from bottom of pan as you stir. Reduce liquid over high heat until just over ½ cup is left, about 5 minutes. Remove pan from heat and whisk in the butter a bit at a time; add the scallions. Spoon a few tablespoons of sauce on warmed plates and top with squab. Serve with rice and snow peas, if desired.

SERVES 6
PREPARATION TIME: 45 minutes, plus marination time
COOKING TIME: 35 minutes

GREEN SALAD WITH SESAME AND WALNUT OIL DRESSING •

3 tablespoons finely chopped shallots
1 tablespoon Chinese white rice vinegar
Salt and freshly ground black pepper

2 teaspoons Oriental sesame oil
2 tablespoons walnut oil
6 cups assorted young salad greens

Combine all dressing ingredients and whisk together. Pour over salad greens and toss thoroughly.

SERVES 6
PREPARATION TIME: 5 minutes
COOKING TIME: None

CHINESE PEAR APPLE WARM COMPOTE WITH CANDIED GINGER À LA MODE •

1 vanilla bean, split lengthwise
½ cup plus 2 tablespoons sugar
1 cup water
2 pounds Chinese pear apples, peeled, cored, and sliced (see Editor's note below)
3 tablespoons unsalted butter, cut into small pieces

2 tablespoons finely chopped candied ginger
1 tablespoon freshly squeezed lemon juice
6 scoops best-quality vanilla ice cream

Scrape out seeds and pulp from vanilla bean and combine well with the 2 tablespoons sugar. Set aside.

In a medium-sized skillet, combine the ½ cup sugar and water. Bring to a boil and reduce by one third, about 7 minutes. Add sliced pear apple and sugar–vanilla seed mixture. Simmer for 5 minutes. Remove from heat and whisk in butter, a few pieces at a time. Add candied ginger and lemon juice. Mix well and cool slightly. Serve over vanilla ice cream.

SERVES 6
PREPARATION TIME: 15 minutes
COOKING TIME: 15 minutes

EDITOR'S NOTE: Chinese pear apples look like apples but have a pearlike texture. They are available in Oriental groceries and some supermarkets during the winter months.

Located in the splendid new Villa Florence Hotel, Kuleto's is a stylish blend of marble, copper, mahogany, and brass. A Cinderella conversion from a seedy old downtown hotel by famed hotelier Bill Kimpton and restaurant designer Pat Kuleto, Kuleto's wins praise from power-breakfast tycoons, luncheon-eager shoppers, and dinnergoers alike.

BAKED CHÈVRE WITH SUN-DRIED TOMATOES AND BASIL
BREAST OF CHICKEN WITH MUSTARD SAUCE AND CREAMY POLENTA
FRESH FRUIT WITH CHAMPAGNE ZABAGLIONE
BISCOTTI DI NICCIOLI

BAKED CHÈVRE WITH SUN-DRIED TOMATOES AND BASIL •

Olive oil
1 8-ounce log of fresh goat cheese
4 ounces oil-packed sun-dried tomatoes, chopped

½ teaspoon chopped garlic
½ cup chopped fresh basil leaves
Cream crackers

Preheat oven to 450°. Oil a small baking dish lightly with olive oil. Place log of cheese in dish and bake for 25 minutes. Mix together the sun-dried tomatoes, garlic, and basil. Top cheese with this mixture, and serve with crackers.

SERVES 6
PREPARATION TIME: 5 minutes
COOKING TIME: 25 minutes

BREAST OF CHICKEN WITH MUSTARD SAUCE AND CREAMY POLENTA

1½ quarts water

1 cup polenta

Salt and pepper

2 tablespoons virgin olive oil

6 skinless and boneless chicken breast halves, about 6 ounces each

2 tablespoons chopped shallot

1 cup chopped mushrooms

⅓ cup dry Madeira

½ cup heavy cream

2 tablespoons whole-grain mustard

2 tablespoons Dijon mustard

Bring the water to a boil and slowly whisk in polenta. Stir constantly for 10 to 15 minutes, or until thick. Season to taste with salt and pepper.

Preheat oven to 450°. Heat olive oil in an ovenproof sauté pan. Season chicken breasts lightly with salt and pepper and lay in pan. Cook for 1 to 2 minutes, until golden. Turn breasts over and add shallot, mushrooms, Madeira, cream, and mustards. Transfer pan to oven and bake for 8 to 10 minutes, until chicken is fully cooked and sauce coats the back of a spoon. Place a large spoonful of polenta in the center of each plate. Lay a portion of chicken on top and cover with sauce.

SERVES 6

PREPARATION TIME: 10 minutes

COOKING TIME: 25 minutes

FRESH FRUIT WITH CHAMPAGNE ZABAGLIONE

5 large egg yolks

5 tablespoons sugar

¾ cup champagne

1 cup heavy cream

4 cups fresh fruit of choice (such as berries, sliced peaches, etc.)

Place egg yolks, sugar, and champagne in the top of a double boiler, or in a bowl. Whisk over simmering water until pale and thick, 12 to 15 minutes. Transfer custard to a stainless-steel bowl. Beat with a wire whisk until bottom of bowl feels cool to the touch.

In a separate bowl, whip cream until soft peaks form. Fold the whipped cream into the zabaglione custard. Refrigerate until ready to serve. Place fruit in stemmed glasses and cover with zabaglione.

SERVES 6

PREPARATION TIME: 30 minutes

COOKING TIME: 15 minutes

BISCOTTI DI NICCIOLI

¼ pound (1 stick) unsalted butter

1½ cups sugar

½ teaspoon vanilla extract

3 eggs, lightly beaten

Grated zest of 1 orange

3¾ cups all-purpose flour

1 tablespoon baking powder

½ teaspoon salt

1 cup whole hazelnuts

Preheat oven to 325°. Cream together butter, sugar, and vanilla. Slowly beat in eggs, then add the orange zest. Combine flour, baking powder, and salt and stir into batter. And hazelnuts last.

Divide dough in half. On a lightly floured surface, roll dough into two logs, each 2½″ in diameter. Bake for 45 to 60 minutes. Slice on the diagonal and return to oven to dry out, but not to get any darker in color, 10 to 12 minutes.

MAKES APPROXIMATELY 40

PREPARATION TIME: 15 minutes

COOKING TIME: about 1 hour

Reminiscent of a rustic Italian *trattoria*, but located in Kentfield, Marin County, this cozy, family-run restaurant features specialties from all over Italy. Owner/chef Jim Brown makes his own pasta; vegetables and herbs are picked in the Browns' spacious garden according to season; poultry, seafood, and meat all come from the surrounding area.

**FETTUCINE CON FUNGHI, PROSCIUTTO, E
 PANNA** (*Noodles with Mushrooms, Ham, and Cream*)
**SCALOPPINE DI VITELLO ALL'OPPORTO E
 PEPE VERDE** (*Scallops of Veal with Port and Green Peppercorns*)
FRAGOLE CON STREGA (*Strawberries with Strega Liqueur*)

FETTUCINE CON FUNGHI, PROSCIUTTO, E PANNA ●

½ pound fresh white mushrooms
4 quarts water
6 tablespoons (¾ stick) butter
½ teaspoon minced garlic
*¼ pound prosciutto, thinly sliced and cut
 into julienne strips*

2 cups heavy cream
Salt
*1 pound good-quality, freshly made
 fettucine*
*1 cup freshly grated imported Parmesan
 cheese*

Wipe mushrooms clean. Trim off ends of stems, slice mushrooms ⅛″ thick, and set aside. Bring the water to a boil while making sauce.

In a sauté pan that will hold the mushrooms loosely in one layer, melt butter over medium-high heat and sauté garlic for a few seconds. Add mushrooms, increase heat, and sauté, stirring constantly, until they release their juices, about 3 minutes. Reduce heat to medium, add prosciutto, and cook for 2 or 3 minutes. Add cream and continue cooking until cream starts to thicken, about 6 to 8 minutes. Set aside.

Add salt to pot of boiling water. Shake off excess flour from fettucine and drop into pot. Cook for 2 or 3 minutes, until just tender to the bite. Drain thoroughly.

Return sauce to burner and heat through. Add fettucine, tossing to coat pasta with sauce. Add cheese and toss again. Serve immediately.

SERVES 4

PREPARATION TIME: 10 minutes

COOKING TIME: 20 minutes

SCALOPPINE DI VITELLO ALL'OPPORTO E PEPE VERDE ●

3 tablespoons virgin olive oil
½ cup all-purpose flour
1 pound veal scallops, thinly sliced and
  pounded ⅛" thick
Salt

½ cup port wine
1 teaspoon green peppercorns, drained
3 tablespoons unsalted butter, softened
Lightly cooked seasonal vegetables for
  garnish

Heat oil in a sauté pan over medium-high heat. Spread flour on a sheet of waxed paper. Flour the veal, shaking off any excess. Sauté scallops a few at a time (do not crowd) for about 30 seconds on each side. Transfer to a warm plate and sprinkle with salt to taste.

Pour off most of the oil from the pan. Increase heat to high and add wine, scraping up any residue in the pan. Boil briskly to reduce wine by half, about 5 minutes. Add green peppercorns and swirl in the butter. Reduce heat and add veal to pan, turning to coat with the sauce. Transfer veal scallops and sauce to warm plates and garnish with seasonal vegetables.

SERVES 4

PREPARATION TIME: 20 minutes

COOKING TIME: 10 minutes

FRAGOLE CON STREGA •

2 baskets ripe strawberries   *3 tablespoons Strega (Italian liqueur)*
Approximately 2 tablespoons sugar

Wash and hull strawberries, and slice in half lengthwise into a bowl. Sprinkle with sugar and Strega and stir gently. Cover bowl with plastic wrap and refrigerate for 30 to 60 minutes.

SERVES 4
PREPARATION TIME: 10 minutes, plus chilling time
COOKING TIME: None

Owned by two Armenians from Lebanon (who married sisters surnamed Lalime), this popular Berkeley bistro serves imaginative Mediterranean cuisine in comfortable, uncomplicated surroundings. Chef Haig Krikorian adds an intriguing dash of Middle Eastern flair to his menus.

> **PICKLED BEETS**
> **SAUTÉED DUCK BREAST WITH CREAMY POLENTA**
> **DRIED FRUIT AND MALAGA COMPOTE WITH A**
> **SHORTBREAD COOKIE**

PICKLED BEETS

15 beets, 2½" to 3" in diameter
2 cups red wine vinegar
2 bay leaves
1 cinnamon stick
2 small shallots, peeled

1 large red onion, peeled and sliced
3 cloves garlic, peeled
2 oranges, peeled and quartered
3 cups freshly squeezed orange juice
1 cup sugar

1½ tablespoons salt

½ tablespoon ground cumin

5 small dried hot chili peppers, left whole

2 cups virgin olive oil

6 large handfuls mixed greens

Trim tops off beets but leave long roots intact to prevent "bleeding." Bring a large pot of water to a boil. Add beets and cook until tender, 30 to 45 minutes for small beets, depending on age. Cool, and remove skin and long roots. (This can be done a day in advance. If so, coat beets lightly with olive oil after peeling, and refrigerate.)

In a large noncorrodible pot, combine all remaining ingredients except olive oil and salad greens. Bring to a boil, reduce heat, and simmer, covered, for 5 minutes. Set aside to cool. Quarter beets and add to brine. Add olive oil. Refrigerate. Bring back to room temperature before serving. Serve on a bed of salad greens.

SERVES 8

PREPARATION TIME: 15 minutes, plus cooling time

COOKING TIME: 30 to 45 minutes

CHEF'S NOTE: These pickled beets will keep for up to a month in the refrigerator. They are also very good served with feta cheese.

SAUTÉED DUCK BREAST WITH CREAMY POLENTA

2 quarts Chicken Stock (page 294) or water

2 cups polenta

2 teaspoons minced garlic

1½ cups heavy cream

½ pound (2 sticks) butter, cut up, plus ¼ pound (1 stick) butter, in flakes, for sauce

Dash ground cumin

8 boneless duck breast halves

Salt and pepper

Peanut oil

2 cups Madeira

Freshly grated Parmesan cheese

Virgin olive oil

Place chicken stock or water in a heavy saucepan and bring to a boil. Pour in polenta in a stream, stirring constantly to avoid lumps. When it starts to bubble, reduce heat to low and cook for 30 minutes, stirring occasionally. Add garlic and continue cooking for another 10 minutes. Stir in cream, cut-up butter, and cumin and heat through. Cover pan and keep warm.

Score the skin of the duck breasts in a crisscross pattern. Season with salt and pepper. Heat a cast-iron skillet, and add enough peanut oil to coat the bottom. Put in duck breasts, skin side down, and cook until dark brown, about 10 minutes. Turn, and cook for 3 to 4 minutes more. Remove and place on a warm platter.

When ready to serve, heat a clean sauté pan and add a light film of peanut oil. Add duck breasts, skin side down, and cook for 3 minutes. Remove and keep warm. Deglaze the pan with Madeira, and add to it the accumulated duck juices from the platter. Bring to a boil and add flakes of butter, stirring fast until melted. Turn off heat.

Pour polenta onto serving plates, and sprinkle with Parmesan and olive oil. Slice duck breasts lengthwise and arrange on the polenta. Pour the sauce on top of the duck breasts.

SERVES 8
PREPARATION TIME: 10 minutes
COOKING TIME: 50 minutes

DRIED FRUIT AND MALAGA COMPOTE WITH A SHORTBREAD COOKIE

2 cups sugar
1 quart water
1½ cups Malaga (dark, sweet Spanish wine from Andalusia)
1 cup freshly squeezed orange juice
Grated zest of 1 orange
2 whole cinnamon sticks
4 bay leaves
Pinch ground allspice

½ teaspoon vanilla extract
2 small hot dried chili peppers, left whole
1 cup dried pear halves
1 cup dried pitted prunes
1 cup dried apricot halves
½ cup golden raisins
½ cup currants, well rinsed
Shortbread Cookies (recipe follows)

In a large stainless-steel saucepan, combine sugar, water, wine, orange juice, orange zest, cinnamon sticks, bay leaves, allspice, vanilla, and chili peppers. Bring to a boil, and reduce to simmer. Add dried pears and simmer for 5 minutes. Add prunes and apricots, and simmer for 10 minutes more. Remove from heat and add raisins and currants. Set aside to cool. Locate and discard cinnamon sticks, bay leaves, and chili peppers. Serve compote with shortbread cookies.

SHORTBREAD COOKIES

½ pound (2 sticks) unsalted butter, softened
½ cup sugar, plus extra for sprinkling
1 teaspoon amaretto

2 cups all-purpose flour
½ cup cornstarch
⅛ teaspoon salt

Cream butter, sugar, and amaretto together until light and fluffy. Mix flour, cornstarch, and salt together. Blend into the butter-sugar mixture just until it holds together. Enclose in plastic wrap and chill for 30 minutes.

Preheat oven to 325°. On a lightly floured surface, or between 2 sheets of plastic wrap, roll dough out into a square, ½" thick. Cut into 1"-×-3" pieces. Prick with a fork and sprinkle with sugar. Place on baking sheet and bake for about 25 minutes, until pale gold and firm to the touch.

SERVES 8
PREPARATION TIME: 15 minutes, plus cooling and chilling time
COOKING TIME: 40 minutes total

EDITOR'S NOTE: If Malaga is hard to find, substitute a good-quality Spanish cream sherry.

Housed in a charming, 100-year-old Victorian tucked away in the town of Larkspur, just across the Golden Gate Bridge, The Lark Creek Inn has been completely refurbished by restaurant consultant Michael Dellar and chef/partner Bradley Ogden. A peaked glass roof over the main dining room shows off the towering redwoods outside, and a new wood-burning brick oven right in the dining room turns out hearty rustic dishes day and night. Bradley Ogden has received consistent acclaim for his exceptional, innovative American cuisine, first at the American Restaurant in Kansas City, later at Campton Place in San Francisco, and now at The Lark Creek Inn.

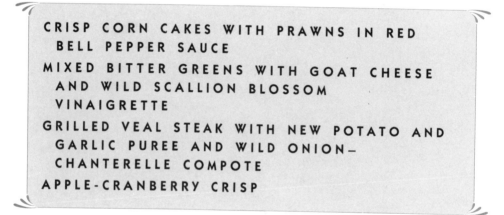

CRISP CORN CAKES WITH PRAWNS IN RED BELL PEPPER SAUCE

MIXED BITTER GREENS WITH GOAT CHEESE AND WILD SCALLION BLOSSOM VINAIGRETTE

GRILLED VEAL STEAK WITH NEW POTATO AND GARLIC PUREE AND WILD ONION—CHANTERELLE COMPOTE

APPLE-CRANBERRY CRISP

CRISP CORN CAKES WITH PRAWNS IN RED BELL PEPPER SAUCE

1 cup virgin olive oil
Juice and grated zest of 3 lemons
1 cup fresh basil leaves, chopped
3½ teaspoons kosher salt
¼ cup freshly cracked black pepper
24 prawns (shrimp), 16 to 20 count,
  shelled and deveined
1⅓ cups yellow stoneground cornmeal
⅔ cup all-purpose flour
½ teaspoon baking powder
¾ teaspoon ground white pepper

1 teaspoon sugar
1½ cups milk
3 large eggs, separated
½ cup freshly shucked corn kernels
¼ cup chopped crisp-cooked bacon
4 tablespoons (½ stick) butter, melted
Clarified Butter (page 291) or bacon fat
Red Bell Pepper Sauce (recipe follows)
6 teaspoons caviar for garnish
12 chives, cut into 2" pieces for garnish

Combine olive oil, lemon juice and zest, basil, 2 teaspoons salt, and pepper. Add prawns and marinate in refrigerator, covered, for 24 hours.

Mix together the cornmeal, flour, baking powder, and remaining 1½ teaspoons salt, pepper, and sugar. Stir milk into egg yolks, add melted butter, and stir into cornmeal mixture. Add corn and bacon. Beat egg whites to stiff peaks and fold into batter. Form into twelve 2" cakes and fry in clarified butter or bacon fat until edges become golden brown, about 3 minutes. Turn and cook for 30 seconds longer. At the same time, grill (or broil) prawns over very hot coals (or under the broiler) until just done, approximately 1½ minutes per side. Remove corn cakes from pan and divide among 6 plates. Top with prawns, and nap with the sauce. Garnish with caviar and chives.

Red Bell Pepper Sauce

2 tablespoons unsalted butter
½ cup freshly shucked corn kernels
1 teaspoon kosher salt
¼ teaspoon ground white pepper
⅛ teaspoon Tabasco sauce
½ cup heavy cream

1 cup Chicken Stock (page 294) or Fish Stock (page 295)
1 red bell pepper, roasted, peeled, seeded (page 291), and pureed
1 whole head garlic, roasted unpeeled, yielding 3 tablespoons garlic pulp

Melt butter in a saucepan. Add corn, salt, pepper, and Tabasco. Cook for 10 minutes, stirring often. Add cream and stock, bring to a boil, reduce heat, and simmer for 10 minutes. Remove from heat and add bell pepper puree and garlic pulp. Blend in a food processor or blender, and strain through a fine mesh strainer.

SERVES 6
PREPARATION TIME: 30 minutes total, plus marination
COOKING TIME: 30 minutes total

MIXED BITTER GREENS WITH GOAT CHEESE AND WILD SCALLION BLOSSOM VINAIGRETTE •

1 head chicory, unblemished
1 bunch young dandelion greens
1 cup mâche
8 scallions or chives with blossoms, cleaned and trimmed, cut diagonally (reserve blossoms for dressing)

1 cup goat cheese, semi-strong domestic, cut into ½" pieces
Wild Scallion Blossom Vinaigrette (recipe follows)

Clean and dry the greens and refrigerate for at least 1 hour so they are well chilled and crisp. Add scallion blossoms and goat cheese to prepared dressing and let stand for 30 minutes before using.

To assemble salad, place chilled greens in a bowl. Separate the goat cheese and blossoms from the dressing. Toss greens with enough dressing to lightly coat the leaves. Arrange attractively on chilled plates. Top with blossoms and goat cheese.

Wild Scallion Blossom Vinaigrette

½ teaspoon dry mustard

2 teaspoons minced garlic

1 teaspoon kosher salt

2 teaspoons freshly cracked black pepper

1 tablespoon lemon juice

¾ cup extra-virgin California olive oil

3 tablespoons red wine vinegar

½ cup thinly sliced shallots

Place mustard, garlic, salt, pepper, and lemon juice in a stainless-steel bowl and whisk together. Then add oil, vinegar, and shallots, mixing well.

SERVES 6

PREPARATION TIME: 20 minutes, plus chilling and marination time

COOKING TIME: None

GRILLED VEAL STEAK WITH NEW POTATO AND GARLIC PUREE AND WILD ONION–CHANTERELLE COMPOTE

6 boneless veal steaks cut from loin, 5 ounces each

Virgin olive oil or Clarified Butter (page 294)

⅛ cup all-purpose flour, seasoned with salt and pepper

Red Potato and Garlic Puree (recipe follows)

1½ pounds chanterelle mushrooms, wiped with a damp cloth and trimmed

18 wild onions or scallions, peeled and cut into long strips (including green tops)

3 red bell peppers, seeded, deribbed, and cut into julienne

2 serrano chili peppers, seeded and cut into julienne

2 teaspoons minced garlic

½ teaspoon kosher salt

½ teaspoon ground black pepper

Place veal steaks between 2 sheets of waxed paper and pound to ¾″ thickness.

Place a large sauté pan over moderate heat with enough oil or clarified butter to coat the bottom. Heat until oil is hot, dust veal steaks with seasoned flour, and place in skillet. Sauté until golden brown on one side, about 2 or 3 minutes, turn, and cook to desired degree of doneness. Place ½ to ¾ cup potato puree in center of warmed dinner plates. Place veal steak over potatoes. Keep warm.

Pour off fat remaining in skillet, leaving only 2 tablespoons. Place pan back over high heat, add chanterelles, and sauté for 1 minute. Add wild onions, bell peppers, chili peppers, and garlic. Sauté for 1 minute more to cook vegetables. Season with salt and pepper.

Garnish veal steaks with chanterelle compote, arranging it on top of meat.

New Potato and Garlic Puree

24 small red potatoes, peeled

2 cups heavy cream

12 cloves garlic, peeled

¼ pound (1 stick) unsalted butter

1 tablespoon kosher salt

1 teaspoon ground white pepper

Preheat oven to 350°. Boil potatoes in salted water until tender, 15 to 20 minutes. Drain and place on a baking sheet. Bake in oven for 10 minutes to dry out completely.

Pour cream into a saucepan and add garlic. Simmer until garlic is very tender, 10 to 15 minutes. Add butter and let it melt. Season with salt and pepper.

Remove potatoes from oven and put through a food mill (or potato ricer) with the cream mixture. Do not use a food processor as this would make the mixture gummy. Taste for seasoning and adjust if necessary. Keep warm in the top of a double boiler over simmering water until needed.

SERVES 6

PREPARATION TIME: 40 minutes total

COOKING TIME: 30 minutes total

APPLE-CRANBERRY CRISP

5 cups peeled and sliced apples (5 or 6)

1 cup cranberries

½ cup brown sugar

5 tablespoons all-purpose flour

1 teaspoon ground cinnamon

Grated zest of 1 lemon

Topping

¾ cup all-purpose flour

¾ cup dark brown sugar, firmly packed

¼ teaspoon salt

¼ teaspoon ground cinnamon

⅛ teaspoon ground ginger

6 tablespoons (¾ stick) unsalted butter

Garnish

Vanilla ice cream or heavy cream

Preheat oven to 375°. Place sliced apples in a bowl and toss gently with the cranberries, brown sugar, flour, cinnamon, and lemon zest until fruit is lightly coated. Set aside.

Topping: In a bowl, mix together the flour, sugar, salt, cinnamon, and ginger. Cut in butter until mixture resembles coarse meal.

Place fruit in a baking dish, cover evenly with topping, and bake for 20 to 30 minutes, or until fruit is soft and the topping is crisp. Serve warm, with vanilla ice cream or heavy cream.

SERVES 6

PREPARATION TIME: 30 minutes

COOKING TIME: 20 to 30 minutes

European country cuisine is the specialty of chef Stephen Silva in this sophisticated, barrel-vaulted, underground restaurant, which was created by renowned restaurant designer Pat Kuleto for proprietor Annette Esser. Named after a cave in France that contains some of the oldest drawings known to man, the room is dominated by a huge handcut French limestone fireplace.

CROSTINI OF WILD MUSHROOMS
CAMPAGNA-STYLE LAMB CHOPS IN
  PARCHMENT
STRAWBERRIES WITH ZABAGLIONE

CROSTINI OF WILD MUSHROOMS •

¼ pound (1 stick) butter
1 small onion, peeled and chopped
1 pound assorted wild mushrooms or a
  mixture of shiitake and regular white
  button mushrooms, sliced
3 cloves garlic, peeled and minced
2 tablespoons sherry vinegar

1 large tomato, peeled, seeded, and
  chopped
4 basil leaves, chopped
Salt and pepper
4 large slices French bread, toasted
Chopped fresh parsley for garnish

Heat butter in a large sauté pan over medium heat. Add onion and cook slowly until golden brown, about 6 minutes. Add mushrooms and garlic, and sauté for 3 minutes. Add vinegar, tomato, and basil, and cook until thick, about 8 minutes. Season to taste with salt and pepper. Spoon onto toast, and garnish with parsley.

SERVES 4
PREPARATION TIME: 5 minutes
COOKING TIME: 15 to 18 minutes

CAMPAGNA-STYLE LAMB CHOPS IN PARCHMENT •

12 small rib lamb chops, very well
   trimmed of fat and membrane
Salt and pepper
¼ cup virgin olive oil, plus extra for
   brushing
4 rounds baking parchment, 16"
   diameter, folded in half and opened
   again

12 large green olives, pitted
12 cherry tomatoes, halved
12 pearl onions, peeled and halved
20 fresh sage leaves

Preheat oven to 500°. Season lamb chops with salt and pepper to taste. Heat olive oil in a large skillet and brown lamb chops well on both sides, about 3 minutes altogether. Allow to cool completely.

When cool, place 3 lamb chops on each round of parchment paper, placing them to one side of the fold. Arrange 3 olives, 3 cherry tomatoes, 3 onions, and 5 sage leaves on top of each chop. Fold paper over to form half circles and crimp the edges tightly together, folding them over and over to seal. Brush parchment packages with olive oil and place on a baking sheet. Bake for 8 to 10 minutes for medium rare. Slide packages onto dinner plates and slit open at the table, in order to savor the good aromas.

SERVES 4
PREPARATION TIME: 10 minutes
COOKING TIME: 10 to 15 minutes

STRAWBERRIES WITH ZABAGLIONE •

1 quart ripe, fragrant strawberries,
   washed and hulled
3 large egg yolks
1½ tablespoons sugar

¼ cup dry Marsala
Grated zest of 1 orange
2 tablespoons chopped toasted hazelnuts

Place strawberries in glass bowls or stemmed glasses. In the top of a double boiler, combine egg yolks, sugar, Marsala, and orange zest. Whip over simmering water until mixture is warm, thick, and fluffy, about 7 minutes. (It will increase greatly in volume.) Pour over berries, garnish with chopped hazelnuts, and serve immediately.

SERVES 4
PREPARATION TIME: 5 minutes
COOKING TIME: 7 minutes

EDITOR'S NOTE: A stainless-steel or unlined copper bowl set over a saucepan of simmering water can be substituted for a double boiler.

Owner/chef Nancy Oakes creates exceptional food at this small, unpretentious but stylish San Francisco restaurant. Located on Geary at Third Avenue—"out in the Avenues"—the ambience is that of a good French bistro, where fine food is taken seriously.

GRILLED QUAIL STUFFED WITH FIGS AND
PROSCIUTTO
GRILLED SWORDFISH WITH PORCINI
VINAIGRETTE, SERVED ON A BED OF
SAUTÉED SPINACH AND RADICCHIO
LEMON TART WITH ALMOND CRUST

GRILLED QUAIL STUFFED WITH FIGS AND PROSCIUTTO

8 quail, about 4 ounces each
⅓ to ½ cup virgin olive oil
2 cloves garlic, peeled and chopped
Black pepper
1 tablespoon chopped fresh sage
2 quarts water

½ pound walnut halves
1½ teaspoons sugar
1 teaspoon kosher salt
8 figs
8 slices prosciutto

Salad

8 handfuls mixed baby greens of choice
3 tablespoons virgin olive oil
1 tablespoon balsamic vinegar

Salt and pepper
¼ pound imported Gorgonzola cheese, crumbled

Place quail in a shallow dish. Combine ¼ cup olive oil, garlic, black pepper, and sage. Pour over quail, turning them to coat all sides. Marinate in refrigerator for at least 2 hours.

Preheat oven to 375°. Bring the water to a boil. Add walnuts, turn off heat, and let soak for 5 minutes. Drain and place on baking sheet. Bake for 7 minutes, or until walnuts are dry. This will eliminate any bitter aftertaste. Heat 1½ tablespoons olive oil in a skillet large enough to hold the nuts in a single layer. Add nuts and toss with sugar and salt. When nuts are coated, drain on paper towels.

Build an intense charcoal fire. Cut figs in half and brush with the remaining olive oil. Grill over coals for about 2 minutes. Wrap 8 fig halves in prosciutto and stuff into cavity of birds, reserving remaining fig halves for garnish. Grill the quail for about 5 minutes on each side; time depends on heat of coals.

Place greens in a bowl and drizzle with olive oil and balsamic vinegar. Season with salt and pepper to taste, and toss well to mix. (Not premixing the dressing keeps the greens shiny, and the taste fresher.) Divide among 8 plates. Top each bed of green with a grilled quail. Sprinkle walnuts and cheese around edge of salad. Cut reserved fig halves into quarters and place on plates near the quail.

SERVES 8

PREPARATION TIME: 30 minutes, plus marination time

COOKING TIME: about 10 minutes

CHEF'S NOTE: Quail can be roasted in a 450° oven instead of grilled on a charcoal fire. Brown quail in olive oil in a hot skillet first; then roast for 10 to 15 minutes, until medium rare.

GRILLED SWORDFISH WITH PORCINI VINAIGRETTE, SERVED ON A BED OF SAUTÉED SPINACH AND RADICCHIO

¼ cup dried porcini mushrooms
1½ cups balsamic vinegar
3 shallots, peeled and finely chopped
2 tablespoons best-quality red wine vinegar
1 teaspoon chopped fresh rosemary
1 cup virgin oil, plus extra for grilling
¼ cup green California olive oil

Salt and pepper
6 to 8 swordfish steaks, 6 to 8 ounces each (or use monkfish, sturgeon, or halibut)
Blanched and sautéed spinach, and radicchio, cored and cut into 6 wedges and separated, seasoned with shallots and garlic to taste

Soak porcini mushrooms in water for 1 hour, then drain, squeeze dry, and chop. In a noncorrodible saucepan, combine balsamic vinegar, mushrooms, and shallots. Bring to a boil and reduce until a little less than ½ cup liquid remains, about 25 minutes.

Pour reduction into a mixing bowl. Add red wine vinegar and rosemary. Whisk in both olive oils, and season to taste with salt and pepper. Adjust tartness by adding more red wine vinegar if required.

Have ready an intense charcoal fire, or preheat broiler. Brush swordfish steaks with olive oil and grill to desired degree of doneness, about 4 minutes per side. Serve on a bed of sautéed spinach and radicchio and spoon vinaigrette on top.

SERVES 6 TO 8
PREPARATION TIME: 30 minutes, plus soaking time
COOKING TIME: about 35 minutes

CHEF'S NOTE: This vinaigrette is also great with grilled chicken.

LEMON TART WITH ALMOND CRUST

Almond Tart Shell (recipe follows)
6 Meyer lemons (substitute other lemons if unavailable) about ¾ cup juice
9 large eggs
1¾ cups sugar
1¼ cups heavy cream

Confectioners' sugar for garnish
Strawberry Coulis (optional) of strawberries pureed with sugar to taste, and strained (see Raspberry Coulis, page 62)

After preparing tart shell, reduce oven temperature to 300°. Wash lemons. Grate the zest into a bowl, then cut lemons in half and squeeze juice into same bowl.

In a separate bowl, lightly beat eggs and sugar together. Whisk in cream, stir in lemon zest and juice, and pour mixture into prepared crust. Bake for

40 minutes. If pastry begins to brown too much, cover edges with a "dough-nut" of aluminum foil. Remove from oven and cool in pan. Remove when still slightly warm, and sprinkle with powdered sugar. Serve with strawberry coulis, if desired.

Almond Tart Shell

10 tablespoons (1¼ sticks) unsalted
   butter, cut into small pieces
¼ cup sugar
2 large egg yolks
2 teaspoons ice water

1 teaspoon best-quality vanilla extract
½ teaspoon salt
½ cup ground blanched almonds
1⅔ cups unbleached all-purpose flour

Preheat oven to 400°. In the bowl of a food processor fitted with a steel blade, chop butter with sugar to pea size. Add egg yolks, water, vanilla, and salt, and pulse machine on and off 2 or 3 times. Add almonds and flour, and process until dough comes together. Do not form into a ball. Enclose in plastic wrap and freeze for 20 minutes.

Roll dough out between 2 sheets of plastic wrap. Lift off top sheet and lay dough upside down in a 10″ tart pan with removable bottom. Peel off second sheet. Gently press dough into fluted sides of pan. Dough will break, but can be pressed and patched back together. Trim edges by pressing top of rim with your thumb. Line tart shell with foil and fill with pie weights, rock salt, or dried beans. Bake for 10 minutes, then gently remove foil.

SERVES 8 TO 10
PREPARATION TIME: 30 minutes total, plus freezing time
COOKING TIME: 50 minutes total

The creation of owner Fritz Frankel, whose professional background includes working for the legendary Claridge's in London, this elegant French restaurant consists of three intimate dining rooms housed within a restored Victorian townhouse. The cuisine reflects the concept perfectly: It's classical, but lightened up to suit contemporary tastes.

BUTTERNUT SQUASH SOUP
ROAST FILET OF BEEF WITH CALVADOS AND CHANTERELLES
RASPBERRIES AND SOUR CREAM

BUTTERNUT SQUASH SOUP

1 butternut squash, about 1½ pounds   *Salt*
6 tablespoons (¾ stick) unsalted butter   *White pepper*
2 medium onions, peeled and quartered   *¼ cup heavy cream (optional)*

Peel the squash, remove seeds, and cut into chunks. Heat butter in a saucepan and soften the onions without browning, about 5 minutes. Add squash and stir together. Add enough water to cover. Season with salt and pepper to taste, and boil gently until the squash is thoroughly cooked, about 30 minutes. Puree the soup in a food processor or blender, and strain. Reheat, and add cream, if desired.

SERVES 4

PREPARATION TIME: 10 minutes

COOKING TIME: 35 minutes

ROAST FILET OF BEEF WITH CALVADOS AND CHANTERELLES

1 center cut filet of beef, 2½ to 3 pounds

Salt and pepper

1 tablespoon virgin olive oil

4 tablespoons (½ stick) butter

2 large shallots, peeled and diced

1 tablespoon Dijon mustard

1 pound chanterelle mushrooms, cleaned and sliced

½ cup plus 1 tablespoon Madeira

2 cups heavy cream

¼ cup Calvados

12 to 16 spears steamed asparagus

Crusty French bread

Preheat oven to 450°. Trim the filet of beef of all gristle and silverskin. Season with salt and pepper. Heat oil in a heavy ovenproof sauté pan. Sear meat on all sides, about 2 minutes, and transfer pan to oven. Roast for 20 to 25 minutes, turning every 5 minutes to brown evenly.

In a separate skillet, heat butter and sauté shallots until softened, about 3 minutes. Add mustard and chanterelles and moisten with 1 tablespoon Madeira. Season with salt and pepper and sauté for 3 to 4 minutes. Leave pan at side of stove.

Remove beef filet from sauté pan and place on a warm platter. Cover loosely with a tent of aluminum foil. Pour off fat from pan, and add remaining ½ cup Madeira. Reduce liquid by half over high heat, about 2 minutes. Add cream and Calvados. Reduce to about ⅔ cup, approximately 10 minutes. Add chanterelles. Stir well and taste for seasoning, adding salt and pepper as needed. Cut filet into 4 portions and add any juices on the platter to the sauce. Serve beef with sauce and steamed asparagus, and offer crusty French bread.

SERVES 4

PREPARATION TIME: 30 minutes

COOKING TIME: about 35 minutes

RASPBERRIES AND SOUR CREAM •

¾ cup dairy sour cream   ¼ cup rum or liqueur of choice
1½ cups vanilla ice cream, softened   2 baskets raspberries

Mix the sour cream with the softened ice cream. Add rum and stir well. Refrigerate for 20 minutes, or until serving time.

Divide raspberries among 4 large wine goblets. Pour sauce over berries just before serving.

SERVES 4
PREPARATION TIME: 5 minutes, plus chilling time
COOKING TIME: None

This Clement Street restaurant, with its working stone hearth, rush-seated chairs, and relaxed ambience, makes you think you might be at some delightful French country inn. The food makes you sure of it. Owner J. B. Lorda likes to call it "modern, classical French cuisine"; Basque chef Gerald Hirigoyen modestly adds, "I try to keep the food simple, but good." The concept has succeeded extremely well for almost twenty years.

ARTICHOKE SOUP WITH HAZELNUTS AND COGNAC
TUNA STEAKS WITH ONION MARMALADE
GOAT CHEESE GÂTEAU

ARTICHOKE SOUP WITH HAZELNUTS AND COGNAC

1½ pounds small artichokes
4 tablespoons (½ stick) butter
½ pound onions, peeled and sliced
2 stalks celery, sliced
4 cups Chicken Stock (page 294) or canned chicken broth
½ pound Idaho potatoes, peeled and quartered
1 cup heavy cream
Salt and pepper
2 tablespoons Cognac
3 tablespoons ground toasted hazelnuts for garnish

Wash and trim the artichokes. Cut into quarters, remove chokes, and cut off stems.

Melt butter in a saucepan. Add onions and celery. Steam gently, covered, for 10 minutes. Add chicken stock, potatoes, and artichokes. Bring to a boil, reduce heat, and simmer for 1 hour. Add cream and cook for another 10 minutes.

Puree mixture in a blender or food processor, then rub through a sieve into a clean saucepan. Add salt, pepper, and Cognac. Reheat gently, and sprinkle with hazelnuts just before serving.

SERVES 4 TO 6
PREPARATION TIME: 20 minutes
COOKING TIME: 80 minutes

TUNA STEAKS WITH ONION MARMALADE •

2 tablespoons virgin olive oil
4 medium onions, peeled and sliced
¼ cup red wine vinegar
½ cup balsamic vinegar
½ cup Veal Stock (page 294)

Salt and pepper
½ cup ventreche (French belly bacon)
  or Italian pancetta, diced and sautéed
  until crisp
4 tuna steaks, about 6 ounces each

Heat 1 tablespoon of olive oil in a skillet, add the onions and sauté until golden brown, about 10 minutes. Add both vinegars and reduce completely, about 5 minutes. Pour in veal stock, and cook for about 5 minutes. Add salt, pepper, and *ventreche*, and remove pan from heat.

In a separate skillet, heat remaining 1 tablespoon of olive oil. Sauté tuna steaks until medium rare, about 2 minutes on each side. (Cooking time depends on thickness.) Transfer to warmed plates, and cover with onion marmalade.

SERVES 4
PREPARATION TIME: 10 minutes
COOKING TIME: 20 minutes

GOAT CHEESE GÂTEAU

6 large eggs
½ pound fresh white goat cheese
⅓ cup sugar

Crème fraîche (optional)
Fresh berries for garnish

Preheat oven to 375°. Butter and flour a 10″ cake pan. Separate eggs and place whites in the bowl of an electric mixer. In a separate bowl, blend goat cheese and sugar. Add egg yolks one by one, beating until the mixture is smooth and creamy. Beat egg whites until they form stiff peaks. Fold very carefully into the cheese–egg yolk mixture. Pour into prepared pan and bake for 30 minutes. Serve cold, with crème fraîche and berries.

SERVES 6
PREPARATION TIME: 15 minutes
COOKING TIME: 30 minutes

Robert Reynolds, chef/proprietor of Le Trou Restaurant and Cooking School, serves earthy French regional fare of great integrity, and conducts cooking classes during the day. Handsome, old-fashioned linens, simple flower arrangements, and casually assembled silverware and china all add to this friendly little restaurant's Gallic charm.

ROQUEFORT CUSTARDS WITH SAUTÉED CHARD
ROAST LEG OF LAMB WITH RED CURRANT SAUCE
EGGPLANT FLAMBÉED IN MARC
PISTACHIO MERINGUE WITH RASPBERRY BUTTERCREAM

ROQUEFORT CUSTARDS WITH SAUTÉED CHARD

Soft butter for molds
4 ounces Roquefort cheese
2 cups half and half
4 large egg yolks

2 tablespoons butter
Salt and pepper
Sautéed Chard (recipe follows)

Preheat oven to 325°. Lightly butter six 4-ounce ovenproof ramekins and bring a kettle of water to a boil.

Press Roquefort through a sieve into a bowl. Place the cream in a blender; add the egg yolks, Roquefort, butter, and salt and pepper. Turn the blender on only long enough to liquefy the ingredients, about 5 seconds. (If eggs are overblended, their binding ability is broken down.)

Like a roasting pan with a double layer of paper toweling, to prevent bottoms of custards from overcooking. Set ramekins on top of towels. Divide the Roquefort mixture evenly among the ramekins and place the roasting pan on middle rack of oven. Pour in enough boiling water to reach halfway up sides of ramekins. Close oven door and reduce heat to 300°. Bake custards for 45 to 60 minutes, until a skewer inserted in the middle comes out clean. Remove from oven and run a knife blade around inside of each ramekin. Invert each custard onto a plate. Garnish with sautéed chard.

Sautéed Chard with Quatre Épices

2 bunches young red or green chard
Salt and pepper
2 to 4 tablespoons butter, in pea-sized
  pieces
2 tablespoons persillade (1½ tablespoons
  chopped fresh parsley and ½
  tablespoon minced garlic, pounded
  together)

Pinch quatre épices (see Chef's Note
  below)
Walnut oil or hazelnut oil

Wash chard leaves and remove ribs. (Reserve for another use.) Plunge leaves into boiling salted water. When the water returns to the boil, blanch chard for 30 seconds. Drain and plunge into cold water to arrest cooking and set the color. Drain and squeeze out any excess water.

When ready to serve, put the blanched chard in a dry skillet, add a light sprinkling of salt, and heat on medium heat until any remaining water has evaporated. Add butter and toss to coat the vegetable. Season with salt and pepper to taste. Stir in *persillade* and *quatre épices*. Transfer to plates and drizzle very lightly with oil of choice.

SERVES 6
PREPARATION TIME: 15 minutes
COOKING TIME: 45 to 60 minutes total

CHEF'S NOTE: *Quatre épices* is available commercially, or you can make your own. Combine 1 teaspoon ground white pepper, a pinch ground cloves, ¼ teaspoon ground ginger, and ¼ teaspoon ground nutmeg, and store airtight.

Sautéed chard can be served as a vegetable in its own right, or with the addition of 1 to 2 tablespoons whole-grain mustard if it is being served with a meat.

ROAST LEG OF LAMB WITH RED CURRANT SAUCE

1 leg of lamb, 5 to 6 pounds
Olive oil
2 cups Veal Stock (page 294)
2 to 4 tablespoons red currant jelly
  (preferably from France), or ½ cup
  fresh red currants if available (see
  Chef's Note below)
4 to 8 tablespoons (½ to 1 stick)
  unsalted butter

1 to 2 tablespoons Dijon mustard
Salt
2 tablespoons fresh mint, cut into tiny
  strips
¼ cup persillade (3 tablespoons chopped
  fresh parsley and 1 tablespoon minced
  garlic, pounded together)
Freshly ground black pepper

Have the butcher remove the hip joint and upper leg bone from the leg of lamb, and then trim off all the fat and silverskin from the entire surface. Tie the boned leg with kitchen string (butcher's twine).

Preheat oven to 400°. Rub the meat with olive oil. Place meat on a rack in a roasting pan and roast for approximately 20 minutes per pound, until a meat thermometer registers 135°. Remove to a warm platter and cover loosely with aluminum foil. Let stand for 10 to 15 minutes for juices to settle.

Place veal stock in a saucepan and reduce over high heat to 1 cup. Whisk in currant jelly. (If you are fortunate enough to have fresh red currants, add them raw as a garnish to the meat after it has been napped with the sauce.) On medium to low heat, whisk in butter a tablespoon at a time, incorporating well each time until you have the desired consistency and taste. Flavor sauce to taste with mustard and a little salt, but do not subject the sauce to too much cooking after adding the mustard as it can become bitter if overcooked. Finish sauce with addition of mint and *persillade,* and give a final grating of black pepper. Carve meat and nap with the sauce.

SERVES 6 TO 8

PREPARATION TIME: 25 minutes

COOKING TIME: about 1¾ hours

CHEF'S NOTE: The red currant jelly should be made from fruit and sugar only, not corn syrup.

EGGPLANT FLAMBÉED IN MARC ●

2 firm purple eggplants, about 1 pound each

Salt

Virgin olive oil for skillet

¼ cup French marc, Calvados, or any eau-de-vie, *or to taste*

Black pepper

Peel eggplant and cut into ¾"-thick slices. Score slices lightly with a knife on both sides several times. Salt well and set on a tray (or a baker's rack) for 30 minutes, to draw off the water. When ready to cook, wash off salt, pat dry with paper towels, and cut eggplant into cubes.

Pour a thin layer of olive oil into a skillet large enough to hold the eggplant in one layer (or use 2 skillets) and set over medium heat. When hot, add eggplant and toss well to coat cubes with oil. (This tossing eliminates the need to add more oil later on.) Brown on all sides so that the eggplant eventually collapses when the last of the moisture evaporates. Pour in the marc, remembering Josephine Araldo's advice on such matters: "If you want the dish to taste of *marc*, add the *marc* until you can taste it . . . none of this two tablespoons business!" Allow to settle for 5 seconds off the heat before igniting the eggplant. Be aware that this is very flammable. Shake the pan to get the marc to burn, and when the flames die out, season with salt and pepper to taste.

SERVES 6 TO 8
PREPARATION TIME: 10 minutes
COOKING TIME: 10 minutes

PISTACHIO MERINGUE WITH RASPBERRY BUTTERCREAM

Cake

3½ ounces (⅞ cup) unsalted pistachios
3½ ounces (almost ½ cup) granulated
  sugar
4 teaspoons cornstarch

8 large egg whites, at room temperature
3¼ ounces (⅓ cup) superfine sugar

Buttercream

13½ ounces (1⅔ cups) sugar
½ cup water
8 large egg yolks
¼ to ½ cup raspberry eau-de-vie
  (framboise)

1½ pounds (6 sticks) unsalted butter, at
  room temperature

Garnish

2 cups fresh raspberries

Unsalted pistachios, finely chopped

Cake: Preheat oven to 350°. Line a 13"-×-20" sheet cake pan with baking parchment, or butter it well and dust with flour. Combine pistachios, granulated sugar, and cornstarch in the bowl of a food processor and grind coarsely.

Whip egg whites until they form soft peaks. Gradually whip in the fine sugar and continue whipping until meringue mixture is very stiff. Dust a third of the nut-sugar mixture over the surface of the meringue and fold in gently. Fold in the remaining two thirds of the nut-sugar mixture, deflating the meringue as little as possible. Spread evenly in prepared pan and bake for 20 to 30 minutes, until top of cake is dry, firm, and light brown. Remove from oven, loosen edges, and cool for 2 minutes before reversing onto a cake rack. Peel off baking parchment, if used, after 1 minute.

Buttercream: combine sugar and water in a heavy saucepan and bring to a boil. Continue to cook until firm-ball stage, or a candy thermometer registers 242°.

Using an electric mixer, beat egg yolks until thick and pale. Slowly pour the hot syrup down the sides of the bowl, beating at low speed at the same time. Be careful not to allow syrup to catch in beaters as this tends to cause it to crystallize. When all the syrup has been incorporated, continue beating at high speed until the mixture cools, about 10 minutes.

When the mixture is cool, flavor to taste with raspberry *eau-de-vie*. Soften the butter with your hands and add it a little at a time, beating it in well with each addition. Continue until all butter is incorporated.

To assemble dessert, trim edges of cake and cut it into three 12"-×-6" rectangles. Place the bottom layer on a sheet of baking parchment or waxed paper set on a flat plate or board and spread with a layer of buttercream. Add second layer of cake, spread with buttercream, and top with third layer. Finish top and sides of cake with a smooth layer of buttercream. Place in refrigerator to harden.

Sprinkle sides with chopped pistachios. Garnish with raspberries just before transferring to a suitable serving platter.

SERVES 8 TO 10
PREPARATION TIME: 45 minutes
COOKING TIME: 20 to 30 minutes

CHEF'S NOTE: The cake is better if made one day in advance, it is excellent if made two days in advance, and sublime if made three days in advance.

Having named his restaurant for the dancing white horses of Vienna, owner/chef Josef Roettig brings something of the same apparently effortless grace to his cuisine. The food is French/Viennese, and every effort is directed towards enhancing the basic flavors of good ingredients. Cream-colored walls, engravings of horses and scenes of old Vienna, lace over dark green tablecloths, and the music of Strauss combine to create a special ambience in this popular Marin restaurant.

BELGIAN ENDIVE WITH WATERCRESS AND PAPAYA

SCALLOPS AND PRAWNS SAUTÉED WITH GREEK OLIVES AND FETA

LINZER TORTE

BELGIAN ENDIVE WITH WATERCRESS AND PAPAYA •

9 heads Belgian endive
2 bunches watercress, stems removed
1 cup walnut halves

Walnut Dressing (recipe follows)
1 large papaya, peeled, seeded, and cut
    into ½" dice, for garnish

Cut endives into 1" slices, cutting solid core into finer slices. Place in a bowl with watercress leaves and walnuts. Toss with walnut dressing and divide among 6 salad plates. Garnish with papaya cubes.

Walnut Dressing

Juice of 3 lemons
2 teaspoons sugar
½ teaspoon freshly ground white pepper
½ teaspoon salt (optional)

2 teaspoons Dijon mustard
1 small bunch chives, finely chopped
½ cup walnut oil

Combine all ingredients except walnut oil. Add oil, beating with a whisk.

SERVES 6
PREPARATION TIME: 15 minutes
COOKING TIME: None

SCALLOPS AND PRAWNS SAUTÉED WITH GREEK OLIVES AND FETA

24 large prawns or jumbo shrimp (16 or 20 to the pound), peeled and deveined
1 pound sea scallops
4 teaspoons finely chopped shallots
3 teaspoons Worcestershire sauce
Juice of 1 lemon
½ teaspoon salt
½ teaspoon freshly ground white pepper
¼ teaspoon cayenne pepper
6 large fresh basil leaves, finely chopped

6 medium tomatoes, cored and quartered
24 Kalamata olives
6 tablespoons (¾ stick) butter
3 cups heavy cream
¼ cup white wine
⅓ cup good Spanish sherry (such as Tio Pepe)
6 ounces feta cheese, crumbled, for garnish
Crusty French bread

In a bowl, combine prawns, scallops, shallots, Worcestershire sauce, lemon juice, salt, white pepper, cayenne, basil, tomatoes, and olives. Toss well and marinate for 5 minutes.

Heat a large skillet and add butter. When very hot, sauté seafood mixture for 20 seconds. Add cream, wine, and sherry. Bring to a boil, stirring constantly, and simmer for 20 seconds. Remove from the flame and set aside to stand for 2 minutes. Divide among 6 soup plates or bowls.

Heat oven to 400°. Reduce juices in skillet to sauce consistency, stirring frequently, about 10 minutes. (Be careful, as cream boils over easily.) Taste for seasoning. Place bowls of seafood in hot oven for 2 minutes. Cover with sauce and garnish with feta cheese. Serve with crusty French bread.

SERVES 6
PREPARATION TIME: 20 minutes
COOKING TIME: about 15 minutes

LINZER TORTE

2 cups all-purpose flour
1⅔ cups (10 ounces) hazelnuts, ground to powder
½ pound plus 4 tablespoons (2½ sticks) unsalted butter, softened, cut up
1⅔ cups (7½ ounces) confectioners' sugar
1 large egg yolk
½ teaspoon ground cloves
1 teaspoon ground cinnamon

Grated zest of 1 lemon
½ cup plus 1 tablespoon (4½ ounces) lingonberry jam (see Editor's Note below)
½ cup plus 1 tablespoon (4½ ounces) raspberry jam
1 egg beaten with 1 teaspoon water, for egg wash
½ cup sliced almonds

Preheat oven to 325°. Combine flour, ground hazelnuts, butter, confectioners' sugar, egg yolk, cloves, cinnamon, and lemon zest in the bowl of an electric mixer. Combine with dough hook until just mixed. Do not overblend. Press two thirds of the dough into a 10″ springform pan to come approximately halfway up sides. Roll remaining third of dough by hand into thin loglike strips for lattice top.

Combine lingonberry and raspberry jam and cover base. Crisscross the strips of dough on top, forming a lattice. Run a knife blade around edge of dough and fold sides over edges of lattice. Brush pastry with egg wash and sprinkle with sliced almonds. Bake for 45 to 50 minutes, until lightly browned and cooked through. Cool in pan for 5 minutes before releasing and removing rim. Cool torte completely on base of pan before removing to a serving plate.

SERVES 8 TO 10
PREPARATION TIME: 30 minutes
COOKING TIME: 45 to 50 minutes

EDITOR'S NOTE: If lingonberry (a kind of European cranberry) jam is unavailable, use all raspberry jam and add a little grated lemon zest for extra tartness. Linzer torte dough is short and crumbly, and is best patted into the pan like a graham cracker crust. If you find that it is too difficult to form into logs for the lattice top, roll out ¼″ thick between 2 sheets of plastic wrap and cut into ⅓″-wide strips. Pick them up on a long narrow pastry spatula or knife blade and set them in position. (Bake any leftover dough as cookies.) The torte may be a little hard at the edges when it comes out of the oven, but will develop a perfect consistency after cooling and then storing for a few hours in an airtight container or under a glass cake dome.

Located in downtown San Francisco and complete with a 1906 marble floor that was uncovered during renovations, The Maltese Grill is the creation of owner and experienced food professional Jo Policastro. Reminiscent of a stylish European trattoria, the restaurant features the casual, hearty, flavorful foods of the northern Mediterranean, with creative menus from chef Amey Shaw.

> HOUSE SMOKED SALMON SALAD
> PORK RAGOUT WITH BALSAMIC VINEGAR AND CÈPES
> WHITE CHOCOLATE MOUSSE

HOUSE SMOKED SALMON SALAD •

2 pounds salmon filet, skin on (see Editor's Note below)
Salt
8 handfuls assorted small garden lettuce leaves
1 English cucumber, peeled and julienned
Vinaigrette (recipe follows)
40 cherry tomatoes
48 Niçoise olives, drained

Let smoker fill with smoke. Sprinkle the salmon with salt and put in smoker. Hot-smoke for 4 minutes. Remove skin and carefully slice and divide into 8 portions.

Toss lettuce leaves and julienned cucumber in the vinaigrette. Arrange on 8 plates. Garnish each plate with 5 tomatoes and 6 olives. Mound the salmon in the center.

Vinaigrette

¼ cup sherry vinegar
Kosher salt
Freshly ground black pepper
6 tablespoons almond oil
½ cup peanut oil

Place vinegar in a bowl, and add salt and pepper to taste. Slowly whisk in oils.

SERVES 8

PREPARATION TIME: 20 minutes

COOKING TIME: 4 minutes

EDITOR'S NOTE: Northwest smoked salmon may be substituted for salmon filets and salt if you do not have access to a smoker.

PORK RAGOUT WITH BALSAMIC VINEGAR AND CÈPES

Virgin olive oil for casserole
6 pounds pork butt, cut into 1½" cubes
Kosher salt
3 large onions, peeled and sliced
8 ounces lean bacon, cut into ½" strips
3 bay leaves

1 cup balsamic vinegar
2 to 3 cups Beef Stock (page 293)
3 ounces dried cèpes
6 ounces fresh shiitake mushrooms,
  stemmed and thickly sliced
Hot cooked polenta or pasta

In a large casserole, add enough olive oil to just coat bottom. Sprinkle pork with salt and brown thoroughly, about 10 minutes. Do this in batches if necessary; do not crowd pan. Remove pork and drain in a colander.

Add more oil to pan if necessary and sauté onions and bacon, about 8 minutes, until onions are lightly browned. Spoon off any excess fat. Add bay leaves and balsamic vinegar. Return pork to casserole and add enough stock to just cover meat. Stir in cèpes and shiitake mushrooms, and bring to a boil.

Cover pan and reduce heat. Simmer for 1½ hours, or until meat is tender. Serve over polenta or pasta, in shallow bowls.

SERVES 8 TO 10

PREPARATION TIME: 30 minutes

COOKING TIME: 2 hours

WHITE CHOCOLATE MOUSSE

*8 ounces best-quality white chocolate,
broken into small pieces*
¼ pound (1 stick) unsalted butter
*6 large eggs, separated, at room
temperature*
1 cup sifted confectioners' sugar

½ cup Frangelico liqueur
2 cups heavy cream, cold
Pinch cream of tartar
*2 cups strawberries, washed and hulled,
for garnish*

Combine white chocolate and butter in a saucepan and melt over very low heat. Set aside.

In a bowl, combine egg yolks and sugar and beat until mixture forms a slowly dissolving ribbon from a lifted beater. Beat in liqueur. Pour mixture into top of double boiler and cook over simmering water, whisking constantly until very thick, about 5 minutes.

Remove to a large mixing bowl. Whisk in the white chocolate mixture and stir until smooth and cold, about 10 minutes.

Beat cream until it forms stiff peaks. In a separate bowl, using clean beaters, beat egg whites with cream of tartar until stiff but not dry. Gently fold egg whites into chocolate mixture; then fold in whipped cream.

Spoon the mousse into a serving dish or individual dishes and chill for at least 2 hours. Garnish with fresh strawberries.

SERVES 10

PREPARATION TIME: 20 minutes, plus chilling time

COOKING TIME: about 5 minutes

Owner/chef Manora Srisopa serves authentic Thai food at this friendly south-of-Market restaurant. Thai carvings and Thai drama paintings on the walls add to the exotic dining experience.

POPIER SOD (*Crab Rolls with Tamarind Sauce*)
GOONG CHU CHEE (*Curried Prawns*)
SIAM GEMS

POPIER SOD

1 Chinese pork sausage, cut into ¼" dice (see Editor's Note below)

¼ pound ground pork, crumbled

2 tablespoons soy sauce

¼ pound tofu, diced

¼ pound raw shrimp meat, deveined, diced

¼ pound Chinese black mushrooms or regular mushrooms, dried

2 sheets fresh edible rice paper skins (available in Oriental grocery stores)

¼ pound crab meat

1 cucumber, peeled, seeded, and cut into julienne

Sauce

¼ cup taramind juice (see Editor's Note below)

2 tablespoons sugar

1 tablespoon black (extra strong) soy sauce

¼ teaspoon salt

1 tablespoons tapioca starch mixed with 1 tablespoon water

Fresh cilantro (coriander) for garnish

Whole red jalapeño peppers for garnish

Fry diced Chinese pork sausage until cooked, about 5 minutes, set aside. Stir-fry ground pork with soy sauce until cooked. Add diced tofu and diced shrimp meat, and stir-fry for 2 minutes. Add diced mushrooms and cook for 2 minutes.

Lay a sheet of rice paper skin out on a work surface. Spread half the cooked mixture on it, leaving a 2″ border at the top. Place half the crab meat, cucumber, and pork sausage on top, distributing evenly. Starting from the bottom, roll the rice skin firmly. Cut roll into 6 pieces. Repeat with second rice paper skin.

Sauce: Combine tamarind juice, sugar, black soy sauce, and salt in a saucepan and stir over high heat until mixture reaches boiling point. Stir in tapioca and water and boil for 3 to 4 minutes, stirring constantly. Cool to room temperature.

Place rolls on serving platter, pour sauce on top, and garnish with cilantro and hot peppers.

SERVES 4 TO 6
PREPARATION TIME: 30 minutes
COOKING TIME: about 20 minutes

EDITOR'S NOTE: Chinese pork sausage, black mushrooms, rice paper skins, black soy sauce, tamarind, and tapioca starch can be found at Chinese and/ or Thai grocery stores.

Tamarind juice is obtained by soaking dried tamarind. The resultant liquid is tangy, and is used like lemon juice or vinegar.

GOONG CHU CHEE •

1 tablespoon Thai red chili paste
1 can coconut milk
2 tablespoons Thai or Chinese fish sauce
1 teaspoon sugar

12 to 15 raw jumbo prawns (shrimp), shelled and deveined
Whole red jalapeño peppers for garnish
Fresh basil leaves for garnish

Combine chili paste, coconut milk, fish sauce, and sugar in a saucepan. Stir over medium-high heat for 15 to 20 minutes.

Broil or grill prawns until just done, about 1½ minutes per side. Place prawns on a serving platter and top with sauce. Garnish with jalapeño peppers and fresh basil leaves.

SERVES 4
PREPARATION TIME: 20 minutes
COOKING TIME: 20 minutes

SIAM GEMS •

¼ pound fresh water chestnuts, peeled and diced

¼ teaspoon red food coloring (available in Vietnamese groceries)

1 tablespoon tapioca starch
1 can coconut milk
¼ cup sugar
Meat from ¼ small young coconut, diced

¼ pound toddy palm seed (palm fruit somewhat similar to coconut in flavor; available in Thai or Vietnamese groceries)

Soak the diced water chestnuts in red food coloring and then stir into tapioca starch. Add to a saucepan of boiling water and boil for 4 to 5 minutes. Drain off water. Add coconut milk to saucepan and add sugar, coconut meat, and toddy palm seed. Serve over crushed ice in sherbet cups.

SERVES 4
PREPARATION TIME: 10 minutes
COOKING TIME: 5 minutes

The standards set by the late master chef Masa Kobayashi have never wavered at this beautifully run San Francisco restaurant, which consistently wins top awards. The banner is now carried by successor chef Julian Serrano, who worked with Kobayashi for three years. The aesthetics of the softly lit burgundy and pale gray decor mesh perfectly with the impeccable contemporary French cuisine.

WARM LOBSTER SALAD WITH CITRUS VINAIGRETTE

LAMB CHOPS WITH HERBED POTATO CRUST

HAZELNUT SOUFFLÉ WITH CRÈME ANGLAISE

WARM LOBSTER SALAD WITH CITRUS VINAIGRETTE

6 Maine chicken lobsters, 1 pound each
3 artichoke bottoms
4 cups vegetable consommé
1 bouquet fresh thyme
3 juniper berries
1 head limestone or butter lettuce
1 head red oak leaf lettuce

1 head curly endive
1 head Belgian endive
Citrus Vinaigrette (recipe follows)
Few drops port wine
Chervil leaves for garnish
Pink peppercorns for garnish

Poach lobsters for 1½ minutes in boiling water. Drain and set aside. Remove meat from shells carefully so as not to break the pieces. Cut tail meat across into ¼″ medallions, holding them together to retain the tail shape. Reserve claws. Braise the artichoke bottoms in vegetable consommé with fresh thyme and juniper berries until tender, about 10 minutes; then cut into julienne strips.

Create a bed of lettuce for the lobster-shaped presentation: For the head, place limestone lettuce leaves in an oval, and center with red oak leaf lettuce topped with curly endive. For the tail, arrange julienned strips of artichoke bottom. Then fan out the Belgian endive leaves. Place the lobster claws on either side of the head section of lettuce. Arrange lobster tail medallions on top of the artichoke strips, to re-create the tail section.

Heat dressing to warm it, being careful not to separate the vinaigrette by getting it too hot. Add a few drops of port wine. Carefully sprinkle warm dressing over lobster and lettuce—they should be shiny, but not saturated. Garnish with chervil leaves and pink peppercorns.

Citrus Vinaigrette

¼ cup freshly squeezed orange juice

¼ cup freshly squeezed lemon juice

¼ cup freshly squeezed lime juice

¼ cup freshly squeezed blood orange or tangerine juice

¼ cup sherry vinegar

1½ cups extra-virgin olive oil

½ cup hazelnut oil

2 tablespoons truffle juice (optional)

Salt and pepper

Sugar

Using separate pans, reduce each fruit juice by a quarter. Combine in mixing bowl and whisk in vinegar, oils, and truffle juice. Add salt, pepper, and sugar to taste, noting that sugar is to soften the acidity of the citrus juices, not to sweeten the dressing.

SERVES 6

PREPARATION TIME: 35 minutes total

COOKING TIME: 10 minutes

CHEF'S NOTE: In season, other fruit juices may be substituted, such as pineapple juice for the blood orange juice.

LAMB CHOPS WITH HERBED POTATO CRUST

3 racks of lamb (6 chops each)
6 large egg yolks
6 medium russet potatoes, peeled and
   grated
1 clove garlic, peeled and minced
½ bunch fresh parsley, destemmed and
   finely chopped

½ bunch fresh chives, finely chopped
½ bunch fresh thyme, destemmed and
   finely chopped
Salt and pepper
6 strips bacon
1 pound snow peas
Virgin olive oil for pan

Sauce

Virgin olive oil for pan
Bones and meat trimmings from racks of
   lamb
2 cloves garlic, peeled and chopped
1 cup heavy red wine
1 medium onion, peeled and diced

1 medium carrot, peeled and diced
2 stalks celery, diced
1 teaspoon chopped fresh thyme
½ teaspoon whole black peppercorns
1 tablespoon tomato paste

Remove all fat from the racks of lamb, and all meat on and between the bones. Set aside bones and meat scraps for the sauce. Cut rack into chops. (Or buy 18 Frenched lamb chops and ask for the bone and meat trimmings.)

In a large mixing bowl, gently mix egg yolks, grated potatoes, garlic, and herbs. Season lightly with salt and pepper. Cover each chop thoroughly with this mixture, top and bottom.

Blanch bacon in boiling water for 1 minute, and chop into 1″ pieces. Trim snow peas, and blanch in boiling salted water for 2 minutes. Drain, plunge into cold water to stop cooking and set color, drain again, and set aside.

Sauce: Heat a heavy sauté pan and film the bottom with olive oil. Sauté reserved bones and meat scraps with garlic until completely brown, about 10 minutes. Drain off any excess fat. Add remaining ingredients, cover with water, and bring to a boil. Reduce heat and simmer for 30 minutes. Strain sauce, and pour into a saucepan. Reduce to desired sauce consistency, about 10 minutes.

Film 2 or more large sauté pans generously with olive oil. Sauté the lamb chops for approximately 6 minutes per side, so that the lamb is cooked medium rare and the potato crust is crispy.

While lamb is cooking, sauté bacon pieces lightly, until cooked but not hard. Toss blanched snow peas in pan with hot bacon.

To serve, place 3 lamb chops on top half of each serving plate, back to back with bones crossed. Arrange snow peas and bacon on bottom left-hand side. Place a portion of the sauce at bottom right, making sure it does not touch the lamb chops, which must remain crispy.

SERVES 6
PREPARATION TIME: 25 minutes
COOKING TIME: 1 hour

HAZELNUT SOUFFLÉ WITH CRÈME ANGLAISE

1 cup (6 ounces) hazelnuts
1¼ cups heavy cream
¼ cup amaretto
2 tablespoons Cognac
½ cup egg whites, from 4 to 5 eggs

½ cup sugar
1½ cups Crème Anglaise (page 297)
Raspberry Sauce (page 114) (optional)

Preheat oven to 350°. Place hazelnuts on a sheet cake pan and roast until lightly colored, about 15 minutes. Rub in a clean kitchen towel to remove loose skins—not every scrap has to come off. Reserve 6 perfect whole nuts for garnish, and grind the remainder to a powder. Secure paper collars around 6 individual soufflé molds or ramekins to extend 1″ above rims.

Combine cream, amaretto, and Cognac. Whip at high speed until mixture forms soft peaks. Combine egg whites and sugar in top of double boiler and heat over simmering water until sugar melts, about 2 minutes. Remove from heat and whip at high speed to soft peaks. Fold ground hazelnuts into cream mixture; then fold in meringue. Transfer to a pastry bag fitted with a large plain tip and pipe into molds. Freeze for at least 4 hours.

Put a little crème anglaise in the middle of each dessert plate and swirl plate to spread sauce. Make a design around the edge with raspberry sauce (optional), and unmold soufflé in the center. Garnish tops with reserved whole hazelnuts.

SERVES 6
PREPARATION TIME: 30 minutes, plus freezing time
COOKING TIME: 25 minutes

Meadowood Resort Hotel is situated in St. Helena, in the heart of the Napa Valley. Sequestered on 250 wooded acres, the hotel hosts the prestigious Napa Valley Wine Auction every June, and offers unique wine and food courses throughout the year. The elegant restaurant is always filled with fresh flowers, and has brocaded armchairs, soft lighting, and crisp white and pink napery. The cuisine reflects an understanding of European culinary traditions artfully blended with Californian innovations.

QUESADILLA OF SMOKED CHICKEN
DUNGENESS CRAB AND AVOCADO SALAD
PEARS IN VELVET

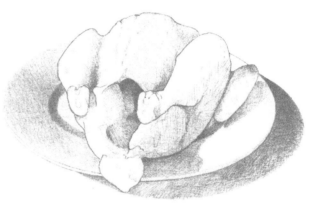

QUESADILLA OF SMOKED CHICKEN •

8 ounces Saint André cheese, rind removed (see Editor's Note below)
8 flour tortillas, 8" diameter
12 ounces smoked chicken meat, shredded

¼ bunch cilantro (coriander) (about 60 leaves), plus extra sprigs for garnish
2 teaspoons freshly ground black pepper
Olive oil for skillet
Salsa (recipe follows)

Spread cheese on tortillas. Top 4 of them with one quarter of the smoked chicken meat, 15 cilantro leaves, and ½ teaspoon pepper each. Cover with remaining tortillas, cheese side down. (Can be refrigerated at this point.)

Heat a large skillet or griddle. Grease with a small amount of olive oil. Sauté filled tortillas for about 1 minute on each side, until cheese melts. Cut into 6 wedges. Place 2 tablespoons salsa on each wedge and garnish with fresh cilantro sprigs.

Salsa

6 halves dry-packed sun-dried tomatoes

¼ cup virgin olive oil

3 ripe tomatoes, peeled, seeded, and chopped

1 small red onion, peeled and chopped

3 scallions, white bulb and most of green tops, chopped

1½ red bell peppers, seeded and chopped

8 cilantro (coriander) leaves, chopped

Marinate sun-dried tomatoes in olive oil for 1 hour or longer and cut into julienne. Transfer to sauté pan and add chopped tomatoes and red onion. Bring to a boil, cover, and sweat over low heat for 3 to 4 minutes to soften tomatoes. Transfer to a bowl and add scallions, bell peppers, and cilantro. Allow mixture to cool for 30 minutes.

SERVES 4

PREPARATION TIME: 15 minutes total, plus marination and cooling time

COOKING TIME: about 15 minutes total

EDITOR'S NOTE: Saint André cheese is a mild, triple-crème French cheese.

CHEF'S NOTE: One cup of cooked black beans may be added to the salsa. Quesadillas may be served with a mixed salad dressed with vinaigrette, using oil from marinating the sun-dried tomatoes.

DUNGENESS CRAB AND AVOCADO SALAD •

6 to 8 generous handfuls mixed salad greens (such as oak leaf, frisée, arugula, etc.)

Honey Grapefruit Dressing (recipe follows)

½ to ¾ pound crab meat

2 avocados, split

1 large grapefruit, peeled and sectioned (page 292)

16 asparagus tips, lightly cooked, cold

1 mango, peeled and julienned

1 vine-ripened tomato, sliced

8 thin rings of red bell pepper (cut straight across)

4 peeled crab claws for garnish (optional)

Place salad greens in a bowl. Toss with enough dressing to just coat the leaves lightly. Arrange on 4 large plates, leaving a space in the center.

Season crab meat with dressing. Fill cavities of avocado halves with crab meat and place 1 half in the center of each plate. Arrange grapefruit sections, asparagus, mango, and sliced tomato decoratively on top of salad greens. Finish by placing 2 red bell pepper rings on top of crab meat. Garnish with crab claw meat, if used.

Honey Grapefruit Dressing

2 tablespoons honey
1 tablespoon Napa Valley or other hot
   sweet mustard
¼ cup freshly squeezed grapefruit juice
¼ onion, peeled and minced
¼ cup freshly squeezed lime juice

¼ teaspoon cayenne pepper
½ teaspoon salt
½ bunch fresh basil, leaves only
1½ cups St. Helena or other virgin olive
   oil

Place all ingredients except oil in a blender or food processor and mix to blend. With motor running, slowly add olive oil. Strain. (Any leftover dressing will keep for 3 days under refrigeration.)

SERVES 4

PREPARATION TIME: 30 minutes total

COOKING TIME: None

PEARS IN VELVET

4 pears, peeled, halved, and cored
1 bottle white wine, 750 ml.
1 cup sugar
2 cinnamon sticks

1 pound bittersweet or semisweet
   chocolate, finely chopped
1 cup heavy cream
11" pastry shell made with Pâte Sucrée
   (recipe follows)

Place pears in a saucepan with wine, sugar, and cinnamon sticks and bring to a boil. Reduce heat and simmer until tender, 10 minutes or more depending on fruit. Cool in the syrup.

Put chopped chocolate in a bowl. Place cream in a saucepan and bring to a boil. Pour over chocolate and let stand for 1 minute. Stir with a whisk until smooth and pour into tart shell.

Drain pears and pat dry. Leave in halves, or slice lengthwise and fan out slightly, retaining the original shape. Sink into the chocolate filling while it is still soft. Chill thoroughly before serving.

Pâte Sucrée

7 ounces (1¾ sticks) butter, cold, cut up   *Pinch salt*
6 tablespoons (3 ounces) sugar   *1 large egg*
1¾ cups (9 ounces) all-purpose flour   *Dash vanilla extract*

Combine butter, sugar, flour, and salt in the bowl of a food processor and process until mixture resembles coarse crumbs. With motor running, add egg and vanilla. Process briefly until dough forms a ball. If mixture is too dry to do this, add a few drops of cold water.

On a lightly floured surface, roll dough ⅛" thick and fit into an 11" fluted tart pan with loose base, without stretching the pastry. With your thumb, gently push dough against sides so that it extends a little above rim of pan, and slightly over the edge. (This prevents sides from falling during baking and eliminates filling shell with weights.) Chill for 30 minutes to relax gluten in flour and firm up the butter.

Preheat oven to 375°. Bake for 25 minutes, or until golden brown. Be sure to check after the first 5 minutes and with the tip of a knife deflate any bubbles that may have formed.

If making dough by hand, combine soft butter and sugar and add egg. When smooth, incorporate flour, salt, and vanilla. Wrap in plastic and chill for 1 to 2 hours. Roll out and fit into tart pan. Line with paper or foil and weight with dried beans. Bake for 15 minutes, then remove paper and beans and continue baking for 10 minutes, until golden brown.

SERVES 12
PREPARATION TIME: 30 minutes total, plus chilling time
COOKING TIME: 35 minutes total

CHEF'S NOTE: Poaching liquid from pears may be used for poaching other fruits, or as a sauce. To make sauce, reduce by half by rapid boiling, or thicken with a little cornstarch dissolved in cold water. Boil until sauce clears and thickens, about 30 seconds.

Apricot-colored walls, wonderful old elk-horn chandeliers, high-backed French Provincial chairs with rush seats, and white napery combine to make this well-established Napa Valley restaurant very inviting. Co-owner/chef Udo Nechutnys blends classic French techniques with subtle Japanese touches, and—in keeping with contemporary tastes—his imaginative cuisine also reflects a concern with healthy eating.

SALAD WITH SALMON AND CAVIAR
VEAL CHOPS WITH SORREL SAUCE
BLUEBERRY-ALMOND TART

SALAD WITH SALMON AND CAVIAR

1 tablespoon butter
2 teaspoons finely chopped shallot
1½ cups Fish Stock (page 295)
1½ cups heavy cream
Salt and pepper
¼ pound thin green beans
1 head Belgian endive
1 head frisée lettuce
1 head radicchio

1 tomato, peeled, seeded, and roughly chopped
½ cup Almond Oil Vinaigrette (recipe follows)
6 thin slices salmon filet, about 1 pound total
3 teaspoons caviar (red, golden, or choice black)

In a saucepan, heat butter and sauté shallot for 1 minute. Add fish stock and boil gently until reduced to 1 cup, about 10 minutes. Add cream and boil for 5 minutes to thicken slightly. Season with salt and pepper to taste and let cool.

Blanch green beans in boiling salted water for 1 minute, or until just tender. (This depends on size.) Drain, refresh in cold water to stop cooking and set color, and drain again. Chill.

Wash and dry salad greens and tear into bite-sized pieces as necessary. In a bowl, combine salad greens, green beans, and tomato. Mix well with almond oil vinaigrette.

Arrange a pool of fish sauce in the center of 6 dinner plates and surround with a wreath of salad greens.

At the last moment, heat a nonstick skillet over high heat and cook salmon slices for 10 seconds on each side. Carefully lift from pan and lay on top of sauce. Garnish each salmon slice with ½ teaspoon caviar.

Almond Oil Vinaigrette

2 tablespoons white wine vinegar   Salt and pepper to taste
6 tablespoons sweet almond oil

Combine all ingredients and blend well.

SERVES 6
PREPARATION TIME: 20 minutes
COOKING TIME: about 20 minutes

VEAL CHOPS WITH SORREL SAUCE •

6 large veal chops, boned and well   2 tablespoons butter
  trimmed, about 5 ounces each (or use   1 tablespoon minced shallot
  choice veal steaks cut from the leg)   ⅓ cup dry white wine
Salt and pepper   1 bunch sorrel (about 36 large leaves),
Flour for dredging   stemmed and deveined, shredded
2 tablespoons virgin olive oil   1½ cups heavy cream

Season veal with salt and pepper to taste and dredge lightly with flour. Do this just before cooking to prevent the coating from becoming soggy.

Heat oil and butter in a heavy skillet and sauté veal until tender, partially covered, about 10 minutes, turning once. Remove meat and keep warm.

In same skillet, simmer minced shallot for 3 minutes. Deglaze pan with wine and add shredded sorrel. Cook for 2 minutes, then add cream. Reduce sauce over medium-high heat until thck enough to coat veal, about 3 minutes.

Place chops on heated serving plates and spoon sauce on top.

SERVES 6
PREPARATION TIME: 10 minutes
COOKING TIME: 18 minutes

BLUEBERRY-ALMOND TART

Pastry Shell (Pâte Sablée)

1¼ cups all-purpose flour
Pinch salt
6 tablespoons sugar

6 tablespoons (¾ stick) unsalted butter,
  cold
2 large egg yolks

Pastry Cream

1 cup milk
1 strip lemon zest
½ vanilla bean

3 large egg yolks
¼ cup sugar
¼ cup all-purpose flour

Almond Filling

6 tablespoons (¾ stick) unsalted butter,
  softened
3 ounces sliced almonds, toasted

¾ cup confectioners' sugar
2 large eggs
2 tablespoons all-purpose flour

Topping

1½ baskets fresh ripe blueberries,
  washed and stemmed

Shell: Sift together the flour, salt, and sugar. Cut in butter until mixture resembles coarse meal. Add egg yolks and knead lightly until dough can be gathered together into a ball. Do not overmix. Enclose in plastic wrap and chill for 1 hour.

Pastry Cream: Place milk in a saucepan with lemon zest and vanilla bean. Bring to a simmer, remove from heat, and take out lemon zest and vanilla bean. Whip egg yolks and sugar together, and add flour. Loosen mixture with a little of the hot milk, then stir in remaining milk. Return entire mixture to saucepan and cook over low heat, stirring, until smooth and thick and floury taste has been cooked out, about 5 minutes. Let cool.

Almond Filling: In the bowl of an electric mixer, beat butter until fluffy. Grind toasted almonds with confectioners' sugar in a food processor. Slowly blend nut mixture into butter. Add eggs, one at a time, beating at low speed. Remove bowl from stand. Sift flour and fold lightly into mixture.

Preheat oven to 375°. On a lightly floured surface, roll dough ⅛″ thick. Fit into a 10″ tart pan with removable base. Bake "blind," or without a filling,

for 15 minutes. (See Editor's Note below.) Blend 2 parts pastry cream with
1 part almond filling (probably not all will be needed) and half fill pastry
shell. Continue baking until pale gold on top and cooked through, about 20
minutes. Cover tart with blueberries and return to oven until berries are
just warmed through, 2 to 3 minutes. Cool on a rack.

SERVES 8 TO 10

PREPARATION TIME: 30 minutes, plus chilling time

COOKING TIME: 45 minutes

EDITOR'S NOTE: To bake a tart shell without a filling, see Standard Prep-
arations, Pastry Shell (page 298).

Owner/chef Jesse Acevedo's imaginative, highly personal interpretation of regional Mexican food is matched by his vibrant design for this Castro neighborhood restaurant: Shades of fuchsia, turquoise, and pink contrast with the black walls; tables are set with pink and yellow cloths and royal blue napkins; tropical plants abound. Lively Latin music contributes to a unique Mexican dining experience.

GREEN SALAD WITH MANGO VINAIGRETTE
CHICKEN MOLE AND BAKED MEXICAN GREEN
   RICE
MEXICAN FLAN

GREEN SALAD WITH MANGO VINAIGRETTE •

3 small heads baby lettuce (such as butter lettuce, limestone lettuce, and arugula)

Mango Vinaigrette (recipe follows)
9 ripe strawberries, halved

Separate, wash, and dry lettuce leaves. Toss with vinaigrette and divide among salad plates. Arrange strawberries around edges of plates.

Mango Vinaigrette

1 ripe mango, peeled and cut into
  chunks
2 tablespoons Oriental sesame oil

2 tablespoons rice vinegar
½ tablespoon Mexican curry powder or
  other curry powder

Combine all ingredients in a blender or food processor and blend well.
SERVES 6
PREPARATION TIME: 10 minutes total
COOKING TIME: None

CHICKEN MOLE WITH BAKED MEXICAN GREEN RICE

3 small dried pasilla chili peppers
3 small dried mulato chili peppers
1½ cups boiling water
¼ cup sesame seeds
3 cloves
1" piece cinnamon stick
¼ teaspoon coriander seeds
⅛ teaspoon aniseseed
¼ cup vegetable oil
¼ cup unblanched almonds
¼ cup seedless raisins
½ cup dried apricots
6 whole chicken legs

¼ teaspoon salt
½ cup coarsely chopped onion
2 cloves garlic, peeled and chopped
1 tablespoon tomato paste
1½ ounces dark Mexican chocolate,
  coarsely chopped
1 cup Chicken Stock (page 294) or
  canned chicken broth
Tomato wedges for garnish
Cilantro (coriander) sprigs for garnish
Baked Mexican Green Rice (recipe
  follows)

Preheat oven to 350°. Roast pasilla and mulato chilies for 20 minutes, then seed and devein. Place in a bowl and cover with boiling water. Leave to stand for 1 hour.

Toast sesame seeds over medium heat in a heavy, dry skillet, stirring frequently, until golden brown, about 30 seconds. Remove and reserve. Combine cloves, cinnamon stick, coriander seeds, and aniseseed. Toast in same skillet over medium heat, stirring frequently, until they start to change color and become very fragrant, about 45 seconds. Remove and reserve. Add oil to skillet and heat until very hot. Add almonds and stir until brown, about 30 seconds. Remove with a slotted spoon to a folded paper towel. When cool enough to handle, chop coarsely. Add raisins and apricots to skillet and cook until raisins are puffed, about 5 minutes. Remove from skillet with slotted spoon.

Sprinkle chicken legs with salt and add to skillet. Cook until brown, about 5 minutes on each side, and remove to a plate. Drain all but 2 tablespoons fat from skillet.

Process raisins and apricots in a blender or food processor until finely ground. Add almonds and process until finely ground. Add onion and garlic and process until finely ground.

Place half the sesame seeds, cloves, cinnamon, coriander, and anise in an electric spice blender and grind to a fine powder. (Or use a mortar and pestle.) Add to mixture in blender. Add chilies and a third of the water to blender, along with tomato paste. Process until smooth. If mixture is too thick, add remaining water a little at a time until blender blades are released.

Reheat skillet containing fat over medium heat. When hot, add chili mixture and cook, stirring constantly, for 5 minutes. Add chocolate and stir until melted, about 2 minutes. Gradually stir in stock and cook, stirring constantly, for another 5 minutes.

Add chicken to skillet, and reduce heat to low. Cover pan and simmer, turning occasionally, until tender, about 45 minutes. Divide chicken among serving plates, top with sauce and remaining toasted sesame seeds. Garnish with tomato wedges and cilantro sprigs. Pass baked rice at the table.

Baked Mexican Green Rice

2 tablespoons vegetable oil

1 cup raw long-grain rice

¼ onion, peeled and finely chopped

2 fresh pasilla chili peppers, roasted, peeled, seeded, deveined, and chopped (for roasting chili peppers, see recipe above)

6 scallions, white bulbs and green tops, thinly sliced

1 clove garlic, peeled and minced

¼ teaspoon salt

¼ teaspoon ground cumin

1¾ cups Chicken Stock (page 294) or canned chicken broth

1½ cups shredded Queso Chihuahua or Monterey Jack cheese

⅓ cup coarsely chopped fresh cilantro (coriander)

Heat oil in a 10″ skillet over medium heat. Add rice and stir until it turns opaque, about 3 minutes. Quickly add onion, and sauté for 1 minute. Add chili peppers, scallions, garlic, salt, and cumin. Sauté for 20 seconds. Add stock and bring to a boil. Reduce heat, cover pan, and simmer for 15 minutes.

Preheat oven to 375°. Remove skillet from heat. Transfer rice to a baking dish, and stir in 1 cup of the cheese. Add cilantro and toss lightly to mix. Bake for 15 to 20 minutes. Top with remaining ½ cup cheese before serving.

SERVES 6

PREPARATION TIME: 1 hour total, plus standing time

COOKING TIME: 1 hour total

MEXICAN FLAN

Caramel

½ cup sugar   ¼ cup water

Custard

2 cups half and half   6 large eggs
1 cup milk   2 large egg yolks
2 teaspoons vanilla extract
½ cup sugar   Small ripe strawberries for garnish

Caramel: Combine sugar and water in a heavy saucepan and boil over medium-high heat until the mixture turns a deep golden-tan color, 350° on a candy thermometer, about 7 minutes. Quickly pour into a ring mold, swirling to spread it up the sides. (Use mitts, as the caramel will be very hot, and will heat the mold.) The caramel will harden almost at once. Cool for 15 minutes.

Custard: Preheat oven to 350°. In a heavy 2-quart saucepan, combine cream, milk, and vanilla. Heat over medium heat until almost simmering. Add sugar and stir to dissolve. In a large bowl, lightly beat whole eggs and egg yolks together until blended but not foamy. Gradually stir in hot milk.

Pour custard into prepared ring mold. Place mold in a shallow roasting pan. Add enough hot water to reach halfway up sides of mold. Bake for 35 minutes, or until a knife blade inserted in center of custard comes out clean.

Remove mold and chill in refrigerator for 1 hour or longer. Loosen inner and outer edges of custard with a knife tip and unmold onto a flat platter with sides. The caramel, which will have softened, will flow over the custard. Garnish with strawberries.

SERVES 6

PREPARATION TIME: 20 minutes, plus cooling and chilling time

COOKING TIME: about 30 minutes

A roadside café on Highway 29 just north of Yountville in the Napa Valley, Mustards opened in 1983 and swiftly became the talk of California, and beyond. Co-owner and chef Cindy Pawlcyn, who is also executive chef of the small Real Restaurants chain (which includes Mustards, Tra Vigne, Bix, and Fog City Diner), creates upscale versions of traditional American cooking, often with exotic Asian and Mexican accents.

EGGPLANT WITH GINGER BUTTER
GRILLED PORK LOIN WITH BLACK BEANS,
PICKLED ONIONS, AND TOMATILLO SALSA
GINGER AND PEAR CAKE

EGGPLANT WITH GINGER BUTTER •

6 Japanese eggplants, 4" to 6" long
Virgin olive oil for grilling
3 red onions, peeled and sliced into
   rounds

Ginger Butter (recipe follows)

Slice eggplants lengthwise almost to the core several times, so they fan out. Brush with olive oil and grill over hot coals, 2 or 3 minutes per side. Brush onion slices with oil and grill at the same time.

Fan eggplants out on plates, inserting a slice of onion between each slice of eggplant. Top with ginger butter.

Ginger Butter

10 tablespoons (1¼ sticks) unsalted
   butter, cut up
1" piece gingerroot, peeled and grated

1 shallot, peeled and minced
¼ teaspoon salt
Ground white pepper to taste

Combine all ingredients in a food processor and mix well.

SERVES 6
PREPARATION TIME: 10 minutes
COOKING TIME: 5 minutes

GRILLED PORK LOIN WITH BLACK BEANS, PICKLED ONIONS, AND TOMATILLO SALSA

1 pound black beans
4½ cups water
¼ pound bacon, chopped
5 medium cloves garlic, peeled and minced
2 medium stalks celery, minced
1 large carrot, peeled and diced
1 medium onion, peeled and diced
1 jalapeño chili pepper, seeded and minced
1 bay leaf
1 tablespoon chili powder

1 teaspoon ground cumin
1 teaspoon cayenne
¾ teaspoon freshly ground white pepper
2 quarts Chicken Stock (page 294) or canned chicken broth
Salt and pepper
1 cup mesquite chips
1 pork loin, about 4 pounds, boned and cut into ¾″ slices
Pickled Onions (recipe follows)
Tomatillo Salsa (recipe follows)

Soak beans in water for 24 hours. Drain. Transfer to a large saucepan and cover with a generous amount of cold water. Boil for 20 minutes. Drain. Rinse beans, and drain again.

In a large, heavy saucepan, cook bacon until golden brown and crisp, stirring frequently, about 5 minutes. Add garlic, celery, carrot, onion, jalapeño chili, and bay leaf. Cook until vegetables are tender, stirring occasionally, about 10 minutes. Add chili powder, cumin, cayenne, and white pepper. Stir until aromatic, about 1 minute. Add beans and stock. Simmer, stirring occasionally, until beans are tender and most of the liquid is absorbed, about 1½ hours. Season to taste with salt.

Build an intense wood or charcoal fire. Soak mesquite chips in water for 30 minutes, and drain. Place pork slices between sheets of waxed paper. Using a mallet or the flat side of a cleaver, pound to a thickness of ½″. Sprinkle pork with salt and pepper to taste. Grease grill rack. Sprinkle coals with mesquite chips. Arrange pork on grill rack and cook until springy to touch, about 2½ minutes per side.

Arrange pork in center of plates. Spoon some salsa on top. Mound pickled onions on one side of pork and black beans on the other.

Pickled Onions

½ cup olive oil
2 pounds white onions, peeled, cut into ⅛″-thick wedges
1½ cups sugar
1 cup red wine vinegar

¼ cup tomato ketchup
2 tablespoons sea salt
2 teaspoons dried red chili flakes
Freshly ground white pepper

Heat oil in a large, heavy saucepan over low heat. Add onions and mix well. Cover and cook until tender, stirring occasionally, about 15 minutes. Add remaining ingredients and simmer for 3 minutes. Serve warm or at room temperature. (Can be prepared 1 day ahead and refrigerated.)

Tomatillo Salsa

½ jalapeño chili pepper, seeded and chopped

¾ pound tomatilloes, peeled

½ cup minced scallions, including part of green tops

¼ cup minced fresh parsley

2 tablespoons olive oil

2 tablespoons fresh lime juice

3 medium garlic cloves, peeled and minced

1 teaspoon grated lime zest

¼ teaspoon salt

¼ teaspoon freshly ground white pepper

Char chili over gas flame or under broiler until skin is blackened and blistered, about 7 minutes. Enclose in a paper bag and steam for 10 minutes. Slip off skin and discard seeds. Rinse and pat dry.

Blanch tomatilloes in boiling salted water for 3 minutes. Drain. Rinse under cold, running water, and drain thoroughly. Transfer to a food processor or blender. Add chili, and remaining ingredients. Puree until smooth. (Can be prepared 1 day ahead and refrigerated.)

SERVES 6

PREPARATION TIME: 1 hour total, plus soaking time

COOKING TIME: 2¼ hours total

CHEF'S NOTE: All the ingredients of this dish marry to make a special treat. The pork is also great served with just the pickled onions.

GINGER AND PEAR CAKE

5 tablespoons unsalted butter
Scant ⅔ cup (5 ounces) sugar
1 extra large egg
¾ cup molasses
2 cups (10 ounces) cake flour

1 teaspoon baking soda
½ teaspoon salt
2 tablespoons peeled and grated
   gingerroot
2 pears, peeled, cored, and grated
1 cup low-fat milk

Preheat oven to 375°. Butter and flour a 9″ square cake pan. Cream butter and sugar together until light and smooth. Beat in egg. Add molasses, stirring until smooth. Sift the flour, baking soda, and salt together, and add to mixture. Combine grated gingerroot, pears, and milk, and add slowly to mixture. Pour into prepared pan. Bake until center springs back to a light touch, about 45 minutes. Cool on a rack.

SERVES 6
PREPARATION TIME: 15 minutes
COOKING TIME: 45 minutes

One of the best-known food figures in the Bay Area, popular talk show host Narsai David of "Narsai & Company" and the "KCBS Saturday Kitchen," has also gained fame as a nationally known television chef. In turn a successful restaurateur, caterer, and developer of his own line of food products, he is frequently called upon to be a wine judge at such events as the Los Angeles County Fair.

GAZPACHO
GRILLED LAMB STEAKS
LIME-RICE PILAF
PEACH SHORTCAKE

GAZPACHO •

1 cucumber, peeled
1 large red onion, peeled
1 large red bell pepper, seeded and deribbed
1 pound tomatoes, peeled
3 or 4 cloves garlic, peeled
3 or 4 sprigs fresh basil
1 cup clam juice, Chicken Stock (page 294), or water

¼ cup wine vinegar
¼ cup virgin olive oil
2 cups tomato sauce
Juice of 1 orange
Tabasco or other hot sauce
Grated zest of ½ orange
Toast or garlic bread

Finely chop ½ cup each of the cucumber, onion, bell pepper, and tomato, and place in a soup tureen.

Place remaining cucumber, onion, bell pepper, and tomato in a blender or food processor. Add garlic and basil. Add as much of the clam juice, stock, or water as needed to obtain a smooth puree; add to soup tureen. Stir in vinegar, oil, tomato sauce, and orange juice. Season with hot sauce to taste. Add orange zest. Cover tureen and refrigerate for 2 or 3 hours to let flavors marry. Serve with toast or garlic bread.

SERVES 6 TO 8
PREPARATION TIME: 20 minutes, plus chilling time
COOKING TIME: None

GRILLED LAMB STEAKS •

6 boneless sirloin lamb or top round
   lamb steaks, 6 ounces each
3 tablespoons Worcestershire sauce

3 cloves garlic, peeled and crushed
3 6" sprigs fresh rosemary, leaves only,
   crushed

Place lamb steaks in a shallow baking pan and rub all over with the Worcestershire sauce, garlic, and crushed rosemary leaves. Set aside to marinate for 1 hour. Wipe off excess marinade and broil to medium rare, about 4 minutes per side.

SERVES 6
PREPARATION TIME: 10 minutes, plus marination time
COOKING TIME: 8 minutes

LIME-RICE PILAF •

2 teaspoons salad oil or butter
1 cup converted white rice
1½ cups Chicken Stock (page 294),
   canned chicken broth, or water

Zest and juice of 1 lime
⅓ cup currants
Salt to taste
¼ cup toasted pine nuts

Heat the oil or butter in a 1-quart pot with a tight-fitting lid. Add rice and stir until it starts to sizzle. Add chicken stock, broth, or water; lime zest and juice; and the currants. Bring to a boil and adjust seasonings with salt, if desired. Lower heat to slowest possible simmer; cover the pan and cook, undisturbed, for 18 to 20 minutes. Remove from heat and set aside to rest until needed. Stir in pine nuts just before serving.

SERVES 6
PREPARATION TIME: 10 minutes
COOKING TIME: about 20 minutes

PEACH SHORTCAKE •

2 cups all-purpose flour
2 tablespoons sugar
4 teaspoons baking powder

¼ pound (1 stick) butter, cut up
1 large egg
⅔ cup milk

Filling

6 medium peaches, peeled, pitted, and thinly sliced	2 tablespoons minced candied ginger
¼ cup sugar	1 cup heavy cream, whipped
¼ cup dark rum	1 to 2 tablespoons confectioners' sugar

Preheat oven to 425°. Mix the flour, sugar, baking powder, and butter in a large bowl until crumbly. Mix in the egg and milk only until barely incorporated. Turn out the dough onto a well-floured board. Gently press dough to form a large ball, coating it well with flour. Pat into a circle about ½″ thick and 8″ in diameter. Cut into 6 or 8 pie-shaped wedges, place on an ungreased cookie sheet, and bake until deep golden brown, about 15 minutes.

Filling: Sprinkle peaches with sugar, rum, and candied ginger. Stir well and refrigerate until ready to serve.

Split cakes in half through the center. Place bottom halves on individual serving plates. Distribute peaches over cakes and divide liquid among them. Top with a large dollop of whipped cream. Cap with top half of cakes and sprinkle with confectioners' sugar.

SERVES 6 TO 8

PREPARATION TIME: 10 minutes

COOKING TIME: 15 minutes

A lively, red-tiled, Italian restaurant located in the wine country town of Yountville, Piatti's has an open kitchen complete with woodburning rotisserie and pizza oven. Chefs Donna Scala and Steffan Terje make full use of local fresh produce, poultry, and seafood, creating authentic Italian food with a touch of Californian ingenuity.

BRUSCHETTA *(Roman Garlic Bread)*

INVOLTINI DI MELANZANE *(Grilled Eggplant Rolls with Goat Cheese)*

ZIMINO CON CAPELLINI *(Steamed Mussels and Clams with Angel Hair Pasta)*

SEMIFREDDO CON NOCE *(Frozen Nut and Chocolate Cream)*

BRUSCHETTA •

8 to 10 ripe tomatoes, peeled, seeded, and cut into ¼" dice

20 large fresh basil leaves, plus extra, julienned, for garnish

1 large clove garlic, peeled and chopped, plus 1 whole head

1 teaspoon chopped fresh oregano, or ½ teaspoon dried

1 cup virgin olive oil (preferably Italian)

Salt and pepper

12 slices crusty Italian bread, 1½" thick

Black olives, Italian, French, or Greek style, for garnish (optional)

Place diced tomato in a bowl and add basil leaves, chopped garlic, oregano, and ½ cup olive oil. Season with salt and pepper to taste. Let stand for 30 minutes at room temperature.

Cut head of garlic in half and rub each slice of bread on both sides. Brush lightly with remaining ½ cup olive oil. Toast under broiler (or better yet, over hot coals) until golden brown, and turn to finish other side.

Arrange garlic toasts on a large platter and divide tomato mixture evenly among them. Garnish with julienned basil leaves and black olives.

SERVES 4
PREPARATION TIME: 15 minutes, plus marination time
COOKING TIME: 3 to 4 minutes

EDITOR'S NOTE: If possible, use a dense and fruity Italian olive oil for this dish, and be sure to use cured Mediterranean-style olives; canned ripe black California olives would be too bland.

INVOLTINI DI MELANZANE

2 large purple eggplants, about 1 pound each

3 cups virgin olive oil (preferably Italian)

4 bay leaves

10 cloves garlic, peeled and coarsely chopped

1 sprig rosemary

8 large leaves arugula

4 to 6 ounces fresh goat cheese, cut into 8 slices

8 slices oil-packed sun-dried tomato

½ cup Chicken Stock (page 294) or canned chicken broth

2 cups Tomato Sauce (recipe follows), hot

Basil leaves, julienned, for garnish

Cut each unpeeled eggplant lengthwise into 4 slices. Grill quickly for a minute on each side, or sear in a hot skillet. Combine olive oil, bay leaves, garlic, and rosemary. Marinate eggplant slices in this mixture for 1 hour at room temperature.

Preheat oven to 450°. Drain eggplant slices well (reserve marinade) and pat dry with paper towels. Top each slice of eggplant with a leaf of arugula, a slice of goat cheese, and a slice of sun-dried tomato. Grease a shallow baking dish lightly with oil from the marinade. Roll up each slice and place in dish. Add chicken stock. Bake, uncovered, for 4 to 5 minutes, until cheese is soft and warmed.

To serve, ladle some tomato sauce onto warmed plates and place 2 eggplant rolls on top. Garnish with some julienned basil and drizzle with olive oil from marinade.

Tomato Sauce

½ cup virgin olive oil (preferably Italian)
4 cloves garlic, peeled and smashed

1 16-ounce can Italian-style tomatoes, including juice

1 cup basil leaves, loosely packed, well   Salt and pepper
    washed and chopped

Heat olive oil in a skillet with garlic and cook until golden, about 5 minutes.
Discard garlic. Add tomatoes and basil. Bring sauce to a boil, then simmer
for 25 minutes. Season with salt and pepper to taste. Puree in a blender or
food processor.

SERVES 4
PREPARATION TIME: 30 minutes total, plus marination time
COOKING TIME: 30 minutes total

ZIMINO CON CAPELLINI •

2 pounds clams (preferably Manila)
2 pounds black mussels (preferably
    Prince Edward Island)
¼ cup virgin olive oil (preferably
    Italian)
Pinch dried red chili pepper flakes
2 cloves garlic, peeled and chopped
½ cup dry white wine
1 16-ounce can Italian-style tomatoes,
    including juice

2 or 3 ripe Roma tomatoes, peeled and
    diced
½ bunch basil, destemmed and chopped
½ bunch Italian flat-leaf parsley,
    destemmed and chopped
Salt
1 pound imported capellini (angel hair
    pasta)
Toasted garlic bread

Scrub clams and mussels well. Bring a pot of water to a boil for the pasta.

Heat oil in a large skillet or pot. Add clams, mussels, chili flakes, and garlic. Sauté for about 30 seconds, then add wine and stir for a minute. Add canned tomatoes, diced fresh tomatoes, basil, and parsley. Bring to a boil, then lower heat and simmer for 2 minutes. Discard any clams or mussels whose shells have not opened. Add salt to pot of boiling water, and then add pasta. Cook for 2 minutes, until *al dente*. Be careful not to overcook. Drain pasta well and toss with shellfish (still in the shells) and tomato sauce. Serve with lots of toasted garlic bread to absorb all the good juices.

SERVES 4

PREPARATION TIME: 15 minutes

COOKING TIME: 6 to 8 minutes

SEMIFREDDO CON NOCE

3 large egg yolks

3 large whole eggs

⅓ cup sugar

⅔ cup ground toasted hazelnuts

⅓ cup ground toasted walnuts

1¾ cups heavy cream, whipped to soft peaks

1 tablespoon Frangelico or brandy

¼ cup grated bittersweet chocolate

Berry Sauce (recipe follows)

Place egg yolks, whole eggs, and sugar in the top of a double boiler. Whisk over simmering water until mixture thickens and reaches 135° on a candy thermometer, about 10 minutes. Transfer to the bowl of an electric mixer and whip at medium-high speed until cold, about 12 minutes. Fold in ground nuts, whipped cream, Frangelico or brandy, and grated bittersweet chocolate. Pour into a loaf pan and freeze until hardened, about 4 hours. (It will not freeze completely.) Unmold by dipping pan into hot water, then inverting onto a flat plate or baking sheet. Enclose in plastic wrap and return to freezer until ready for use.

To serve, cut the semifreddo into ½"-thick slices and serve on a pool of berry sauce.

Berry Sauce

4 cups fresh strawberries (washed and hulled) or raspberries

¼ cup sugar

Juice of 1 lemon

1 cup water

Combine all ingredients in a food processor or blender and puree. Strain.

SERVES 8 TO 10

PREPARATION TIME: 30 minutes, plus freezing time

COOKING TIME: 10 minutes

Wolfgang Puck's new restaurant in San Francisco is an elegant, peach-colored, beribboned fantasy. The elaborate staircase makes watching new arrivals part of the evening's entertainment. Puck and executive chefs Anne and David Gingrass, who moved here from Spago in Los Angeles, present contemporary California cuisine that successfully blends professional expertise with pure whimsy.

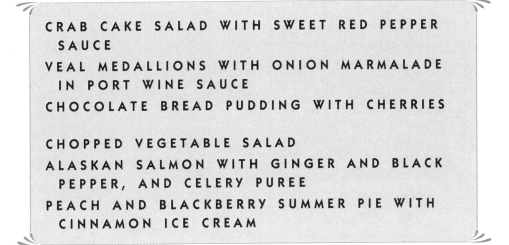

CRAB CAKE SALAD WITH SWEET RED PEPPER SAUCE

VEAL MEDALLIONS WITH ONION MARMALADE IN PORT WINE SAUCE

CHOCOLATE BREAD PUDDING WITH CHERRIES

CHOPPED VEGETABLE SALAD

ALASKAN SALMON WITH GINGER AND BLACK PEPPER, AND CELERY PUREE

PEACH AND BLACKBERRY SUMMER PIE WITH CINNAMON ICE CREAM

CRAB CAKE SALAD WITH SWEET RED PEPPER SAUCE

2 teaspoons extra-virgin olive oil
2 tablespoons finely diced red onion
1 tablespoon finely diced red bell pepper
1 tablespoon finely diced yellow bell pepper
½ cup heavy cream
⅛ jalapeño pepper, seeded and minced
1 teaspoon chopped fresh chives
1 sprig thyme, leaves only
1 teaspoon chopped Italian flat-leaf parsley
Pinch cayenne pepper
1 large egg, lightly beaten

½ cup fine dry white bread crumbs
½ cup ground blanched almonds
Salt
10 ounces fresh crab meat (preferably Louisiana blue crab)
Equal quantities extra-virgin olive oil and butter for frying crab cakes
4 to 6 handfuls arugula or mixed lettuces
Balsamic Vinaigrette (recipe follows)
Bell Pepper Cream Sauce (recipe follows)

Heat olive oil in a sauté pan. Sauté onion and bell peppers until onion is translucent, about 3 minutes. Transfer to a mixing bowl and cool. Combine cream and jalapeño pepper in a saucepan and reduce over medium-high heat until ¼ cup liquid remains. Set aside to cool. When cold, pour cream into onion and bell pepper mixture. Stir in chives, thyme, parsley, cayenne, egg, a third of the bread crumbs, a third of the ground almonds, and salt to taste. Add crab meat and mix thoroughly.

Combine remaining bread crumbs and ground almonds on a plate. Shape crab meat mixture into 12 small round cakes. Coat with the bread crumb–almond mixture and refrigerate for at least 2 hours.

Just before serving time, heat enough oil and butter in a large skillet to reach a depth of ¼″. Fry crab cakes for about 4 minutes on each side. Remove to paper towels to drain.

Toss arugula leaves with vinaigrette and arrange in center of plates. Pour a ribbon of sauce around salad. Top salad with 2 or 3 crab cakes.

Bell Pepper Cream Sauce

5 tablespoons unsalted butter	2 sprigs thyme, leaves only
½ red onion, peeled and diced	½ cup white wine
½ large red bell pepper, seeded, deribbed, and diced	1 cup heavy cream
	Salt and pepper
2 cloves garlic, peeled and mashed	Juice of ½ lemon

In a saucepan, heat 3 tablespoons of butter until foaming. Add onion, bell pepper, garlic, and thyme. Sauté until onion is transparent, about 5 minutes. Deglaze pan with white wine and reduce until thick, about 5 minutes. Add cream and bring to a boil. Puree in blender or food processor until smooth. Add remaining 2 tablespoons of butter, salt and pepper to taste, and lemon juice. Strain and keep warm.

Balsamic Vinaigrette

3 tablespoons extra-virgin olive oil	Salt and pepper
1 tablespoon balsamic vinegar	

Whisk oil and balsamic vinegar together, and season to taste with salt and pepper.

SERVES 4 TO 6
PREPARATION TIME: 45 minutes total, plus chilling time
COOKING TIME: 11 minutes total

VEAL MEDALLIONS WITH ONION MARMALADE IN PORT WINE SAUCE

2 large onions, peeled and cut into
   eighths
Salt and pepper
2 tablespoons virgin olive oil
1 tablespoon good-quality red wine or
   sherry vinegar
½ cup Chicken Stock (page 294) or
   canned chicken broth
½ cup port

1 cup heavy cream
1½ pounds boneless veal loin, cut into 6
   medallions, 3 ounces each
½ cup Veal Stock (page 294) or Beef
   Stock (page 293)
2 tablespoons unsalted butter, cut up
Fresh herb sprigs (such as thyme,
   chervil, etc.) for garnish
Sautéed baby vegetables of choice

Season onions with salt and pepper to taste. Heat 1 tablespoon of oil in a sauté pan. Add onions, and stir over medium-high heat until translucent, about 5 minutes. Add vinegar, chicken stock, and ¼ cup of port wine. Cook over moderate heat until liquid is reduced to a thick sauce, 15 to 20 minutes. Add cream, and season to taste with salt and pepper. Reduce over medium heat to half its original volume, about 10 minutes.

Season veal with salt and pepper. Heat a heavy skillet, and add remaining 1 tablespoon of oil. When oil is smoking hot, sauté the veal medallions until seared golden brown on both sides, but still pink inside, 3 to 4 minutes per side. Remove to a plate and keep warm.

Deglaze pan with remaining ¼ cup of port. Add veal stock. Season to taste with salt and pepper, and reduce over moderate heat until sauce has thickened, about 6 minutes. Whisk in pieces of butter until sauce is smooth.

Divide onion mixture among 6 warmed serving plates. Top onion with veal medallions, and spoon sauce on top. Garnish with fresh herbs, and serve with baby vegetables.

SERVES 6

PREPARATION TIME: 15 minutes

COOKING TIME: 45 to 50 minutes

CHOCOLATE BREAD PUDDING WITH CHERRIES

½ cup kirsch

½ cup dried cherries

8 slices day-old brioche, cut into cubes

¾ cup heavy cream

6 ounces bittersweet chocolate, cut into small pieces

11 tablespoons (almost 1½ sticks) unsalted butter, softened

5 large eggs, separated

1 cup blanched almonds

1 cup sugar

1 cup heavy cream, whipped to soft peaks, for garnish

Preheat oven to 350°. Butter six 1-cup molds. In a small saucepan, warm the kirsch. Soak cherries in warm kirsch until ready to use.

Place brioche cubes in a mixing bowl. Add cream and let stand for 10 minutes, or until cream has been absorbed. Melt chocolate over hot water.

Cream butter in a large mixing bowl. Add egg yolks, almonds, ¾ cup of sugar, the brioche, and melted chocolate. Mix well. Whip egg whites to soft peaks, then gradually whip in remaining ¼ cup of sugar. Continue to whip until soft, shiny peaks form. Stir a quarter of beaten egg whites into chocolate mixture, then gently fold in remainder. (It is better to have a little of the whites showing than to overfold.)

Chop cherries fine. Divide the pudding mixture among the molds, sprinkling chopped cherries between layers. Place molds in a roasting pan, add enough boiling water to reach halfway up sides of molds, and cover loosely with buttered aluminum foil. Bake until puddings are set, about 45 minutes. Unmold on dessert plates, cool a little, and decorate with a little whipped cream.

SERVES 6

PREPARATION TIME: 30 minutes

COOKING TIME: 45 minutes

CHOPPED VEGETABLE SALAD

½ cup diced carrots
½ cup diced green beans
½ cup diced red onion
½ cup diced radicchio
½ cup fresh corn kernels
½ cup diced celery
½ cup diced fresh artichoke bottoms,
  cooked al dente

½ cup diced ripe avocado
¼ cup peeled, seeded, and diced tomato
Mustard Vinaigrette (recipe follows)
4 teaspoons grated Parmesan cheese
1 cup mixed greens of choice (such as
  curly endive, chicory, chopped lettuce,
  etc.)

Blanch the carrots and green beans separately in boiling salted water for 1 minute. Drain, and plunge into cold water to stop the cooking and set the color, and cool. Drain again.

In a large bowl, combine the onion, radicchio, corn kernels, celery, carrots, green beans, and artichoke. When ready to serve, add the avocado and tomato. Reserving a little of the vinaigrette, toss salad with dressing. Sprinkle with grated cheese and toss again.

Divide the salad greens among 4 plates. Mound the chopped salad in the center, and drizzle remaining vinaigrette over the border of the salad greens.

Mustard Vinaigrette

1 tablespoon Dijon mustard
3 tablespoons sherry vinegar
½ cup virgin olive oil

½ cup almond or safflower oil
Salt and pepper

Combine the mustard and vinegar in a small bowl. Slowly whisk in the oils. Season to taste with salt and pepper.

SERVES 4
PREPARATION TIME: 35 minutes
COOKING TIME: 1 minute

ALASKAN SALMON WITH GINGER AND BLACK PEPPER, AND CELERY PUREE

4 filets Alaskan king salmon, about 6
    ounces each
Salt and pepper
3 tablespoons finely chopped gingerroot

3 tablespoons cracked black pepper
Virgin olive oil for grilling
Celery Puree (recipe follows)

Sauce

6 tablespoons (¾ stick) unsalted butter
1 shallot, peeled and chopped
1 clove garlic, peeled and minced
1 ripe tomato, peeled, seeded, and
    chopped

½ bottle Cabernet Sauvignon
2 tablespoons balsamic vinegar
1 cup Chicken Stock (page 294) or
    canned chicken broth
Salt and pepper

Season the salmon filets with salt and pepper to taste, and set aside. Combine ginger and black pepper on a plate, and have olive oil at hand.

Sauce: Heat 2 tablespoons of butter in a sauté pan until foamy. Add shallot, garlic, and tomato and sauté for 5 minutes, or until shallot is translucent. Add wine and vinegar, and continue cooking over moderate heat until reduced by half, about 15 minutes. Add chicken stock and again reduce by half, about 10 minutes. Cut remaining 4 tablespoons of butter into pieces and whisk into sauce until desired consistency is reached. Season to taste with salt and pepper, and keep warm.

Have ready a hot charcoal fire, or heat a large sauté pan and film the bottom with olive oil. Bread salmon filets with the ginger-pepper mixture, and sprinkle with olive oil if planning to grill. Grill or sauté salmon until medium done, about 4 minutes per side.

Divide sauce among 4 warmed dinner plates. Spoon celery puree in center of plates. Place salmon on top.

Celery Puree

2 medium baking potatoes, peeled
1 large celery root, peeled
1 cup heavy cream

4 tablespoons (½ stick) unsalted butter
Salt and pepper

Cut potatoes and celery root into 1″ cubes—there should be equal amounts. Boil in salted water until tender, about 15 minutes. Drain off water, and return vegetables to pan. Add cream and simmer for about 15 minutes over moderate heat until thickened, stirring occasionally to prevent sticking. Remove from heat, add butter, and season to taste with salt and pepper. Process in a food mill until creamy but not gluey.

SERVES 4

PREPARATION TIME: 20 minutes total

COOKING TIME: 35 to 45 minutes total

PEACH AND BLACKBERRY SUMMER PIE WITH CINNAMON ICE CREAM

Fruit

2 pounds (about 6 or 7) ripe but firm peaches

3 tablespoons maple or brown sugar

3 tablespoons freshly squeezed lemon juice

2 tablespoons peach brandy

Pinch grated nutmeg

3 tablespoons all-purpose flour

2 baskets blackberries, raspberries, or blueberries

Streusel

½ cup (3 ounces) unpeeled almonds

6 tablespoons (¾ stick) unsalted butter, chilled, cut up

2 tablespoons brown sugar

2 tablespoons white sugar

2 tablespoons ground cinnamon

1 teaspoon grated nutmeg

¼ teaspoon ground cardamom

½ cup rolled oats

½ cup all-purpose flour

Shortcake Biscuits

2¾ cups all-purpose flour

9 tablespoons unsalted butter, cut up

6 tablespoons sugar, plus extra for brushing

1 tablespoon plus 1 teaspoon baking powder

1 teaspoon salt

1 cup heavy cream, plus extra for brushing

Cinnamon Ice Cream (recipe follows)

Fruit: Drop peaches in boiling water, drain, and slip off skins. Discard pits and slice. Mix well with remaining fruit ingredients. Set aside.

Streusel: Preheat oven to 350°. Place almonds on a baking sheet and toast for 10 minutes. Grind to a powder. In the bowl of a food processor, combine ground almonds and remaining streusel ingredients. Process just until mixture comes together. Set aside.

Shortcake Biscuits: In a food processor, combine dry ingredients. Grind until very fine. Add cream and process just until dough comes together. On a lightly floured surface, roll out biscuit dough to about ¼″ thick. Using a 3½″ round cutter, cut 8 circles from dough.

Divide fruit mixture among 8 ramekins or small bowls, about 4″ in diameter and 4″ deep. Sprinkle fruit with the streusel. Top each ramekin with a biscuit. Brush biscuits lightly with cream and sprinkle generously with sugar. Bake at 350° until biscuits are golden, about 15 to 18 minutes. Serve immediately with cinnamon ice cream.

Cinnamon Ice Cream

2 cups milk	*10 large egg yolks*
2 cups heavy cream	*6 tablespoons sugar*
2 sticks cinnamon	*Pinch ground cinnamon*

Combine milk, cream, and cinnamon sticks in a saucepan and bring to a simmer. Turn off heat, cover, and let stand for 30 minutes.

Whisk together egg yolks and sugar until sugar is dissolved. Reheat cream mixture to a simmer, add to egg yolks and sugar, and return whole mixture to saucepan. Stir with a wooden spoon over medium heat until mixture coats spoon, about 7 minutes, and reaches 165° on a candy thermometer. Pour through a fine mesh strainer into a bowl, and refrigerate until cold.

Stir cinnamon into mixture. Process in an ice cream maker according to manufacturer's instructions. Makes 1 quart.

SERVES 8

PREPARATION TIME: 1 hour total, plus chilling and freezing time

COOKING TIME: 25 to 28 minutes total

RAF's interior was designed by Amy McGill. Exposed beams, faux tree branches, and unbaked clay formed into floral wreaths twined around large mirrors combine to form a surrealistic interpretation of a Tuscan villa. The cuisine is regional Italian, reinterpreted in an exciting, modern style.

STUFFED SQUASH BLOSSOMS
GRILLED CHICKEN SPIEDINI WITH BALSAMIC ONIONS
BISCUIT TORTONI

STUFFED SQUASH BLOSSOMS

3 ounces mozzarella cheese, grated
6 fresh basil leaves, chopped
3 tablespoons slivered prosciutto
2 tablespoons slivered oil-packed sun-dried tomatoes, drained

12 fresh zucchini blossoms, stamens removed

Beer Batter

1 cup beer
1 cup all-purpose flour
1 large egg
½ teaspoon salt

¼ teaspoon cayenne pepper

Vegetable oil for deep-frying
Lemon wedges for garnish

Combine mozzarella, basil, prosciutto, and sun-dried tomatoes. Wash and dry zucchini blossoms, and stuff with this mixture, bringing petals back over stuffing.

Beer Batter: Combine batter ingredients and mix until smooth.

Heat vegetable oil to 350°. (If you do not have a thermometer, toss in a 1" cube of bread. It should turn golden brown on a slow count of 60 when oil is at the right temperature.) Dip stuffed blossoms in batter, then deep-fry 4 at a time until golden, about 3 minutes. Serve with lemon wedges.

SERVES 6 TO 8
PREPARATION TIME: 25 minutes
COOKING TIME: 8 to 9 minutes

GRILLED CHICKEN SPIEDINI WITH BALSAMIC ONIONS

1 cup balsamic vinegar

2 large red onions, unpeeled and halved
through the stem

2 whole chicken breasts, skinned, boned,
and cut into 24 pieces (6 per half
breast)

6 slices pancetta, quartered

Virgin olive oil

Salt and pepper

Preheat oven to 400°. Pour vinegar into a baking pan large enough to hold the onions in one layer. Place onions in baking pan, cut side down. Cover with aluminum foil and bake for 35 to 40 minutes. Cool, then remove skins and cut onions into 24 chunks.

Thread chicken, pancetta, and onion alternately onto 6 skewers. Brush with olive oil and sprinkle with salt and pepper to taste. Grill over hot coals, turning often, for 5 to 6 minutes, or quickly sear in olive oil in a sauté pan, then finish in a 400° oven 4 to 5 minutes.

SERVES 6

PREPARATION TIME: 30 minutes

COOKING TIME: 45 minutes

BISCUIT TORTONI •

1½ cups heavy cream

¼ cup sugar

⅓ cup blanched almonds, toasted and
chopped

3 tablespoons dark rum

14 ounces amaretti, or almond
macaroons, crushed

Fresh Raspberry or Strawberry Coulis
(page 62 or 16)

Whip cream and add sugar. Stir in almonds and rum. Cover the bottom of an 8"-×-8" baking pan with half the macaroon crumbs. Cover crumbs with cream mixture, smoothing it with a spatula. Press remaining crumbs on top. Cover with plastic wrap and freeze for at least 4 hours. Spoon berry coulis onto dessert plates and top with a square of tortoni.

SERVES 6 TO 8

PREPARATION TIME: 20 minutes, plus freezing time

COOKING TIME: None

Chef-proprietor Regina Charbonneau, a Louisiana native of French-Creole descent, presents spicy yet sophisticated interpretations of Creole classics in charming surroundings located on theater row. The restaurant is decorated with a stunning collection of *commedia* masks and theatrical costume drawings; but the food takes center stage.

WILD RICE AND CORN CHOWDER
PEPPERED OYSTERS ON TOAST
STRAWBERRIES WITH SOUR CREAM AND RUM SAUCE

WILD RICE AND CORN CHOWDER

½ pound bacon, diced
2 small onions, peeled and diced
1 large red bell pepper, seeded, deribbed and diced
4 stalks celery, peeled with vegetable peeler and diced
3 cloves garlic, peeled and minced
1½ quarts Chicken Stock (page 294) or canned chicken broth

1 cup raw wild rice
1 tablespoon chopped fresh thyme
1 tablespoon chopped fresh basil
½ to 1 teaspoon dried red pepper flakes
2 cups heavy cream
2 cups yellow corn kernels (fresh or frozen)
Salt

In a skillet, sauté bacon until almost crisp. Add onion, bell pepper, celery, and garlic and cook with bacon for 5 minutes at medium heat. Drain off excess fat.

In a large soup pot, heat chicken stock to a boil and add wild rice. Add bacon and vegetable mixture, thyme, basil, and pepper flakes. Simmer for 45 minutes. Add cream and corn and cook for 15 minutes longer. Add salt to taste.

SERVES 6
PREPARATION TIME: 20 minutes
COOKING TIME: about 1¼ hours
CHEF'S NOTE: I recommend making this chowder the day before it is to be served, both for convenience and so that the flavors can mellow.

PEPPERED OYSTERS ON TOAST •

9 slices egg bread, toasted, crusts
    removed, and cut in half on the
    diagonal
18 tomato slices
18 lemon slices
18 basil leaves, plus 4 tablespoons
    chopped basil
Julienned zest of 1 lemon
½ pound (2 sticks) butter

1 tablespoon minced fresh garlic
2 to 4 tablespoons cracked black pepper
1 cup Worcestershire sauce
¼ cup virgin olive oil
4 dozen shucked fresh oysters (preferably
    Eastern or Gulf)
2 tablespoons chopped fresh chives for
    garnish

Place 3 triangles of toast on each plate. Garnish toasts with a slice of tomato, a slice of lemon, a basil leaf, and a pinch of lemon zest.

In a deep skillet or sauté pan, combine butter, chopped basil, garlic, pepper, Worcestershire sauce, and olive oil. Heat until butter melts.

When ready to cook oysters, bring sauce to a boil and add about 10 oysters at a time. Cook for 2 minutes or less and remove to a bowl with a slotted spoon. When all the oysters are cooked, place 2 or 3 on each toast triangle, then spoon the pepper sauce on top. Sprinkle chopped chives over all.

SERVES 6
PREPARATION TIME: 20 minutes
COOKING TIME: 5 minutes

STRAWBERRIES WITH SOUR CREAM AND RUM SAUCE •

2 cups dairy sour cream
2 cups brown sugar
1 teaspoon ground cinnamon
¼ cup Myers's dark rum

1 quart fresh ripe strawberries, hulled
    and halved lengthwise
6 fresh mint sprigs for garnish

Whisk together the sour cream, brown sugar, cinnamon, and rum until very smooth. Refrigerate for at least 1 hour.

Place a little of this sauce in the bottom of 6 stemmed glasses. Divide strawberries among glasses, then top with remaining sauce. Garnish with mint sprigs.

SERVES 6
PREPARATION TIME: 5 minutes, plus chilling time
COOKING TIME: None

This handsome ninety-seat restaurant is housed inside one of the two brick kilns still standing in California. Built by the Remillard family in 1891, the Larkspur kiln and landmark smokestack baked most of the brick that rebuilt San Francisco after the 1906 earthquake and fire. The kiln closed in the 1930s, but has recently been restored to its original beauty and transformed into a restaurant. Partner/chef Emile Waldteufel, formerly chef at Le Castel for several years, creates classical food in the great French tradition, but lightens it up to suit contemporary tastes.

> BAY SHRIMP WITH ENDIVE AND SESAME OIL
> SAUTÉED MINUTE STEAK WITH CONFIT OF
> ONION AND BOILED RED POTATOES
> FRESH PEACHES AND PEACH ICE CREAM
> WITH CARAMEL SAUCE AND TOASTED
> ALMONDS

BAY SHRIMP WITH ENDIVE AND SESAME OIL •

½ pound peeled bay shrimp, cooked
½ red bell pepper, seeded, deribbed, and finely diced
6 fresh chives, finely cut
Juice of ½ lemon
Mayonnaise
1 teaspoon hot Oriental sesame oil (sesame oil with chili)

2 heads Belgian endive
Small basil leaves for garnish
12 snow peas, deveined
1 head radicchio, quartered
1 large tomato, cut into 12 segments
6 to 8 small mushrooms, sliced
1 slice bacon, crisp fried and crumbled
Red Wine Vinaigrette (recipe follows)

Combine shrimp, bell pepper, chives, and lemon juice with just enough mayonnaise to bind them together. Add hot sesame oil. Fill 8 larger leaves of endive with shrimp mixture and garnish with basil leaves.

Blanch snow peas in boiling salted water for 15 seconds, drain, plunge into cold water, and drain again. Put a quarter head of radicchio in the center of each plate. Arrange 3 slices of tomato, 3 snow peas, and mushroom slices around radicchio. Sprinkle with bacon chips. Spoon vinaigrette over salad and place 2 endive boats on each plate.

Red Wine Vinaigrette

¼ cup best-quality red wine vinegar   Salt and freshly ground black pepper
⅔ cup virgin olive oil

Whisk vinegar with oil and season to taste with salt and pepper.

SERVES 4
PREPARATION TIME: 20 minutes
COOKING TIME: None

SAUTÉED MINUTE STEAK WITH CONFIT OF ONION AND BOILED RED POTATOES

12 boiling onions, peeled
⅓ to ½ pound (1¼ to 2 sticks) butter
8 egg-sized red potatoes
Salt
4 sirloin steaks, about 8 ounces each, ¼" to ⅓" thick
Freshly ground black pepper

Virgin olive oil for skillet
½ cup water
Juice of 1 or 2 lemons
1 bunch parsley, destemmed and finely chopped
1 cup dairy sour cream

Preheat oven to 450°. Place whole onions on a sheet of foil with 1 tablespoon of butter. Enclose tightly so that neither juice nor steam can escape. Bake until tender, about 30 minutes. Cook potatoes in their skins in lightly salted boiling water until tender, about 15 minutes. Season steaks on both sides with salt and pepper.

Heat a large skillet and moisten the bottom with olive oil. Sear the steaks over high heat for 30 seconds per side. Place in a row on a heated serving platter.

Drain potatoes of all water and cut a cross in the top of each, like a baked potato. Arrange along one side of the steaks. Remove onions from foil, reserving juice, and place along other side of steaks. Pour off any fat from skillet, deglaze with the water, and add deglazing to the onion liquor. Add remaining butter to skillet. When lightly browned, add lemon juice, chopped parsley, and the onion liquor and water. Taste for seasoning, adding more lemon juice, salt, or pepper as needed. Spoon over the steaks and potatoes. Accompany with sour cream for potatoes.

SERVES 4
PREPARATION TIME: 15 minutes
COOKING TIME: 35 minutes

FRESH PEACHES AND PEACH ICE CREAM WITH CARAMEL SAUCE AND TOASTED ALMONDS •

⅓ cup sugar

⅔ cup heavy cream

4 scoops best-quality peach ice cream

2 ripe peaches, peeled and halved

¼ cup sliced almonds, toasted in oven until medium brown

Pour sugar into a heavy saucepan, place over moderate heat, and melt sugar without stirring until it caramelizes, about 3 minutes. Add cream, remove from heat, and stir.

To assemble, place a scoop of ice cream in each dessert dish. Add ½ peach, spoon a teaspoonful of caramel sauce on top, and sprinkle with toasted almonds.

SERVES 4
PREPARATION TIME: 10 minutes
COOKING TIME: 3 minutes

Owner/chef Kurt Grasing, ably abetted by pastry chef Phil Ogiela, has created an exceptional French restaurant in San Mateo on South Ellsworth. The surroundings are comfortable, welcoming, and feature modern art and banks of fresh flowers, washed by subtle lighting. This backdrop perfectly complements the creative, contemporary interpretations of French classics on the menu.

SMOKED SALMON AND NEW POTATO SALAD
SQUAB WITH QUINCE
SOUFFLÉ GLACÉ AU CHOCOLAT

SMOKED SALMON AND NEW POTATO SALAD •

6 medium red potatoes, unpeeled
Salt
4 large handfuls mixed greens (such as arugula, frisée, watercress, baby spinach leaves, etc.)
1 tablespoon virgin olive oil

1 shallot, peeled and finely chopped
2 tablespoons capers, drained
1 teaspoon each chopped fresh chives, tarragon, and thyme
Vinaigrette (recipe follows)
½ pound smoked salmon, thinly sliced

Wash potatoes and cook slowly in salted water until tender, 15 to 20 minutes, and slice. Place well washed and dried salad greens in a large bowl.

Heat olive oil in a sauté pan, and lightly sauté potatoes until starting to turn golden, about 5 minutes. Add shallot, capers, and herbs. Remove from heat. Toss greens with enough vinaigrette to lightly coat the leaves, and arrange on plates. Top with warm potatoes and drape with slices of smoked salmon.

Vinaigrette

1 small shallot, peeled and finely chopped
1 tablespoon lemon juice
1 tablespoon champagne or other white wine vinegar

½ cup virgin olive oil
Salt and pepper

Place chopped shallot in a small mixing bowl, and add lemon juice and vinegar. Whisk in olive oil slowly. Season to taste with salt and pepper.

SERVES 4

PREPARATION TIME: 10 minutes

COOKING TIME: 20 minutes

SQUAB WITH QUINCE

2 large quince, peeled, quartered, and cored

Juice of 1 lemon

½ cup sugar

3 tablespoons cider vinegar

4 squab (baby pigeons), about 1 pound each

Salt and pepper

2 tablespoons butter

Preheat oven to 300°. Slice quince. Toss with lemon juice. Melt sugar in a heavy casserole and boil until it turns a light golden caramel color, about 7 minutes. Add quince. Toss gently to cover with syrup and add vinegar. Cover casserole and place in oven. Bake until quince slices are soft, about 30 minutes. Remove from oven and increase heat to 450°. Heat a roasting pan at the same time.

Remove giblets, liver, and heart from squab. Pat birds dry and season with salt and pepper. Melt butter in a skillet over medium heat. Brown squab on all sides. When nicely browned, transfer to a roasting pan and roast for 12 minutes. Remove from oven and cool a little. Carefully remove meat from bones without tearing the meat. Arrange quince slices on plates with their juices, and top with 2 reassembled squab halves.

SERVES 4

PREPARATION TIME: 20 minutes

COOKING TIME: 45 minutes

CHEF'S NOTE: If quince are not in season, you may substitute pears or tart green apples for a different dish. They may need less sugar.

SOUFFLÉ GLACÉ AU CHOCOLAT •

4 ounces best-quality semisweet or bittersweet chocolate, chopped

1 ounce (1 square) unsweetened chocolate, chopped

2 large egg whites

½ cup sugar

2 cups heavy cream

Grated or shaved semisweet chocolate for garnish

Confectioners' sugar for garnish

Combine semisweet and unsweetened chocolate in the top of a double boiler and melt over simmering water. Remove from heat.

Place egg whites and sugar in a metal bowl. Place over a pan of simmering water and stir until mixture is warm to the touch. Remove from heat and beat until mixture holds soft peaks. Stir a little of this meringue into the chocolate to loosen it, then fold in the remainder. Whip cream until it starts to hold soft peaks (do not whip too stiff or it will not amalgamate nicely). Fold cream into chocolate-meringue mixture. Spoon into 8 ramekins. Cover with plastic wrap and freeze on coldest setting for 3 to 4 hours, until solid. To serve, garnish with grated or shaved chocolate and a light dusting of confectioners' sugar.

SERVES 8

PREPARATION TIME: 20 minutes, plus freezing time

COOKING TIME: 10 minutes

Housed in a former Berkeley train depot, the elegantly low-key Santa Fe Bar and Grill specializes in perfectly cured seafood, meat, and game, smoked on the premises over alderwood, and mesquite-grilled to a turn. New owner and chef Fazol "Faz" Poursohi has revitalized one of the earliest purveyors of what has come to be known as California cuisine, and given it a spanking new look and taste all its own.

GRILLED PASILLA PEPPERS WITH SALSA
PETALUMA DUCK WITH POMEGRANATE SAUCE
AND BASMATI RICE
ALMOND PRALINE MOUSSE WITH A CARAMEL
CROWN

GRILLED PASILLA PEPPERS WITH SALSA •

4 to 8 pasilla peppers, depending on size
4 ounces Roquefort cheese
4 ounces white jack cheese
4 ounces sharp Cheddar cheese
Juice of 1 lemon
Salsa (recipe follows)

Have ready an intense mesquite charcoal fire. Cut caps from peppers and set them aside. Deseed peppers and blanch in boiling water for 2 minutes. Immediately plunge into ice water, drain, and dry.

Chop Roquefort, jack, and Cheddar cheeses together, and add lemon juice. Stuff peppers with cheese mixture and cover with reserved caps. Grill over mesquite for 3 to 4 minutes, until cheese is melted. Serve with salsa.

Salsa

½ red onion, peeled and chopped
1 ripe beefsteak tomato, peeled, seeded, and diced
1 jalapeño pepper, chopped very fine
¼ bunch fresh cilantro (coriander), chopped
1 avocado, peeled and pitted
Juice of 2 lemons
¼ cup virgin olive oil
Salt and pepper

Combine onion, tomato, jalapeño, and cilantro. Chop avocado and add to mixture with lemon juice. Add olive oil, and season to taste with salt and pepper.

SERVES 4
PREPARATION TIME: 15 minutes total
COOKING TIME: 5 to 6 minutes

PETALUMA DUCK WITH POMEGRANATE SAUCE AND BASMATI RICE

1 fresh Petaluma or other domestic
  duck, 5 to 6 pounds
1 cup honey
1 cup soy sauce
2 tablespoons chopped fresh gingerroot

Pomegranate Sauce (recipe follows)
2 cups cooked basmati rice

If using a smoker, use alderwood as fuel, and set smoker at 350°. Alternatively, preheat oven to 325°.

Fill a pot with enough water to cover the duck and bring to a boil. Place duck in boiling water and simmer for 15 minutes. (This helps to remove the fat.) Drain, and lightly pierce skin of duck with a fork over entire surface. Combine honey, soy sauce, and gingerroot. Using a pastry brush, apply liberally all over duck. Smoke or roast duck for 2 hours, checking every half hour, and basting with marinade. Remove duck from smoker or oven and cool.

When duck has cooled, split in half and remove meat from carcass. Remove as much remaining fat as possible from under skin, but do not break or pierce skin. Serve with pomegranate sauce and basmati rice.

Pomegranate Sauce

1 cup sugar
1 cup water
2 cups Duck Stock (page 295)

2 cups pomegranate juice (available at
  Middle Eastern grocery stores)
Salt and pepper

Combine sugar and water in a heavy saucepan and bring to a boil. Boil until mixture thickens and turns golden brown, about 8 minutes. Remove from heat and, using a wire whisk to avoid spattering, very slowly add duck stock.

Add pomegranate juice and return pan to heat. Bring to a boil and reduce to preferred consistency. Season to taste with salt and pepper.

SERVES 4

PREPARATION TIME: 20 minutes total

COOKING TIME: 2 hours total

ALMOND PRALINE MOUSSE WITH A CARAMEL CROWN

Almond Praline

⅓ cup blanched almonds

⅓ cup sugar

⅓ cup water

Amaretto Mousse

6 large egg yolks, at room temperature

⅓ cup confectioners' sugar, sifted

½ cup amaretto

½ cup orange juice

1 cup heavy cream

½ cup slivered well-toasted almonds

Caramel Crown

1 cup sugar

½ cup light corn syrup

Almond Praline: Preheat oven to 325°. Place almonds on a baking sheet and toast until brown, about 20 minutes. In a food processor or blender, grind until coarsely chopped. Grease a baking sheet.

Place sugar and water in a heavy saucepan and cook over low heat until sugar melts. Continue boiling until mixture turns golden brown and caramelizes, 7 to 8 minutes. Stir in almonds. Quickly pour onto greased baking sheet, smoothing with a metal spatula. Before mixture sets, press in a 2″ fluted cookie cutter to make 4 "flowers." When praline has hardened, cut the flowers out. Grind remaining praline in a food processor or blender and set aside.

Amaretto Mousse: Beat egg yolks and confectioners' sugar together until mixture is pale and thick, and forms a slowly dissolving ribbon from a lifted beater. Beat in amaretto and orange juice and transfer to a heavy saucepan. Place pan over low heat and whisk until mixture is very thick. Set aside to cool. Beat cream until it is stiff. Stir one quarter into cooled egg yolk mixture to loosen it. Gently fold in remaining cream. Cover and refrigerate overnight.

Caramel Crown: Combine sugar and corn syrup in a heavy saucepan. Cook over low heat until mixture caramelizes, about 8 minutes. Do not stir, just swirl pan by its handle to mix ingredients. Remove from heat and allow caramel to cool.

To Assemble: Layer mousse into 4 goblets, dividing layers with an even sprinkling of reserved powdered praline and slivered almonds. Leave 1″ clearance at top of goblet. Dip fork into caramel and drizzle over mousse. Top each with a praline flower. Let stand in a cool place—not the refrigerator—for 15 minutes before serving.

SERVES 4

PREPARATION TIME: 30 minutes, plus chilling time

COOKING TIME: 40 minutes

Silks is a quietly opulent restaurant with brocade armchairs, soft lighting, and extravagant floral displays. The central focus of the room is an octagonal copper and brass table laden with a display of fresh fruits and vegetables, breads, wines, and liqueurs. Executive chef Richard Hoff and new chef David Kinch create menus that are light, seasonal, and constantly changing. The cuisine, which emphasizes fish and seafood, is best described as California cooking with colorful Asian accents.

WATERCRESS AND PEAR SALAD
LOBSTER, SCALLOPS, AND CLAMS WITH CORN AND GINGER CREAM
CHOCOLATE SOUFFLÉ

WATERCRESS AND PEAR SALAD

2 bunches watercress, well washed and
  dried, stems removed
1 perfect pear
4 slices bacon, crisply cooked
¼ cup coarsely chopped, lightly toasted
  walnuts

Honey-Mustard Vinaigrette (recipe
  follows)
2 ounces best-quality Roquefort cheese,
  crumbled

Place watercress in a large bowl. Quarter the pear lengthwise, remove core, and then cut pear wedges crosswise into thin slices. Add pear slices to watercress. Crumble bacon over pears and watercress, and then add walnuts. Add vinaigrette and toss salad. Divide among 4 plates and garnish with crumbled Roquefort cheese.

Honey-Mustard Vinaigrette

2 tablespoons honey
¼ cup Dijon mustard
3 tablespoons sherry vinegar
¼ cup hazelnut or walnut oil

½ cup virgin olive oil
Salt and pepper
Dash Tabasco
2 tablespoons water

In a mixing bowl, combine honey, mustard, and vinegar. Whisk in the oils, adding them in a slow stream. Add salt, pepper, and Tabasco to taste, and thin with water as needed to dressing consistency.

SERVES 4

PREPARATION TIME: 15 minutes total

COOKING TIME: None

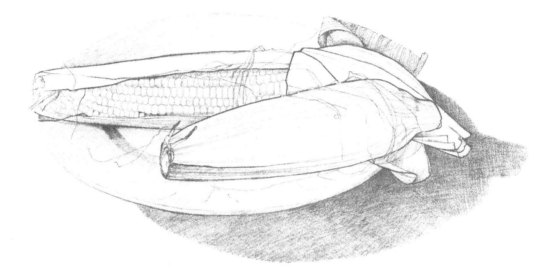

LOBSTER, SCALLOPS, AND CLAMS WITH CORN AND GINGER CREAM

4 lobsters, 1 to 1½ pounds each
Salt
6 ears of corn
3 tablespoons butter
½ onion, peeled and diced
1 cup dry white wine
1 pound clams in the shell
2" piece gingerroot, peeled and sliced
2 cups Chicken Stock (page 294) or
canned chicken broth

1 quart heavy cream
½ pound sea scallops, halved
horizontally if very large
2 tablespoons chopped fresh parsley
Salt and pepper
Dash Tabasco
Crusty French bread for dipping
(optional)

Plunge lobsters into a large pot of boiling salted water. Cover and cook for approximately 5 minutes. Lobsters will be only semicooked at this point.

Remove from pot and, when cool enough to handle, remove tails and claws. Crack claws and remove shell. Split the tail in half lengthwise and remove meat from shell. Reserve lobster meat. Place shells in a plastic bag and crush with a rolling pin. Reserve for making corn and ginger cream.

Scrape corn kernels off the cobs, working over a bowl to catch the corn milk. Cut cobs into 1″ pieces.

In a large saucepan, heat 1 tablespoon of butter and sauté onion until soft, about 5 minutes. Add wine and clams. Cover pot and steam until clams open, about 2 minutes. Remove clams from pan and set aside, discarding any that do not open.

To the saucepan add corn cobs, lobster shells, gingerroot, and chicken stock. Add enough water to cover. Simmer until almost no liquid remains, approximately 1 hour. Add cream and bring to a boil. Remove pan from heat and strain cream into another large saucepan. Press hard on the shells and cobs to extract as much flavor as possible, and discard them.

Add corn kernels and any corn milk to cream and simmer until sauce consistency is reached, about 10 minutes. Put lobster pieces into sauce with clams and simmer gently until lobster is cooked through, about 5 minutes. Add scallops and simmer for a few moments until cooked. Add parsley, remaining 2 tablespoons of butter, and season with salt, pepper, and Tabasco to taste. Serve piping hot in a large bowl or covered terrine and let diners serve themselves into soup bowls. Accompany with crusty French bread, if desired.

SERVES 4
PREPARATION TIME: 30 minutes
COOKING TIME: 1½ hours

CHOCOLATE SOUFFLÉ

5 ounces bittersweet chocolate (preferably Callebaut), cut up and ground in food processor
Butter and sugar for molds
4 large eggs

¼ cup freshly brewed double espresso coffee
1 tablespoon granulated sugar
Confectioners' sugar for decoration, in a sifter
1 cup heavy cream, whipped

Put ground chocolate in a metal bowl and cover with aluminum foil. Place 2″ of water in a small saucepan and bring to a boil. Remove from heat and set covered bowl of chocolate in the saucepan. Keep in a warm place for approximately 30 minutes, until chocolate is melted.

Preheat oven to 400°. Butter four 5-ounce individual soufflé molds and dust with sugar. Have 4 plates ready on which to put the very hot soufflé molds.

When chocolate is melted, but not before, separate 4 egg whites into one immaculately clean and dry bowl. Place 3 of the yolks in another clean bowl, reserving the extra yolk for another use.

Add the espresso to the melted chocolate and whisk it in. (If you must use instant espresso, so be it. Just be sure that it is *very* hot.) Whisk in the egg yolks. With a very clean and dry whisk, or an electric mixer, whip the whites until a ribbon will fall from a lifted beater. Add granulated sugar and whisk a few more beats. *Do not beat to soft-peak stage!*

With a rubber spatula, fold the egg white mixture into the chocolate mixture until just incorporated. There should still be a few tiny white streaks. Pour mixture to the top of the prepared molds, being careful not to touch the inside of the mold with a finger, spoon, etc., as this would spoil the fine sugar crust that will develop. Place in oven for 9 to 10 minutes, until the very center of the soufflé is no longer liquid. Dust with confectioners' sugar. Serve immediately with whipped cream.

SERVES 4
PREPARATION TIME: 45 minutes
COOKING TIME: 10 minutes

Proprietor/chef Joyce Goldstein, yet another very successful Chez Panisse alumna, presents an eclectic, international menu at her functional, contemporary restaurant overlooking Sidney Walton Park, near the Golden Gateway. The name implies fresh beginnings every day, and in fact everything is made fresh daily, including breads, pasta, ice creams, and pastries. In 1986, Joyce's son and co-proprietor Evan Goldstein became, at twenty-five, the youngest American member of the British Master Court of Someliers.

PUMATE-PROVOLONE SALAD
SWORDFISH WITH SESAME OIL, GINGER, AND GARLIC
MEYER LEMON TARTLETS

PUMATE-PROVOLONE SALAD •

6 large handfuls arugula leaves, about 6 ounces

10 to 12 tablespoons coarsely chopped fresh mint

10 to 12 tablespoons coarsely chopped fresh basil

Champagne Vinaigrette (recipe follows)

36 julienne strips oil-packed sun-dried tomatoes (pumate), drained (6 per portion)

¼ pound imported Italian provolone cheese, cut into ⅛"- × -2"- × -½" strips (approximately 7 or 8 per portion)

In a large bowl, combine arugula, mint, and basil. Toss with 2 to 3 tablespoons of the vinaigrette. Divide among 6 plates. Top with strips of sun-dried tomato and cheese, and drizzle with vinaigrette.

Champagne Vinaigrette

6 tablespoons champagne vinegar
6 tablespoons champagne

Salt and pepper
1 cup virgin olive oil

Place vinegar and champagne in a bowl and dissolve the salt in the mixture. Add pepper. Whisk in olive oil and taste for seasoning.

SERVES 6

PREPARATION TIME: 20 minutes

COOKING TIME: None

SWORDFISH WITH SESAME OIL, GINGER, AND GARLIC •

3 cloves garlic, peeled

3" piece gingerroot, peeled

2 tablespoons strong Dijon mustard

¼ cup soy sauce

1 tablespoon sugar

½ cup white wine or rice vinegar

⅓ cup Oriental sesame oil

⅓ cup peanut oil, plus additional for fish

6 swordfish steaks, 6 ounces each

Salt and pepper

1 bunch scallions, white bulbs and most of green tops, minced

3 tablespoons sesame seeds, toasted in a dry pan until they "pop"

Sautéed spinach or Swiss chard, or broiled Japanese eggplant, for garnish

Make charcoal fire in grill or preheat broiler to very hot.

In the bowl of a food processor, place garlic, ginger, mustard, and soy sauce. Process until blended. Add sugar and vinegar and process again. Gradually add sesame and peanut oils and process until the sauce emulsifies.

Brush swordfish steaks lightly with peanut oil and sprinkle with salt and pepper. Broil for 3 to 4 minutes per side.

Place swordfish on warmed plates. Spoon the sauce over the fish and sprinkle with scallions and sesame seeds. Garnish with vegetable of choice.

SERVES 6

PREPARATION TIME: 20 minutes

COOKING TIME: 6 to 8 minutes

MEYER LEMON TARTLETS

3 tablespoons cornstarch

¼ cup milk

6 whole large eggs

9 large egg yolks

Grated zest of 6 Meyer lemons (approximately ¼ cup)

Juice of 7 Meyer lemons (1¾ cups)

1 cup sugar

8 tablespoons (1 stick) unsalted butter

12 tablespoons (1½ sticks) salted butter

8 prebaked Pâte Brisée Tartlet Shells (recipe follows)

Dissolve the cornstarch in the milk. In a heavy saucepan, combine whole eggs, yolks, lemon zest and juice, sugar, milk-cornstarch mixture, and all butter. Stirring constantly, cook over medium heat until the custard is thick and coats the back of a spoon, about 7 minutes. Pour into a bowl and cool, stirring occasionally.

Preheat oven to 375°. Pour custard into prebaked tartlet shells. Bake for 10 to 15 minutes, or until the custard just starts to brown.

Pâte Brisée Tartlet Shells

1½ cups all-purpose flour
½ teaspoon sugar
12 tablespoons (1½ sticks) salted butter, frozen

2 tablespoons Crisco (solid vegetable shortening), frozen
2 tablespoons ice water
2 teaspoons lemon juice

In a bowl, combine flour and sugar. Cut butter and shortening into small pieces and work them into the dry ingredients. Add ice water and lemon juice and mix the dough until it just holds together. Do not overwork! Enclose dough in plastic wrap and refrigerate for at least 30 minutes.

Preheat oven to 325°. On a lightly floured surface, roll dough out ⅛" thick. Press dough into eight 4" individual tartlet pans. Line with foil and beans and bake for 8 to 10 minutes.

SERVES 8
PREPARATION TIME: 30 minutes total, plus chilling time
COOKING TIME: about 30 minutes total

CHEF'S NOTE: These tartlets may be made with Meyer lemons, blood oranges, tangerines, or regular lemons. Adjust sweet and acid ratio according to flavor of citrus fruit.

Much-publicized chef/owner Jeremiah Tower, who first gained fame with Alice Waters at Chez Panisse, has created what he likes to call an American brasserie near San Francisco's civic and cultural center, where he plays to a full house. The restaurant is big, bustling, and cheerfully noisy, with high ceilings, star-studded green carpeting, and polished wood and brass accents. The food is original and innovative, and changes constantly with the seasons.

RED AND YELLOW TOMATO SALAD WITH
   GOAT MOZZARELLA, PANCETTA, AND FRIED
   OKRA
ROAST SALMON WITH FRENCH LENTILS AND
   SAFFRON SAUCE
VANILLA WAFERS WITH FRESH BERRIES AND
   CHAMPAGNE SABAYON

RED AND YELLOW TOMATO SALAD WITH GOAT MOZZARELLA, PANCETTA, AND FRIED OKRA •

2 vine-ripened red tomatoes, peeled
2 vine-ripened golden tomatoes, peeled
12 slices pancetta or lean bacon
Vinaigrette with Fresh Herbs (recipe follows)
4 rounds goat mozzarella, cut ⅜" thick

Basil Mayonnaise (recipe follows)
Vegetable oil for deep-frying
1 pound fresh okra, sliced into ¼" rounds
½ cup cornmeal

Cut each tomato into at least 4 slices, discarding the core and stem ends. Cook pancetta or bacon until crisp, drain well, and keep warm.

Divide red and yellow tomato slices among 4 plates. Spoon vinaigrette over tomatoes. Place a round of cheese in the center, with a spoonful of basil mayonnaise on top.

Heat vegetable oil to 375°. (If you do not have a thermometer, test by tossing in a 1" cube of bread. If it turns golden brown on a slow count of

60, the oil is at about the right temperature.) While oil is heating, coat okra with the cornmeal, shaking off any excess. Just before serving, fry okra until lightly golden, about 2 minutes. Drain on paper towels and then divide among the 4 plates. Place 3 slices of pancetta around each plate.

Vinaigrette with Fresh Herbs

1 tablespoon balsamic vinegar
½ cup olive oil
1 teaspoon finely chopped mixed fresh
   herbs (thyme, tarragon, marjoram,
   etc.)

Salt and pepper

Combine vinegar, olive oil, and herbs, and season to taste with salt and pepper.

Basil Mayonnaise

1 bunch fresh basil, leaves only
½ cup mayonnaise

1 tablespoon lemon juice
Salt and pepper

Blanch basil leaves in boiling, salted water for 10 seconds, drain, and plunge into cold water. Drain again, and puree in a food processor or blender. Mix with mayonnaise and lemon juice. Season with salt and pepper to taste.

SERVES 4
PREPARATION TIME: 25 minutes total
COOKING TIME: 2 minutes

ROAST SALMON WITH FRENCH LENTILS AND SAFFRON SAUCE

1 cup small green lentils, imported from
   France
1 quart Fish Stock (page 295)
Bouquet garni (small carrot, ½ onion,
   ½ stalk celery, bay leaf, and sprig
   thyme, tied up in cheesecloth)
8 tablespoons (1 stick) unsalted butter

Salt and pepper
¼ teaspoon saffron threads
1 teaspoon lemon juice
4 salmon filets, skin on, about 6 ounces
   each
2 tablespoons virgin olive oil
Buttered young green beans

Pick over lentils for any small stones etc., rinse well, and place in pot with fish stock. Add bouquet garni. Bring to a boil, reduce heat, and simmer lentils until tender, about 30 minutes, adding more stock if necessary. Drain off most of the cooking liquid, reserving ½ cup for sauce, and discard bouquet garni. Add 2 tablespoons of butter to the lentils, and season with salt and pepper. Keep warm.

Place reserved ½ cup of stock in a small saucepan and add saffron. Reduce by rapid boiling to half the original quantity, about 5 minutes, and reduce heat to low. Whisk in remaining 6 tablespoons of butter, a little at a time, to form a liaison. Season with salt, pepper, and lemon juice. Keep warm over warm water.

Preheat oven to 450°. Season salmon with salt and pepper. In a well-seasoned cast-iron pan, heat oil until very hot but not smoking. Place salmon in pan, skin side up, and cook until lightly colored, about 2 minutes. Turn filets over to crisp the skin. Turn salmon skin side up again and transfer pan to oven. Bake until cooked to medium, about 6 minutes. Spoon sauce over 4 warmed plates. Put lentils in center, and place salmon on top, skin side up. Garnish with buttered young green beans.

SERVES 4
PREPARATION TIME: 15 minutes
COOKING TIME: 45 minutes

VANILLA WAFERS WITH FRESH BERRIES AND CHAMPAGNE SABAYON

Vanilla Wafers

⅓ cup egg whites (about 3)
½ cup plus 1 tablespoon sugar
6 tablespoons (¾ stick) unsalted butter, melted and cooled to lukewarm

½ teaspoon vanilla extract
½ cup plus 1 tablespoon all-purpose flour

Champagne Sabayon

3 large egg yolks
¼ cup sugar
Small pinch salt

½ cup champagne
½ cup heavy cream

Fruit Filling

1 cup each raspberries, blackberries, and strawberries, hulled and quartered

2 tablespoons sugar
Confectioners' sugar for garnish

Vanilla Wafers: Preheat oven to 350°. Line a baking sheet with baking parchment. Whip egg whites and sugar together until smooth. Add melted butter and vanilla, then sift flour on top of mixture and fold it in. Place by tablespoons on prepared baking sheet, spacing well apart. Spread each spoonful of batter into a 4″ circle; there should be at least 8. Bake until golden brown, about 7 minutes. Cool on baking sheet, then remove with a metal spatula. Cookies can be made early in the day and stored airtight.

Champagne Sabayon: Combine egg yolks, sugar, salt, and champagne in a stainless-steel mixing bowl. Place over simmering water and whisk vigorously until mixture is thick and pale yellow, about 10 minutes. Place bowl in a large bowl filled with ice. Whisk sabayon occasionally until cold. Whip cream to soft peaks, and fold into the sabayon. Refrigerate until ready to use; this can be made a day ahead, if desired.

To Assemble: Toss berries with sugar. Place a wafer cookie on each dessert plate and spoon some berries and champagne sabayon over it. Place another cookie on top, and sprinkle with confectioners' sugar.

SERVES 4

PREPARATION TIME: 30 minutes, plus cooling time

COOKING TIME: about 15 minutes

A San Francisco institution, Tadich Grill dates back to the Gold Rush, having originally opened its doors in 1849. Owners Bob and Steve Buich were presenting simply grilled fish dressed with light sauces long before the term "California cuisine" became fashionable, and have retained the original look of the restaurant—which was moved to its present location about twenty-five years ago—by keeping the decor as straightforward as the food.

HEARTS OF ROMAINE SALAD
FILET OF SOLE AMANDINE
BAKED ROME BEAUTY APPLES

HEARTS OF ROMAINE SALAD •

2 small, tight heads romaine lettuce, left whole, well washed and dried
1 tablespoon red wine vinegar
1 tablespoon freshly squeezed lemon juice
½ teaspoon dry mustard powder
¼ teaspoon salt
¼ teaspoon pepper
½ cup virgin olive oil

Peel away dark outer leaves of romaine, and cut off tips of leaves. Cut heads in half lengthwise and then in half again, to make quarters.

Combine remaining ingredients in a bottle and shake for 1 minute, until creamy.

Arrange 2 lettuce quarters on each plate and dress with vinegar and oil mixture.

SERVES 4
PREPARATION TIME: 10 minutes
COOKING TIME: None

FILET OF SOLE AMANDINE •

12 filets of sole, about 2 pounds total
Flour for dredging
½ cup virgin olive oil
Salt and pepper

4 tablespoons (½ stick) butter

2 tablespoons slivered blanched almonds

Lemon wedges for garnish

Parsley sprigs for garnish

Lightly cooked sliced carrots and/or boiled new potatoes (optional)

Just before cooking, dredge filets of sole lightly in flour.

Heat olive oil in a large skillet. Add the filets one by one, sprinkle with salt and pepper, and cook for 2 minutes. Turn with a spatula and cook on second side for another 2 minutes. Remove sole and divide among 4 heated plates.

Discard oil in pan and add butter and almonds. Stir for 1 minute, until almonds are light gold. Immediately pour over sole and garnish the plates with lemon wedges and parsley sprigs. Accompany with carrots and new potatoes, if desired.

SERVES 4

PREPARATION TIME: 5 minutes

COOKING TIME: 5 minutes

BAKED ROME BEAUTY APPLES

4 Rome Beauty Apples

4 teaspoons raisins

3 cups water

1 cup brown sugar

4 perfect bay leaves

4 cloves

1 large pinch ground cinnamon

2 slices lemon

Preheat oven to 350°. Wash apples, cut out core, and stuff cavity with the raisins. Place in a shallow baking dish. Combine remaining ingredients and pour over apples. Bake for 30 to 40 minutes, until tender. Serve apples warm or cold, using a bay leaf on each for garnish.

SERVES 4

PREPARATION TIME: 10 minutes

COOKING TIME: 30 to 40 minutes

An exceptionally beautiful mountain resort situated on a ridge above the northern Sonoma coastline, Timberhill Ranch is an oasis of tranquility, with secluded cottages for guests hidden among the trees. The main lodge has a spacious dining room with huge windows for viewing the panorama outside. The sophisticated nouvelle California cuisine suits the surroundings perfectly.

TIMBERHILL PROSCIUTTO ROLL
DUCK BREAST ORIENTALE
POACHED PEARS WITH WHITE CHOCOLATE
AND RASPBERRIES

TIMBERHILL PROSCIUTTO ROLL

4 cups raw sushi rice (covered with glucose)
6 sheets sushinori (roasted seaweed)
16 slices prosciutto

4 avocadoes, peeled and sliced
Wasabi mustard, prepared from Japanese wasabi powder
Grape leaves

Prepare rice according to package directions and cool. On a bamboo sushi roller or a piece of waxed paper, lay out 1 sheet of seaweed. Moistening hands with water to handle it more easily, press a thin layer of rice onto the seaweed. About one third of the way in from the edge closest to you, place 1 slice prosciutto, then another. Lay slices of avocado end to end. Smear a very thin line of wasabi next to this and roll the whole thing up tightly to form a log. Repeat this process with the other 5 sheets of seaweed, and refrigerate until ready to use.

Line a plate with grape leaves. Slice logs into 1½" pieces and arrange on top. Serve with additional wasabi. Roll the remaining 4 strips of prosciutto and slice very thin. Use as garnish on the plate.

SERVES 8
PREPARATION TIME: 30 minutes
COOKING TIME: 20 minutes

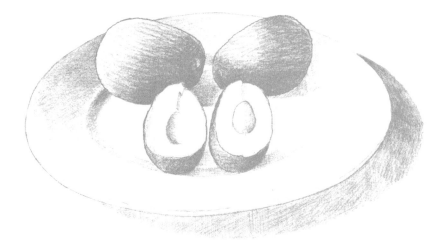

DUCK BREAST ORIENTALE

8 *duck breast halves, boneless but with skin*
3 *tablespoons sugar*
2 *teaspoons chopped shallot*
2 *cups heavy red wine*

1 *10-ounce jar red currant jelly*
1 *cup Major Grey Chutney (or homemade mango or plum chutney)*
2 *teaspoons cornstarch*
Blanched snow peas and slivered carrots for garnish

Preheat oven to 400°. Heat a heavy, ovenproof skillet to very hot. Brown the duck breasts, skin side down, for about 1 minute. Turn them over and transfer pan to oven. Bake for 8 minutes, until the meat is firm to the touch. If skin is not desired, remove *after* baking to preserve juiciness and flavor. Put to rest in a warm place for a few minutes.

While duck breasts are baking, slowly melt sugar in a heavy saucepan. Stirring constantly, add shallot and wine. The sugar will crystallize, but will melt down again during cooking. Add red currant jelly and chutney and bring to a boil. Reduce heat and simmer for 5 minutes. Dissolve cornstarch in a little water and stir into sauce. Cook until sauce clears and thickens, 30 seconds or less.

Slice duck breasts on the diagonal. Spoon a pool of sauce onto heated dinner plates and top with a sliced duck breast. Garnish with snow peas and slivered carrot.

SERVES 8
PREPARATION TIME: 20 minutes
COOKING TIME: 15 minutes

POACHED PEARS WITH WHITE CHOCOLATE AND RASPBERRIES

8 well-shaped Bartlett or Bosc pears,
  firm but not hard, with stems
1 quart strained fresh orange juice
1 cup dry white wine
1 cup sugar
2 cinnamon sticks

½ teaspoon fennel seeds
½ pound white chocolate, chopped small
½ cup milk
Raspberries for garnish
Mint sprigs for garnish

Using a vegetable peeler, peel pears evenly, leaving stems intact. Trim bottom so that pears will stand upright. Combine orange juice, wine, sugar, cinnamon sticks, and fennel seeds in a saucepan or skillet large enough to hold the pears without pears touching one another or sides of pan. Add pears. Liquid should cover them. If it does not, add more orange juice and wine. Poach for 12 to 15 minutes, until just tender. Remove and stand on paper towels to drain. (Reserve poaching liquid to poach other fruits, or reduce to make a delicious sauce for another dessert.)

Combine chocolate with milk and melt over very low heat. Work with a rubber spatula until smooth, then spoon this sauce onto 8 dessert plates. The sauce should cover the plate. Place pear upright on sauce and sprinkle sauce with raspberries. Garnish pear with a mint sprig at the stem. Serve with a knife and fork.

SERVES 8
PREPARATION TIME: 15 minutes
COOKING TIME: 20 minutes

Founded in Oakland in 1893, and still in the same family, this colorful Sacramento Street restaurant has authentic links with the history of California. Since its beginnings, the restaurant has specialized in true early California cuisine—the *ranchero* food of Spanish California. The founder of the original Tortola acquired a collection of handwritten early California recipes through a bequest from an elderly cook to one of the original Spanish land-grant families. Today, the spirit of the past prevails, though dishes are lightened and are more California/Southwest in nature, with the emphasis on very fresh ingredients.

BLACK BEAN SOUP WITH LIME CREAM
FLANK STEAK QUESADA
MOCHA CUSTARDS

BLACK BEAN SOUP WITH LIME CREAM

2 pounds black beans
3 cloves garlic, peeled and chopped
4 carrots, peeled and chopped
2 cups chopped celery
1 bunch fresh cilantro (coriander), chopped
1 large red onion, peeled and chopped

½ cup peeled, seeded, and diced tomato, or tomato sauce
Chicken Stock (page 294) or water
1½ tablespoons salt
Black pepper
Lime Cream (recipe follows)

Pick over and rinse beans. Cover with cold water and soak overnight. Drain beans and place in a large stockpot. Add all the remaining ingredients except chicken stock, salt, pepper, and lime cream. Pour in enough stock or water to cover. Bring to a boil, reduce heat, and simmer, partially covered, for 1½ hours, or until beans are tender but not mushy. Add more stock or water if needed to keep the beans covered. Add the salt and pepper to taste during last 15 minutes of cooking. Puree 2 cups of beans with some of the broth, and return to pot. Thin soup with stock or water if desired and adjust seasoning. Serve in soup bowls, and top with a dollop of lime cream.

Lime Cream

1 lime
1 cup dairy sour cream

Salt and freshly ground black pepper

Wash lime. Grate zest and combine with juice. Mix with sour cream. Add salt and black pepper to taste.

SERVES 6
PREPARATION TIME: 30 minutes total, plus overnight soaking
COOKING TIME: 1½ hours

FLANK STEAK QUESADA

1 pound flank steak
12 whole wheat tortillas
6 ounces jack cheese, sliced
2 red bell peppers, grilled, seeded, and
  sliced

1 bunch fresh cilantro (coriander)
6 ounces Teleme cheese
Vegetable oil

Grill steak to medium rare and slice thin. Divide into 6 portions.

Lay 6 tortillas on a work surface. Top with slices of steak, jack cheese, bell peppers, and cilantro. Spread 6 remaining tortillas with Teleme cheese. Place on top of filled tortillas, cheese side down, sandwich fashion. Grease a heavy skillet with oil and heat tortillas on both sides, about 2 minutes per side.

SERVES 6
PREPARATION TIME: 20 minutes
COOKING TIME: 15 minutes

MOCHA CUSTARDS

2 cups heavy cream
2 tablespoons sugar
½ cup whole coffee beans
½ vanilla bean, split

6 large egg yolks
8 ounces semisweet chocolate, cut up
1 ounce unsweetened chocolate, cut up

In a saucepan, combine cream, sugar, coffee beans, and vanilla bean. Heat, but do not allow to boil. Let stand for 1½ hours, and then strain.

Blend egg yolks together and add to strained cream mixture. Combine semisweet and unsweetened chocolate in top of double boiler and melt over simmering water. Cool slightly and add to egg yolk–cream mixture.

Preheat oven to 325°. Pour custard mixture into 6 custard cups and place in a shallow roasting pan. Add enough very hot water to reach halfway up sides of cups. Cover loosely with aluminum foil and bake for 20 to 25 minutes. Remove custard cups from water bath and cool. Serve at room temperature.

SERVES 6

PREPARATION TIME: 15 minutes, plus steeping

COOKING TIME: 25 minutes

Located in a fine old stone building, this popular St. Helena restaurant has a crisply stylized, neo-Gothic look, complemented by ash tables and rush-seated chairs. The vine-covered brick courtyard is a delightful place for dining out of doors. Co-proprietor/chef Michael Chiarello says his cuisine is "American food prepared with the head, hands, and heart of an Italian," and everything is made on the premises, from prosciutto to gelati.

PIZZETTA CON AGLIO *(Pizza with Olive Oil and Roasted Garlic)*
SPIEDINI DI GAMBERI *(Grilled Jumbo Shrimp with Chardonnay Scallion Butter Sauce)*
BISCOTTI *(Almond Dipping Cookies)*
FRAGOLE PAZZE *(Strawberries with Balsamic Vinegar)*

PIZZETTA CON AGLIO

⅞ ounce fresh compressed baker's yeast, or 1 package dried granular yeast
1 cup warm water (110°)
1 large egg
9 tablespoons virgin olive oil
3½ cups unbleached bread flour

4 teaspoons fresh rosemary, minced
4 cloves garlic, peeled and minced
4 tablespoons grated imported Italian Parmesan cheese
Roasted Garlic (recipe follows)

Place yeast (crumbled, if fresh), water, egg, and 1 tablespoon of olive oil in the bowl of an electric mixer. Mix with the dough hook for 30 seconds. Add flour and mix until dough is supple and elastic, 10 to 15 minutes. Dough should be slightly wet. Turn out onto a lightly floured surface. Knead by hand for 1 minute. Place in a clean bowl and let rise until doubled in bulk, about 1½ hours. Punch down and cut into 4 pieces. Roll each piece into a ball. Place on a baking sheet, brush lightly with olive oil, and let rise until doubled in size, about 1 hour.

Preheat oven to 500° and heat a baking stone if available. Work one ball of dough with your hands from the middle of it to the outside, pressing with your thumb and forefinger and rotating the dough in your hand until it is all the same thickness, and approximately 10" in diameter. Repeat with remaining balls of dough. Brush each with 2 tablespoons olive oil, and sprinkle with rosemary, minced fresh garlic, and Parmesan. Place in oven and bake until a deep, golden brown, about 20 minutes. Put dish of roasted garlic heads in oven at the same time, uncovered, for 10 minutes. Cool a little and separate cloves. When pizzetta are ready, squeeze roasted garlic pulp on top, and spread out over surface. Cut pizzetta into quarters and serve at once.

Roasted Garlic

4 whole heads garlic (preferably red garlic)
1 cup virgin olive oil
2 tablespoons minced fresh thyme
2 tablespoons minced fresh rosemary
Salt
White pepper

Preheat oven to 350°. Shear tops off heads of garlic, exposing the cloves. Brush liberally with olive oil and place in a shallow baking dish with remaining oil. Sprinkle with thyme, rosemary, salt, and white pepper. Cover and bake for 1 hour, until very soft and mellow, and garlic pulp starts to squeeze out by itself.

SERVES 4
PREPARATION TIME: 30 minutes total, plus rising time
COOKING TIME: about 1½ hours total

SPIEDINI DI GAMBERI

1 pound fresh jumbo shrimp, in the shell (24 count)
¼ pound pancetta, sliced paper thin
¼ cup virgin olive oil
Salt and pepper
2 shallots, peeled and minced
¾ cup Chardonnay
4 scallions
1 tablespoon heavy cream
6 tablespoons (¾ stick) unsalted butter, softened
½ lemon
Simple sautéed vegetable of choice

Build an intense charcoal fire. Soak 4 bamboo skewers in water for 20 minutes, to prevent them from burning.

Peel and devein shrimp, leaving tail on. Wrap each shrimp in a half piece of pancetta, and thread onto skewer, allowing 6 per skewer. Coat lightly with olive oil and season with salt and pepper. Set aside at room temperature while making sauce.

Put shallot, pepper to taste, and wine in a noncorrodible saucepan. Reduce over medium heat until less than ½ cup remains, about 8 minutes. Coarsely chop green tops from scallions and add to pan. Reserve white bulbs. Continue to reduce until 3 to 4 tablespoons remain. Strain through a fine mesh strainer into another pan. Add cream, bring to a boil, and whisk in butter, 1 tablespoon at a time, over very low heat, to form a liaison. Finish with a squeeze of lemon juice and salt to taste.

Grill shrimp for 2 minutes on each side, until cooked through. Slice white bulbs of scallions thin, on the bias. Put ¼ cup of sauce on each plate, arrange shrimp on top, and sprinkle with white scallion. Serve with vegetable of your choice.

SERVES 4
PREPARATION TIME: 30 minutes
COOKING TIME: 20 minutes

EDITOR'S NOTE: The shrimp can be broiled if a grill is not available, but the result will be different.

BISCOTTI

¼ pound (1 stick) unsalted butter, softened
1 cup sugar
⅔ cup almonds, ground
1 large egg

3 egg yolks
2 cups all-purpose flour
2 tablespoons aniseseed
¾ teaspoon baking powder

Preheat oven to 350°. In the bowl of an electric mixer, cream butter and sugar together. Beat in ground almonds. At slow speed, beat in whole egg and egg yolks. When mixture is smooth, add flour, aniseseed, and baking powder. Turn dough out onto a lightly floured surface and roll into two 1½"-wide-by-9"-long logs. Transfer to a baking sheet (logs will increase considerably in size, so set well apart from one another) and bake for approximately 1¼ hours. Transfer to a cooling rack. When logs are cold, cut on the diagonal into ½"-thick slices. Place on baking sheet and bake for 7 minutes at 400°. Cool on rack.

MAKES APPROXIMATELY 40
PREPARATION TIME: 20 minutes
COOKING TIME: 1½ hours

FRAGOLE PAZZE •

2 tablespoons sugar

3 tablespoons balsamic vinegar

½ teaspoon freshly ground black pepper

2 cups ripe strawberries, washed and hulled

4 teaspoons grated bittersweet chocolate

In a stainless-steel bowl, mix the sugar, vinegar, and black pepper together. Stir in strawberries and marinate for 5 minutes. Transfer to serving bowls and garnish with grated chocolate.

SERVES 4

PREPARATION TIME: 5 minutes

COOKING TIME: None

Lynn Bergeron, son of the late Victor Bergeron, is the proprietor of this famous old dining spot. (Dubbed "Trader" Vic for his early habit of exchanging goods for services, Vic Bergeron's original restaurant opened in Oakland in 1934, and was to be the first of a whole fleet.) The cuisine, now in the hands of executive chef Klaus Selb, is a unique mixture of Chinese, Polynesian, and Indian, and the decor is equally colorful and exotic.

FRESH CRAB WITH ORANGE DRESSING
MONGOLIAN LAMB CHOPS
APPLE FRITTERS

FRESH CRAB WITH ORANGE DRESSING •

1 tablespoon peanut oil	*1 Dungeness crab, cooked and cracked*
4 shiitake mushrooms	*12 asparagus tips, cooked and cooled*
¼ teaspoon chopped gingerroot	*8 orange sections (page 292)*
½ teaspoon soy sauce	*Orange Dressing (recipe follows)*
1 tablespoon sherry	

In a small skillet, heat peanut oil and add mushrooms, gingerroot, soy sauce, and sherry. Cook for about 3 minutes, and set aside to cool. Remove crab meat from shell, and reserve legs.

Arrange 3 asparagus tips on each of 4 plates, radiating from the center with tips at the rim. Place 2 orange sections to one side of the asparagus. Put a quarter of the crab meat in center of each plate, and fan crab legs out from center. Coat with orange dressing, and place 1 shiitake mushroom in center.

Orange Dressing

2 oranges, peeled and sectioned (page
   292), without pith, membrane, or pits
2 limes, peeled and sectioned (page
   292), without pith, membrane, or pits
½ cup virgin olive oil

Pinch ground cumin
Salt and pepper
5 fresh basil leaves, julienned
1 ripe tomato, peeled, seeded, and
   chopped

In a blender or food processor, combine orange sections, lime sections, olive oil, and cumin. Add salt and pepper to taste. Blend to a creamy consistency. Stir in basil and tomato, and set aside.

SERVES 4

PREPARATION TIME: 25 minutes total

COOKING TIME: 5 minutes (using ready-cooked crab)

MONGOLIAN LAMB CHOPS

12 rib lamb chops
2 onions, peeled and sliced

3 tablespoons hoisin sauce (available in
   Chinese markets)
1 teaspoon sesame oil

Sauce

Lamb chop trimmings
1 carrot, peeled and chopped
1 onion, peeled and chopped
1 clove garlic, peeled and chopped
2 tablespoons hoisin sauce
½ cup Chicken Stock (page 294) or
   canned chicken broth

4 handfuls frisée lettuce leaves
4 handfuls oak leaf lettuce leaves
8 leaves Belgian endive
Cilantro Dressing (recipe follows)
Cooked baby vegetables of choice for
   garnish

Trim lamb chops of all fat and membrane, exposing bones. (Save trimmings.) Combine sliced onions, hoisin sauce, and sesame oil. Add lamb chops, turning to coat well, and marinate for 2 to 3 hours.

Sauce: Sauté lamb chop trimmings (including a little fat) with chopped carrot, onion, and garlic until golden brown, about 7 minutes. Add hoisin sauce and chicken stock, and simmer for 30 minutes. Strain.

Remove lamb chops from marinade and grill to medium rare, 3 to 4 minutes on each side. Toss lettuce leaves with enough cilantro dressing to coat lightly, and arrange on one half of each plate. (Place the Belgian endive leaves pointing outwards, spoke fashion.) On the other half of plate, pour 2 tablespoons of sauce and 2 tablespoons of cilantro dressing. The two sauces should be side by side. Place lamb chops on top of the sauces, and garnish plates with baby vegetables.

Cilantro Dressing

1 bunch fresh cilantro (coriander), destemmed
¼ cup white wine vinegar
1 cup peanut oil

¼ cup heavy cream
Salt and pepper

Combine cilantro leaves, vinegar, and oil in a blender or food processor; blend to a smooth consistency. Add cream and season to taste with salt and pepper. Blend until creamy.

SERVES 4
PREPARATION TIME: 1 hour total, plus marination time
COOKING TIME: 40 minutes

APPLE FRITTERS

Mild vegetable oil for deep-frying
2 crisp green apples, peeled, cored, and diced
2½ tablespoons apricot jam
Dash fresh lime juice
12 round won ton wrappers

Approximately 1 cup Crème Anglaise (page 297)
24 fresh raspberries for garnish
4 sprigs mint for garnish
Confectioners' sugar

Pour about 2″ of vegetable oil into a heavy skillet and heat to 370° on a deep fat/candy thermometer.

Combine diced apples, apricot jam, and lime juice. Place a spoonful in the center of each won ton wrapper and brush edges with water. Fold in half and press edges together to seal. Deep-fry until golden brown, about 3 minutes.

Pour a little crème anglaise onto each dessert plate and swirl plate to spread sauce over the surface. Arrange 3 apple fritters in a flower shape in the center. Garnish with raspberries and mint, and dust with confectioners' sugar.

SERVES 4
PREPARATION TIME: 30 minutes
COOKING TIME: 5 minutes

Carlo and Lisa Middione's unique delicatessen, catering service, and café is housed in a long, narrow building on upper Fillmore. Bustling, white-jacketed cooks make fresh pasta, roast meats, cut vegetables, and prepare desserts in the open-plan kitchen, in full view of interested diners at linen-covered tables. Everything is prepared by hand in the authentic, uncomplicated Italian style.

SICILIAN-STYLE EGGS
SCALLOPS OF BREAST OF FOWL WITH LEMON AND CAPERS
STUFFED ZUCCHINI
APRICOT SOUFFLÉ

SICILIAN-STYLE EGGS •

2 medium vine-ripened tomatoes	*2 tablespoons virgin olive oil*
4 large eggs, fresh as possible	*Plain toasted Italian bread*

Drop tomatoes into boiling water for 15 seconds and slip off skins. Core and cut into small dice; do not discard seeds or juice. Crack eggs into a bowl and beat them, using only 3 or 4 strokes. There should be a few streaks of white showing; do not overbeat.

Heat oil in a 9″ skillet until quite hot but nowhere near smoking. Put in diced tomatoes with their seeds and juice. Stir them around for a little less than 2 minutes. Add beaten eggs. After about 5 seconds, gently stir the mass around the pan until the eggs are just set. They should be very moist but set in rather large curds. The dish should look very pretty and appetizing, a bit like a stained glass window. Serve immediately on hot plates, and pass plain toasted Italian bread at the table.

SERVES 4
PREPARATION TIME: 10 minutes
COOKING TIME: about 5 minutes

CHEF'S NOTE: Fine ingredients are critical to this very old, traditional dish. When made correctly, it needs no salt, pepper, or herbs.

SCALLOPS OF BREAST OF FOWL WITH LEMON AND CAPERS

1½ pounds chicken, turkey, or duck breasts, skinned and boned
Salt and pepper
Flour for dredging
8 to 10 tablespoons (1 to 1¼ sticks) butter

¼ cup finely chopped fresh Italian flat-leaf parsley
Juice from 2 lemons
1½ tablespoons capers with a little of their juice
Dry white wine, as needed

To facilitate cutting the breasts if they are whole, place them on a tray over ice and let them get very cold and firm, or put them in the freezer for 30 minutes or so. With a sharp blade, slice cleanly about ⅜″ thick. Place between 2 sheets of plastic wrap or waxed paper and hit them gently with the flat side of a meat cleaver, or use a meat bat. Be careful not to hit them too hard and thereby tear them. Make the scallops ¼″ thick. Season with salt and pepper and dredge lightly in flour just before cooking.

Using a 10″ skillet, heat the butter until it just begins to sizzle, but do not allow it to brown. Sauté the scallops for about 1½ minutes on each side; do not overcook. Do this in batches if necessary, and keep warm in a low oven. Add more butter to the pan if required, and stir in parsley, lemon juice, and capers. The pan sauce should be glossy and there should not be much of it—just enough to flavor the meat. If there is not enough sauce, add some dry white wine, and reduce it a bit. Place scallops on hot plates and serve at once.

SERVES 4
PREPARATION TIME: 20 minutes
COOKING TIME: 12 to 14 minutes

STUFFED ZUCCHINI

¼ ounce dried porcini mushrooms
2 zucchini, about 6″ long by 1″ diameter
Salt
½ cup grated Reggiano Parmesan cheese
½ cup coarse white bread crumbs
1 large egg

Freshly ground black pepper
4 leaves fresh basil, finely chopped
2 slices soprassata or Toscana salami, thinly sliced and finely chopped
2 tablespoons virgin olive oil, or more if needed

Soak porcini mushrooms in warm water for 20 minutes, squeeze dry, and chop fine.

Preheat oven to 400°. Simmer the whole zucchini in salted water for about 5 minutes. Remove and cool in a bowl of cold water. Dry zucchini and split in half. Scoop out pulp and chop fine. Place pulp in a bowl with ¼ cup of Parmesan, the porcini, bread crumbs, egg, salt and pepper to taste, basil, and salami. Mix well.

Lightly coat a baking dish with a little olive oil. Stuff zucchini with the mixture, mounding it up. Sprinkle with remaining ¼ cup grated Parmesan and drizzle with remaining olive oil. Bake for 25 minutes, until tops are golden brown. Serve hot.

SERVES 4

PREPARATION TIME: 25 minutes

COOKING TIME: 30 minutes

CHEF'S NOTE: This dish can be prepared up to the point of baking the day before and refrigerated, tightly covered. Bring to room temperature before baking. Save the flavorful water from the soaked mushrooms and add to soups or stocks.

APRICOT SOUFFLÉ •

1 ounce dried apricots	*3 tablespoons unsalted butter, softened,*
2 tablespoons dry Marsala wine	*for molds*
2 tablespoons brandy	*Sugar for molds*
2 tablespoons sugar	*3 large egg whites, at room temperature*

Put apricots in a small bowl and sprinkle with Marsala and brandy. Macerate for 2 or 3 hours in a warm place. When fruit is soft, remove from bowl, squeeze out liquid. Chop apricots fine and return to liquid. Stir in 1 tablespoon of sugar.

Place rack in lower third of oven and preheat oven to 350°. Lightly butter four 4″-diameter ramekins and dust with sugar. Set aside, and have ready a baking sheet. Whisk egg whites until very frothy and drizzle in remaining tablespoon of sugar. Continue beating at medium speed to firm but supple peaks. Stir about ½ cup of egg whites into fruit mixture to loosen it; then fold in remaining egg whites. Quickly spoon the soufflé mixture into the prepared ramekins and place on baking sheet for easier handling. Bake for 12 to 14 minutes, until they puff 1″ to 1½″ above rims of molds. Serve at once.

SERVES 4

PREPARATION TIME: 15 minutes, plus maceration time

COOKING TIME: 12 to 14 minutes

Co-proprietor/executive chef Mary Etta Moose creates original, contemporary Italian food for this popular North Beach restaurant. A longtime favorite with newspaper writers, politicians, sports stars, and sports fans, the "Washbag" is cheerful, noisy, and friendly, and as the proprietors are lovers of classical jazz, the upright piano against the back wall does not go unplayed.

PENNE, FLAGEOLETS, AND CAVIAR
MARINATED ROAST RACK OF LAMB, OKU
BAKED FIGS CHARTREUSE

PENNE, FLAGEOLETS, AND CAVIAR •

8 ounces imported penne (short tubular pasta)

1 14-ounce can flageolets verts (pale green French kidney beans, canned Italian white beans, or cannellini can be substituted)

2 large scallions, white bulbs and part of green tops, sliced

2 tablespoons chopped fresh chives

Juice of 1 lemon

2 tablespoons unsalted butter, at room temperature

2 to 3 ounces choice black caviar

Kosher salt (optional)

Cook pasta in plenty of boiling salted water until just tender, or *al dente*. While pasta is cooking, drain beans of most of their liquid and gently heat beans through. Off heat, stir in scallions, chives, and lemon juice.

Toss drained pasta with butter, then with the bean mixture. Gently fold in caviar and taste for seasoning. Sprinkle with a few grains of kosher salt if necessary. Divide among 4 heated serving bowls.

SERVES 4

PREPARATION TIME: 10 minutes

COOKING TIME: 10 to 12 minutes

MARINATED ROAST RACK OF LAMB, OKU

1 rack of lamb, 8 ribs
1 tablespoon honey
½ cup soy sauce
½ cup Jack Daniel's whiskey
4 cloves garlic, peeled and smashed
1" piece gingerroot, peeled, sliced, and
   smashed

1 red onion, peeled and chopped
2 jalapeño chili peppers, seeded and
   chopped
1½ cups water
1 purple globe eggplant, about 1 pound,
   unpeeled, sliced ¼" thick

Have butcher French cut the rack of lamb (remove chine bone, expose rib bones, and remove all but ¼"-thick layer of fat), and give you the chine bone.

Combine honey, soy sauce, whiskey, garlic, ginger, onion, jalapeño peppers, and water. Place the lamb and this mixture in a plastic bag set in a dish and refrigerate overnight.

Remove lamb from bag, reserving marinade for basting eggplant. Wipe dry of all clinging bits and let air-dry until room temperature.

Preheat oven to 450°. Wrap rib ends of lamb in foil. Grease a small roasting pan with lamb fat and position lamb in it fat side up, resting on the foil tips and severed chine bone. Roast for 10 minutes, then reduce heat to 350° and continue to cook for a total, including the first 10 minutes, of 10 minutes per pound—about 30 minutes for a 3-pound rack. A meat thermometer should register 140° for medium rare. Let meat rest in a warm place under a tent of foil for 15 minutes after it comes from the oven.

While meat is resting, broil eggplant slices for 2 or 3 minutes per side, basting with marinade mixture. (There is no need to salt them first.) Carve meat into 2-chop portions and serve with broiled eggplant.

SERVES 4
PREPARATION TIME: 10 minutes, plus marination overnight
COOKING TIME: about 35 minutes

BAKED FIGS CHARTREUSE

8 ripe figs, unpeeled
1 stick cinnamon, broken up
1 tablespoon finely julienned orange zest

1 tablespoon dark brown sugar, tightly
    packed
4 ounces mascarpone cheese
4 teaspoons green Chartreuse

Preheat oven to 250°. Arrange whole figs upright in a shallow dish. Surround with pieces of cinnamon, orange zest, brown sugar, and enough water to reach halfway up the figs. Bake until tender, basting frequently with pan juices, about 40 minutes. Set aside to cool. (This may be done the day before figs are to be served.)

At serving time, cut a cross into each fig and open it up like a flower. Mix mascarpone cheese with Chartreuse and stuff each fig with about 1 tablespoon of the mixture. Re-form the figs. Arrange 2 figs in each serving dish, and spoon the pan sauce over all, discarding the cinnamon.

SERVES 4
PREPARATION TIME: 15 minutes
COOKING TIME: 40 minutes

A thoroughly authentic Shanghai restaurant with definite touches of sophisticated Hong Kong about it, but located in downtown San Francisco, Wu Kong serves dazzling food in elegant surroundings. White linen–covered tables, black lacquer chairs with blue upholstered seats, and crystal chandeliers form a suitable backdrop for impeccable Chinese cuisine.

TOSSED BEAN CURD SALAD
FRESH SCALLOPS WITH GARLIC SAUCE
BRAISED NAPA CABBAGE WITH CREAMY
  WHITE SAUCE
SWEET SHANGHAI CREPES WITH RED BEAN
  PASTE

TOSSED BEAN CURD SALAD •

6 dried black Chinese mushrooms
3 tablespoons soy sauce
4 teaspoons Oriental sesame oil
1 teaspoon sugar
¼ teaspoon crushed red pepper flakes
½ teaspoon hot pepper sauce (optional)

1 small carrot, peeled and cut into
  matchsticks
1 8-ounce package plain or seasoned
  pressed bean curd, cut into
  matchsticks
2 stalks celery, cut into matchsticks

Soak mushrooms in warm water to cover for 20 minutes. Cut off and discard stems. Slice caps thin, and set aside.

In a small bowl, combine soy sauce, sesame oil, sugar, red pepper flakes, and hot pepper sauce, if used.

Cook carrot in boiling water for 1 minute. Drain and rinse in cold water. Set aside.

Place sliced mushrooms, carrot, bean curd, and celery in a bowl. Add dressing and mix well. Chill before serving.

SERVES 4
PREPARATION TIME: 20 minutes, plus chilling time
COOKING TIME: 1 minute

FRESH SCALLOPS WITH GARLIC SAUCE •

2 tablespoons vegetable oil
1 teaspoon minced gingerroot
3 cloves garlic, peeled and minced
¾ pound fresh sea scallops
2 scallions, minced, including green tops
1 tablespoon soy sauce

1 teaspoon chili paste
1 teaspoon chopped fresh jalapeño chili
 pepper, seeded
1 teaspoon Oriental sesame oil
1 teaspoon cornstarch mixed with 2
 teaspoons cold water

Place wok over high heat until very hot. Add oil, swirling to coat sides. Add ginger and garlic; cook, stirring, until fragrant, about 20 seconds. Add scallops and stir-fry until they turn opaque, about 2 minutes. Add scallions, soy sauce, chili paste, chili pepper, sesame oil, and cornstarch mixture. Cook, stirring, until sauce thickens slightly, about 20 seconds.

SERVES 4
PREPARATION TIME: 5 minutes
COOKING TIME: 4 minutes

EDITOR'S NOTE: On most Western-style electric stoves, it is better to use a flat-bottomed wok or a heavy sauté pan for the best heat contact.

BRAISED NAPA CABBAGE WITH CREAMY WHITE SAUCE •

1 pound Napa cabbage
½ cup milk
¼ cup Chicken Stock (page 294) or
 canned chicken broth
1 teaspoon vegetable oil
½ teaspoon sugar

½ teaspoon salt
⅛ teaspoon white pepper
2 teaspoons cornstarch mixed with 4
 teaspoons water
2 tablespoons finely diced Smithfield or
 Virginia ham for garnish (optional)

Cut cabbage in half lengthwise. Blanch cabbage in boiling salted water for 4 minutes. Drain and rinse under cold water. Transfer to a serving platter.
   In a saucepan, combine milk, chicken stock, vegetable oil, sugar, salt, and pepper. Bring to a boil over medium heat, stirring constantly. Add cornstarch mixture and cook, stirring, until slightly thickened, about 1 minute. To serve, pour sauce over cabbage. Garnish with diced ham, if desired.

SERVES 4
PREPARATION TIME: 5 minutes
COOKING TIME: 5 minutes

SWEET SHANGHAI CREPES WITH RED BEAN PASTE

Crepes

1 cup all-purpose flour
1 large egg, lightly beaten
1 cup water

2½ tablespoons butter or margarine, melted

Date Paste

¼ pound pitted dates, coarsely chopped
½ cup sweet red bean paste (available at Chinese markets)

Vegetable oil
2 tablespoons chopped unsalted roasted peanuts

Crepes: Place flour in a bowl. Using a fork, blend egg into flour until mixture is crumbly. Add water, a few tablespoons at a time, stirring well after each addition. Add butter and beat until batter becomes smooth and silky. Let stand for 15 minutes.

Date Paste: In a food processor or blender, whirl dates and bean paste into a smooth paste. Place in a bowl and set aside.

Place a wide, nonstick frying pan over medium-high heat until hot. Add 1 teaspoon oil and wipe with a dry paper towel. Pour ¼ cup of batter into center of pan. Tilt pan in all directions to spread batter and form a 6″ to 7″ crepe. Cook for 45 seconds, or until batter is completely set and the surface feels dry. Loosen edges with a spatula, turn over, and cook for 30 seconds. Repeat with remaining batter. Stack crepes on a platter as they are cooked.

Spread 1 tablespoon of date-bean paste across center of each crepe, leaving about 1″ exposed on each end. Sprinkle paste with ¼ teaspoon of peanuts. Fold exposed ends over filling, then fold each side over, completely enclosing filling. Repeat with remaining crepes.

Place a wide, nonstick frying pan over medium-high heat until hot. Add 2 teaspoons oil, swirling to coat surface. Cook filled crepes, a few at a time, for 1½ minutes on each side, or until golden brown, swirling pan over heat to brown evenly. Serve hot crepes whole or cut into bite-sized pieces.

MAKES 24 TO 27
PREPARATION TIME: 30 minutes
COOKING TIME: about 30 minutes

A far cry from the typical old-style San Francisco Chinese eating house, Henry Chan's award-winning Yank Sing is a sophisticated Financial District restaurant with open spaces, etched glass partitions, and crisp white napery. Chef Helen Chan—who has been with the restaurant for over twenty years— prepares exceptional Chinese food that matches the surroundings: Flavors and textures are equally crisp and distinct.

PHOENIX SHRIMP
MANDARIN BEEF
ELEGANT ORANGE SLICES

PHOENIX SHRIMP

12 medium-sized raw shrimp, in the
  shell
1 tablespoon cornstarch
¾ teaspoon sugar
¼ teaspoon salt
⅛ teaspoon white pepper

Shrimp Paste (recipe follows)
½ cup fine bread crumbs
1 quart vegetable oil
2 ripe tomatoes, sliced, for garnish
2 lemons, sliced, for garnish

Shell shrimp, leaving tails intact, then devein and clean well in cold water. Pat dry with paper towels. Combine cornstarch, sugar, salt, and pepper. Dredge shrimp in this mixture.

Wet one hand. Scoop up one twelfth of the shrimp paste onto your palm. Place 1 shrimp on top of paste. Wrap paste around shrimp, excluding tail, and mold the paste so that it is consistent with the shape of the shrimp. Dip in bread crumbs. Repeat with remaining 11 shrimp.

Pour oil into wok and heat to 350° (see Editor's Note following Mandarin Beef recipe, page 280). Deep-fry shrimp a few at a time until golden brown, approximately 1 minute. Drain on wire rack or paper towels. Arrange on a platter and garnish with tomato and lemon slices. Serve hot.

Shrimp Paste

10 medium-sized shrimp, peeled, deveined, and finely chopped
1 tablespoon cornstarch
⅛ teaspoon white pepper
¼ teaspoon salt

¾ teaspoon sugar
1 small onion, peeled and finely chopped
1 sprig fresh cilantro (coriander), finely chopped

Mix all ingredients together until they form a paste, then refrigerate for 30 minutes.

SERVES 4
PREPARATION TIME: 30 minutes total, plus chilling time
COOKING TIME: about 5 minutes

MANDARIN BEEF •

1 pound lean beef (such as flank steak)
2 tablespoons cornstarch
2 cups plus 2 tablespoons vegetable oil
1 clove garlic, peeled and minced
1 teaspoon minced gingerroot

1 red bell pepper, seeded, deribbed, and sliced ⅛" thick
1 green bell pepper, seeded, deribbed, and sliced ⅛" thick
Seasoning Sauce (recipe follows)
2 scallions, white bulbs and green tops, cut into 1" pieces

Cut beef across the grain into 1"-×-¼"-×-⅛" strips. Add cornstarch and 1 tablespoon of oil. Mix well and set aside.

Pour approximately 2 cups of oil into a wok and heat to 350°. Add beef and stir-fry for 30 seconds. Remove beef from oil and set aside. Drain hot oil from wok. Reheat wok and add 1 tablespoon of fresh oil. Add garlic, ginger, and bell peppers and stir-fry for 30 seconds. Add seasoning sauce and cook for another 30 seconds before adding beef and scallions. Toss for a few seconds to heat through before serving.

Seasoning Sauce

3 tablespoons A-1 steak sauce
1 tablespoon dry sherry
2 tablespoons Worcestershire sauce
2 tablespoons hoisin sauce

2 tablespoons Kikkoman soy sauce
1 tablespoon sugar
½ teaspoon black pepper

Mix all ingredients together and stir again before using.

SERVES 4

PREPARATION TIME: 25 minutes

COOKING TIME: 3 to 4 minutes

EDITOR'S NOTE: A traditional round-bottomed wok set on a ring does not get hot enough on the typical electric Western-style stovetop—the heat source is too far away. Use a flat-bottomed wok or a heavy sauté pan for better heat contact. If you do not have a deep-fat frying thermometer to check the temperature of the oil, test by tossing in a 1″ cube of bread. The bread should turn golden brown in approximately 60 seconds.

ELEGANT ORANGE SLICES •

4 large oranges

2 cups water

1 6-ounce package orange Jell-O

Cut oranges in half. Scoop cut orange segments, being very careful not to break or puncture the orange rinds. Rinse orange rind cups, drain, and set aside.

Place orange segments in a food processor or blender and puree. Strain and measure liquid. Bring water to a boil and stir into Jell-O. Add 2 cups of strained orange pulp. Place orange rind cups in muffin tins to keep them level. Fill to the rims with liquid gelatin. Refrigerate until firm. Cut each orange half into 2 quarters and serve.

SERVES 4

PREPARATION TIME: 15 minutes, plus chilling time

COOKING TIME: None

A comfortable simplicity and fresh flowers contribute to the feeling of friendly intimacy in this neighborhood restaurant. Larry Bain runs the front of the house, while his wife, chef Catherine Pantsios, and co-chef Rachel Gardner create contemporary Mediterranean food with a California influence.

FRESH TOMATO AND HERB TARTS
ROAST POUSSIN WITH TARRAGON BUTTER AND POTATOES
FRESH STRAWBERRIES WITH RASPBERRY COULIS

HERB-MARINATED SALMON WITH MUSTARD SAUCE
FREE-RANGE VEAL LOIN WITH MOREL MUSHROOMS
ROASTED FIGS WITH VANILLA ICE CREAM

FRESH TOMATO AND HERB TARTS

¾ teaspoon granulated yeast
1½ tablespoons warm water
1 cup all-purpose flour
Salt
1 tablespoon butter, cold, cut up
1 large egg
4 ripe tomatoes, cut into 6 slices each

1 tablespoon coarsely chopped fresh marjoram
1 tablespoon coarsely chopped fresh oregano
Freshly ground black pepper
¼ cup virgin olive oil

In a small bowl, dissolve yeast in water. Let stand until bubbly, about 5 minutes. Place flour and ½ tablespoon salt in bowl of a food processor. Add butter and process briefly. With motor running, add egg, then yeast mixture, and process until dough forms into a ball. On a lightly floured surface, knead dough briefly by hand. Divide into 4 equal portions, form into balls, and let rise at room temperature until doubled in bulk, about 1½ hours.

Preheat oven to very hot, 550°. Roll out tart dough in circles approximately ¼″ thick and place on a baking sheet. Overlap 6 tomato slices on each tart.

Sprinkle with herbs, salt, and pepper. Drizzle with olive oil. Bake for 10 minutes, until edges are brown. Cut each tart into 4 wedges.

SERVES 4

PREPARATION TIME: 20 minutes, plus rising time

COOKING TIME: 10 minutes

ROAST POUSSIN WITH TARRAGON BUTTER AND POTATOES

¼ pound (1 stick) butter, softened, plus 2 tablespoons butter, melted

¼ cup chopped fresh tarragon

Grated zest and juice of 1 orange

Salt and pepper

4 poussins (baby chickens), about 1½ pounds each

2 pounds all-purpose potatoes, peeled and cut into 1" dice

1 cup Chicken Stock (page 294) or canned chicken broth

Preheat oven to 500°. In the bowl of a food processor, combine softened butter, tarragon, orange zest and juice, and salt and pepper to taste. Separate skin from breasts of poussins with your fingers and stuff all but 2 tablespoons of the tarragon-flavored butter under skin. Place in a shallow roasting pan and roast in hot oven for 20 minutes.

Toss diced potatoes with melted butter, season with salt and pepper, and place in a separate roasting pan. Roast alongside poussins until golden and tender, 15 to 20 minutes more.

Remove poussins from oven and keep warm. Deglaze roasting pan with chicken stock and reduce by half over medium-high heat, about 5 minutes. Whisk in remaining 2 tablespoons of tarragon butter. Cut poussins in 4, place on warmed plates, and pour sauce on top. Garnish with roast potatoes.

SERVES 4

PREPARATION TIME: 15 minutes

COOKING TIME: 40 to 45 minutes

EDITOR'S NOTE: Cornish game hens can be substituted for the poussins, if these are unavailable.

FRESH STRAWBERRIES WITH RASPBERRY COULIS •

1 quart fragrant ripe strawberries

2 cups fresh raspberries

1 teaspoon sugar

1 tablespoon kirsch

Fresh mint leaves for garnish

Wash and hull strawberries, and cut in half. Place in a bowl.

Combine raspberries, sugar, and kirsh in the bowl of a food processor. Puree, and then strain. Pour over strawberries and let stand for 30 minutes. Garnish each portion with a fresh mint leaf.

SERVES 4

PREPARATION TIME: 10 minutes, plus marination

COOKING TIME: None

HERB-MARINATED SALMON WITH MUSTARD SAUCE •

½ pound fresh salmon filet

½ cup freshly squeezed lime juice

½ cup virgin olive oil

2 tablespoons mixed chopped fresh
chives, tarragon, and parsley

Salt and pepper to taste

Mustard Sauce (recipe follows)

Cut salmon on an angle into 8 very thin slices. Lay in a shallow dish. Whisk together the lime juice, olive oil, herbs, salt, and pepper. Pour over salmon, cover, and refrigerate for 2 hours.

Place 2 slices of salmon on each plate, and drizzle mustard sauce on top.

Mustard Sauce

1 tablespoon Dijon mustard

3 tablespoons heavy cream

2 tablespoons freshly squeezed lemon
juice

Salt and pepper to taste

Whisk all ingredients together.

SERVES 4

PREPARATION TIME: 10 minutes, plus marination time

COOKING TIME: None

FREE-RANGE VEAL LOIN WITH MOREL MUSHROOMS

1 veal loin, free-range if possible

1 tablespoon butter

2 shallots, peeled and chopped

3 cloves garlic, peeled and chopped

½ pound fresh morel mushrooms (see
Editor's Note below)

Salt and pepper

1 tablespoon chopped fresh tarragon

1 tablespoon virgin olive oil

1 cup Veal Stock (page 294)

Wild rice

Have your butcher bone and butterfly the loin of veal, leaving the flap on. Preheat oven to 450°.

Heat half the butter in a small saucepan. Add chopped shallot and garlic and sweat, covered, until translucent, about 5 minutes. Roughly chop mushrooms and add to saucepan. Cover and cook gently until tender, about 8 minutes. Season with salt, pepper, and tarragon.

Lay veal loin out on a work surface and flatten slightly with the side of a meat cleaver. Season lightly with salt and pepper. Lay stuffing on top and press down to compact it. Roll up loin and tie with butcher's twine, like a rolled roast. Heat olive oil and remaining butter in an ovenproof skillet. Sear roast on all sides over high heat. Transfer to oven and roast, basting occasionally with pan juices, for 25 minutes, or until meat registers an internal temperature of 110° on a meat thermometer. Remove roast and keep warm.

Pour off fat and place pan over high heat. Deglaze with veal stock and reduce by half. Let veal rest for 10 minutes, then slice and serve with pan juices and wild rice.

SERVES 4
PREPARATION TIME: 20 minutes
COOKING TIME: 40 minutes

EDITOR'S NOTE: If fresh morels are unavailable, substitute ¼ pound fresh white mushrooms and 1 to 2 ounces dried morels, soaked in warm water for 20 minutes.

ROASTED FIGS WITH VANILLA ICE CREAM •

12 fresh figs
½ cup sugar

1 pint best-quality vanilla ice cream

Preheat oven to 350°. Dip each fig in water, then in sugar. Place in a small roasting pan. Roast for 25 to 30 minutes, until tender and syrupy. Serve 3 figs in a bowl with a scoop of vanilla ice cream. Drizzle with warm syrup from pan.

SERVES 4
PREPARATION TIME: 5 minutes
COOKING TIME: 25 to 30 minutes

Multileveled space, whitewashed walls, blond woods, and a few Navajo rugs here and there form a suitable backdrop for chef Judy Rodgers's eclectic, ever-changing menu. Her culinary apprenticeship in southern France, followed by a three-year stint with Alice Waters in Berkeley, is clearly reflected in the California/Mediterranean style of food.

GREEN BEANS AND PECORINO
SALMON BRAISED IN VERNACCIA
ASSORTED FIGS WITH RASPBERRIES AND
  FRESH ALMONDS

FENNEL, PEAR, AND WALNUT SALAD
ROASTED QUAIL WITH BITTER GREENS AND
  POLENTA WITH WHITE TRUFFLES
DATES AND PARMESAN CHEESE

GREEN BEANS AND PECORINO •

*1 pound tender young green beans
  (preferably Blue Lake)*
*Extra-virgin olive oil from Tuscany or
  Umbria*

Kosher salt
½ pound piece Pecorino Romano cheese
Black pepper

Bring a large pot of salted water to a boil. Pinch off stems from the green beans and tail them as necessary. Drop beans into rapidly boiling water and cook until just tender—they must not taste grassy or raw—5 to 7 minutes. Cooking time depends on size of beans; test by biting into one. Drain well and toss with just enough olive oil to lightly coat beans, and season with a pinch of kosher salt. Pile onto a warm platter and, using a vegetable peeler, shower the beans abundantly with shavings of Pecorino (the whole piece of cheese will not be required). Season with a grind of black pepper. Serve while the beans are still warm.

SERVES 4

PREPARATION TIME: 15 minutes

COOKING TIME: 5 to 7 minutes

SALMON BRAISED IN VERNACCIA

1½ pounds salmon filet, skinned and boned, cut into 4 pieces

Kosher salt

⅓ cup Vernaccia (see Chef's Note below)

⅓ cup vermouth

⅓ cup Chicken Stock (page 294)

Few branches fresh thyme

12 tablespoons (1½ sticks) unsalted butter

Salt-Roasted Finnish Potatoes (recipe follows)

Preheat oven to 400°. Season salmon pieces liberally with kosher salt. Place in a wide, heavy-bottomed, ovenproof sauté pan and moisten with the wine, vermouth, and chicken stock. Tuck in the thyme branches and dot with 8 tablespoons of butter. Bake for 10 to 12 minutes, or until salmon is medium rare. Remove pan from oven (leave a potholder folded over the handle as a reminder that it will be very hot). Lift the fish gently from the braising liquid and keep warm. Reduce braising liquid by one half over high heat and whisk in remaining 4 tablespoons of butter to make an emulsion, adding additional salt to taste. Spoon over salmon and garnish with potatoes.

Salt-Roasted Finnish Potatoes

Rock salt

12 to 16 small yellow Finnish potatoes

Preheat oven to 400°. Cover the bottom of a small roasting pan with rock salt. Lay potatoes on top and add more salt, burying them completely. Place in oven and bake for approximately 45 minutes, or until meltingly tender.

(These potatoes have a rich flavor and exceptional texture when cooked this way.)

SERVES 4

PREPARATION TIME: 15 minutes total

COOKING TIME: 45 minutes total

CHEF'S NOTE: The Vernaccia grape makes a very distinctive wine, which is lovely for braising fish. At Zuni, we use a Vernaccia from San Gimignano, an inland Tuscan village (which is something of an oddity in itself, as the idea for the dish comes from Sardinia, where the grape is cultivated extensively).

ASSORTED FIGS WITH RASPBERRIES AND FRESH ALMONDS •

12 to 16 assorted ripe figs (such as Kadota, Black Mission, Brown Turkey, Desert Jewel, Adriatic, etc.)

1 basket ripe and fragrant red and/or yellow raspberries

1 pound almonds, freshly shelled (see Chef's Note below)

¾ cup heavy cream, whipped

Lavender honey

Arrange figs, raspberries, and almonds on 4 large dessert plates. Place a mound of whipped cream drizzled with honey on each plate.

SERVES 4

PREPARATION TIME: 5 minutes

COOKING TIME: None

CHEF'S NOTE: Almonds are especially sweet and flavorful in the early fall, when newly ripened. They should be shelled just before serving.

FENNEL, PEAR, AND WALNUT SALAD •

4 small firm, round heads fennel

2 firm, ripe Bosc pears

¼ cup virgin olive oil

2 tablespoons balsamic vinegar

½ cup walnut halves, freshly shelled (see Chef's Note below)

Trim and core fennel and slice paper thin. Divide among salad plates. Peel and core the pears and slice into thin wedges. Layer the ribbons of fennel with wedges of pear. Drizzle with olive oil and sprinkle with balsamic vinegar. Garnish with walnuts.

SERVES 4
PREPARATION TIME: 10 minutes
COOKING TIME: None

CHEF'S NOTE: Sweet, fruity, fresh walnuts are a luxury of the late fall. Ask your grocer for fresh, ungassed walnuts—or cultivate a friend with a walnut tree.

For this dish, splurge on a vintage balsamic vinegar of excellent quality.

ROASTED QUAIL WITH BITTER GREENS AND POLENTA WITH WHITE TRUFFLES

8 quail
Kosher salt
Freshly cracked black pepper
Few branches fresh thyme
8 juniper berries
Few drops grappa or Armagnac
2 quarts water
2 cups polenta or coarse yellow cornmeal

8 tablespoons (1 stick) unsalted butter, softened
¼ cup aged red wine vinegar
Salad of Bitter Greens (recipe follows)
Few drops hazelnut oil
4 heaping tablespoons mascarpone cheese
1 fresh white truffle

Buy quail 2 days before you plan to serve them. Place in a shallow dish and toss with a pinch of kosher salt, pepper, and thyme branches. Place 1 crushed juniper berry inside each bird and drizzle the quail with grappa or Armagnac. Cover dish with a damp towel and refrigerate for 2 days.

An hour or so before eating, make the polenta: Bring water to a boil in a heavy stainless-steel saucepan. Whisk in the polenta in a thin stream. Reduce heat to simmer and add kosher salt to taste. Stir regularly with a wooden spoon for 40 minutes, until polenta is tender and creamy. Do not undercook. Stir in 6 tablespoons of butter and hold polenta over warm water until required.

Preheat oven to 425°. Rub quail with remaining 2 tablespoons of butter and place in a heavy ovenproof sauté pan just large enough to hold them in one layer without crowding. Roast for 10 to 15 minutes. They should be medium rare. Remove birds to a warm platter. Place pan over high heat and deglaze with red wine vinegar. Pour this over the greens and toss well. Season with a few drops of hazelnut oil. Pile the greens around the birds and serve them family-style.

Provide each person with a wide plate of polenta topped with a generous spoonful of mascarpone cheese. Pass a white truffle with a truffle peeler (or vegetable peeler) so that each diner may garnish his polenta at will. Eat the birds, polenta, and salad at the same time.

Salad of Bitter Greens

4 heads bitter greens (choose from radicchio, dandelion, chicory, escarole, watercress, endive, frisée, etc.)
¼ cup virgin olive oil

Pinch kosher salt
Freshly ground black pepper

Separate lettuce leaves and wash and dry well. Toss with olive oil, kosher salt, and pepper.

SERVES 4
PREPARATION TIME: 15 minutes total, plus 2 days to marinate birds
COOKING TIME: 1 hour

DATES AND PARMESAN CHEESE •

6 to 8 different varieties of fresh dates, on the branch if possible (see Chef's Note below)

1 pound piece of best-quality imported Parmesan cheese (Parmigiano-Reggiano)

Arrange the dates, still on the branch if possible, on a large platter and garnish with chunks of Parmesan. The combination of the sticky, nutty, caramel-like fruit with the dry, nutty sweetness of the Parmesan is stunning.

SERVES 4
PREPARATION TIME: 5 minutes
COOKING TIME: None

CHEF'S NOTE: Starting in late November, a variety of ripe dates with fabulous Arabic names arrive in the market; look especially for the slightly salty black ones.

Techniques

TO ROAST AND PEEL BELL PEPPERS

Preheat oven to 400°. Place bell peppers on a baking sheet and bake until skin is evenly charred and blistered, turning several times, about 45 minutes. Remove peppers from oven and place in a paper bag. Steam for 10 minutes. Skins should then slip off quite easily. Cut in half, remove, and discard seeds and ribs. (The peppers will be fully cooked.)

TO BROIL AND PEEL BELL PEPPERS

Preheat broiler. Cut bell peppers in quarters. Remove and discard seeds and ribs. Flatten pepper pieces with your hand, and broil until skin is charred and blistered, about 7 minutes. Place pepper pieces in a paper bag and steam for 10 minutes, then slip off skins. (The pepper pieces will retain their crunchy texture.)

TO BONE A POUSSIN, CHICKEN, OR OTHER BIRD

Place bird on a cutting board. Using a short-bladed, very sharp knife, cut off wings at second joint. Turn bird over and slit the skin along the backbone. Start scraping the meat away from the carcass, starting at the backbone and working down. Do this on both sides. Find the ball joint of each thigh and cut through the tendon to disconnect. Repeat for shoulders. Scrape meat away from breastbone and disconnect the keel bone (soft cartilage) without cutting through the skin. Keep scraping with the knife blade against the bony carcass until it can be lifted away from the now-flat bird. Scrape meat away from thigh bones and cut through joint. Leave drumstick bone in place or not, as desired, but chop off the knobby joint and expose the bone slightly by scraping with the knife.

TO CLARIFY BUTTER

Place ¼ pound (or more) unsalted or lightly salted butter in the top of a double boiler set over simmering water. Melt, remove from heat, and let stand until the milky substances settle at the bottom, about 15 minutes. Strain the clear golden liquid through cheesecloth into a container. As the milk solids have been removed, clarified butter does not burn easily, so it is good for cooking. It will keep almost indefinitely in a covered container in the refrigerator.

TO SECTION AN ORANGE, LEMON, LIME, OR GRAPEFRUIT
Cut off all the peel and white pith, exposing the juicy flesh. Working over a bowl, to catch the juice, hold the fruit in one hand and slice down between the membranes. Rotate the fruit as you go, letting the freed sections fall into the bowl. Pick out any seeds.

Stocks and Glazes

BEEF STOCK

2 tablespoons virgin olive oil

4 pounds meaty beef shanks, sliced 2" thick

1 veal shank, cut into 2" pieces

1 calf's foot, split (optional)

1 onion, peeled and coarsely chopped

1 carrot, peeled and coarsely chopped

1 stalk celery, coarsely chopped

1 bay leaf

3 sprigs parsley

6 black peppercorns

3 quarts water

½ cup tomato puree

Preheat oven to 375°. Pour olive oil into a shallow roasting pan and heat in oven for 5 minutes. Add beef bones, veal shank, and calf's foot. Brown in oven for 30 minutes, turning pieces over after 15 minutes. Transfer to a large pot. Pour a little water into the roasting pan and scrape up any coagulated bits, and add to pot. Add remaining ingredients to pot and bring to a boil. Boil briskly for 5 minutes, skimming off the cloudy scum on the surface. Reduce heat and partially cover pot. Simmer slowly for 4 hours, adding more water if necessary to maintain the original level.

Line a colander with several thicknesses of dampened cheesecloth. Strain stock through cheesecloth into a bowl. Cool in the refrigerator. When stock is cold, remove the solid layer of fat that will have formed on the surface. Stock will keep for 3 days in the refrigerator, or can be frozen for several months. (Freeze in small containers, and be sure to label and date.)

MAKES APPROXIMATELY 2 ½ QUARTS

PREPARATION TIME: 15 minutes

COOKING TIME: about 4½ hours

Beef Glaze

Place 1 quart Beef Stock (see above) in a saucepan and bring to a boil. Reduce to 1 cup by boiling over medium-low heat, until a thick, very flavorful amber syrup forms. This will solidify to a very firm jelly when chilled. This jelly can then be cut into eight 1-ounce squares, wrapped individually, and frozen.

VEAL STOCK

Proceed as for Beef Stock (page 293), substituting 4½ pounds meaty sliced veal shanks for the beef shanks.

Veal Glaze

Proceed as for Beef Glaze (page 293), using Veal Stock (above) instead of Beef Stock.

CHICKEN STOCK

4 pounds chicken necks and backs, or carcasses, cut up
1 yellow onion, unpeeled, halved
1 leek, well washed, trimmed, and coarsely chopped
1 carrot, peeled and coarsely chopped
1 stalk celery, coarsely chopped

2 cloves garlic, unpeeled
1 bay leaf
3 sprigs parsley
3 sprigs fresh thyme, or ½ teaspoon dried
6 black peppercorns
4½ quarts water

Combine all ingredients in a large pot and bring to a boil. After 5 minutes, skim off cloudy froth from surface. Boil rapidly for another 15 minutes, skimming often. Reduce heat and simmer, uncovered, for approximately 2 hours.

Line a colander with several thicknesses of dampened cheesecloth. Strain the stock through the cheesecloth into a bowl, pressing down on the solids to extract all the liquid. Cool in the refrigerator. When stock is cold, remove the layer of solidified fat that will have formed on the surface. Stock will keep in the refrigerator for 3 days, or can be frozen for several months. (Freeze in 1-cup amounts, or in ice cube trays, and be sure to label and date.) Note that this chicken stock does not contain salt. Salt is added later, when the stock is used in sauces or soups.

MAKES APPROXIMATELY 3 QUARTS
PREPARATION TIME: 10 minutes
COOKING TIME: about 2¼ hours

DUCK STOCK

4 duck carcasses
1 yellow onion, unpeeled, halved
1 carrot, peeled and coarsely chopped
4½ quarts water

2 stalks celery, cut up
1 bay leaf
3 sprigs parsley
6 crushed peppercorns

Preheat oven to 375°. Break up duck carcasses and place in a roasting pan. Roast for 1 hour. Add onion and carrot and roast for an additional 30 minutes, until bones are well browned. Using a slotted spoon, transfer bones and vegetables to a stockpot. Pour fat off roasting pan and discard. Add 2 cups of water and scrape up brown residue from bottom of pan. Pour liquid into stockpot. Add remaining 4 quarts of water, celery, bay leaf, parsley, and peppercorns and bring to a boil. Boil briskly for 5 minutes, skimming off any cloudy scum from surface. Reduce heat and simmer, uncovered, for 3 hours, adding more water if necessary to maintain original level.

Line a colander with several thicknesses of cheesecloth. Strain the stock through the cheesecloth into a bowl, pressing down on the solids to extract all the liquid. Cool in the refrigerator. When stock is cold, remove layer of solidified fat from surface. Stock will keep in the refrigerator for 3 days, or can be frozen for several months.

MAKES APPROXIMATELY 4 QUARTS
PREPARATION TIME: 15 minutes
COOKING TIME: 4½ hours

Duck Glaze

Place 1 quart Duck Stock (see above) in a saucepan and bring to a boil. Reduce to 1 cup by boiling over medium-low heat, until a thick, very flavorful amber syrup forms. This will solidify to a very firm jelly when chilled. It can then be cut into eight 1-ounce (2 tablespoon) squares, wrapped individually, and frozen.

FISH STOCK

2 pounds fish frames (skeletons), with heads, from white fish only	6 parsley stems
	4 peppercorns
1 onion, peeled and sliced	1 cup dry white wine
2 stalks celery, sliced	1 quart water

Combine all ingredients in a stockpot. Bring to a boil, skim, and simmer for 30 minutes.

Line a colander with several thicknesses of cheesecloth. Strain stock through cheesecloth into a bowl and chill in refrigerator. Freeze if not using immediately.

MAKES APPROXIMATELY 1 QUART
PREPARATION TIME: 10 minutes
COOKING TIME: 30 minutes

BÉCHAMEL SAUCE •

1 tablespoon butter	*1 tablespoon heavy cream*
1 tablespoon all-purpose flour	*Salt*
1 cup milk	*White pepper*
1 thin slice onion	*Dash grated nutmeg*
1 sprig parsley	

Melt butter in a small, heavy saucepan. Stir in flour and cook for a few minutes, stirring, to eliminate raw flour taste, without allowing mixture to brown. In a separate saucepan, combine milk, onion, and parsley. Heat until bubbles form around the edge. Strain hot milk into flour mixture, whisking constantly. Add cream, bring to a boil, and cook slowly for 5 minutes. Season to taste with salt, pepper, and nutmeg.

MAKES 1 CUP
PREPARATION TIME: 5 minutes
COOKING TIME: 10 minutes

BROWN SAUCE

2 tablespoons butter	*1 cup dry white wine*
2 tablespoons all-purpose flour	*Pinch dried thyme*
2 cups Beef Stock (page 293)	*1 tablespoon tomato puree*
1 tablespoon diced salt pork	*½ cup Madeira or Spanish sherry (such*
1 tablespoon finely chopped onion	*as Dry Sack)*
1 tablespoon finely chopped carrot	

Melt butter in a heavy saucepan and stir in flour. Cook until golden brown, stirring constantly. Add beef stock and bring to a boil, whisking constantly. Reduce heat and continue simmering.

Heat a skillet and brown salt pork lightly. Add onion and carrot and cook until golden, stirring occasionally, about 7 minutes. Pour off fat. Add wine, thyme, and tomato puree. Add this mixture to the stock mixture. Simmer for 1 hour. Stir occasionally, and skim off any fat. Puree in a food processor or blender, and add Madeira or sherry. The brown sauce should be thick enough to coat a spoon; if too thin, cook a little longer; if too thick, add a little beef stock.

MAKES APPROXIMATELY 2 1/2 CUPS
PREPARATION TIME: 20 minutes
COOKING TIME: 1¼ hours

CRÈME ANGLAISE •

2 cups milk
½ vanilla bean

7 large egg yolks
¼ cup sugar

Place milk in a saucepan and add vanilla bean. Bring to a boil and turn off heat. Remove vanilla bean.

In a bowl, whisk egg yolks with sugar until smooth. Pour a quarter of the milk mixture over yolks, stir well, then return entire mixture to pan. Stir with a wooden spatula over low heat until mixture thickens slightly and reaches 165° on a candy thermometer. It should coat the back of the spatula. Pour through a sieve into a bowl and cool. Crème anglaise will keep for 2 or 3 days in the refrigerator.

MAKES APPROXIMATELY 3 CUPS
PREPARATION TIME: 10 minutes
COOKING TIME: 10 minutes

EDITOR'S NOTE: After infusing, rinse vanilla bean in water, pat dry, and store in a container of sugar. It will perfume the sugar, and can be reused until the aroma fades.

CRÈME FRAÎCHE

2 cups heavy cream

2 tablespoons buttermilk

Combine cream and buttermilk, cover, and let stand at cool room temperature for 24 hours, until thickened. (Let stand for 4 to 6 hours only if room is warm.) Store tightly covered in refrigerator—it will keep for 4 to 5 days.

MAKES APPROXIMATELY 2 CUPS
PREPARATION TIME: 1 minute, plus standing time
COOKING TIME: None

PASTRY SHELL (Pâte Brisée)

2 cups (10 ounces) all-purpose flour
½ teaspoon salt
10 tablespoons (1¼ sticks) unsalted
  butter, chilled, cut up

1 large egg
2 tablespoons cold water

Place flour, salt, and butter in the bowl of a food processor. Process until mixture resembles coarse meal. With motor running, add egg and water through feed tube. Pulse machine on and off until mixture starts forming into a ball. Divide dough in half. Working with one half at a time, roll out on a lightly floured surface into an 11″ circle. Fit into a 9″ fluted tart pan with removable base. Repeat with remaining dough.

To semi-bake or bake fully without a filling, push sides of dough very slightly above and over edge of rim. This will prevent sides from shrinking and falling down. Bake for 5 minutes at 350°, then deflate any air bubbles with knife tip. For a semi-baked shell, continue baking for 10 or 15 minutes more, until pale gold and crisp. For a fully baked shell, bake for 20 to 25 minutes longer, or until golden brown.

Alternatively, line unbaked tart shell with baking parchment or aluminum foil and fill with dried beans or pie weights. Remove beans after baking at 350° for 15 minutes. Continue baking for 15 minutes longer, until golden brown, for a fully baked shell.

MAKES TWO 9-INCH TART SHELLS
PREPARATION TIME: 10 minutes
COOKING TIME: 15 to 30 minutes

EDITOR'S NOTES: It saves time to make 2 tart shells at once, as the second one can be frozen in the pan (wrapped in plastic wrap) and then baked without thawing. If halving ingredients for 1 shell, beat egg lightly and use only half of it.

If making dough by hand, have butter at room temperature. Rub lightly into flour, then add liquid ingredients, with a little extra water if necessary. Wrap and chill dough for 30 minutes before rolling out.

For a sweet tart shell, add 1 tablespoon sugar to flour and salt.

Appendix

Alphabetical List of Restaurants

Allegro
1701 Jones Street
San Francisco, CA   94109
(415) 928-4002

Amelio's
1630 Powell Street
San Francisco, CA   94133
(415) 397-4339

Auberge du Soleil
180 Rutherford Hill Road
Rutherford, CA   94573
(707) 963-1211

Bay Wolf Café and Restaurant
3853 Piedmont Avenue
Oakland, CA   94611
(415) 655-6004

Bix
56 Gold Street
San Francisco, CA   94133
(415) 433-6300

The Blue Fox
659 Merchant Street
San Francisco, CA   94111
(415) 981-1177

Bua Thong Kitchen
1320 Broadway
Burlingame, CA   94010
(415) 347-4340

Butler's
625 Redwood Highway
Mill Valley, CA   94941
(415) 383-1900

Café Beaujolais
961 Ukiah
Mendocino, CA   95460
(707) 937-5614

Café Majestic
1500 Sutter Street
San Francisco, CA   94109
(415) 776-6400

Café 222
222 Mason Street
San Francisco, CA   94102
(415) 394-1111

Caffé Freddy's
901 Columbus Avenue
San Francisco, CA   94133
(415) 922-0151

California Café Bar and Grill
The Village at Corte Madera
1736 Redwood Highway
Corte Madera, CA   94925
(415) 924-2233

California Culinary Academy
625 Polk Street
San Francisco, CA   94102
(415) 771-3500

Campton Place
340 Stockton Street
San Francisco, CA   94108
(415) 781-5155

Chevys Mexican Restaurant
150 Fourth Street
San Francisco, CA   94133
(415) 543-8060

Chez Chez
1715 Union Street
San Francisco, CA   94123
(415) 921-0036

Chez Panisse
1517 Shattuck Avenue
Berkeley, CA   94701
(415) 548-5049

China Moon Café
639 Post Street
San Francisco, CA   94109
(415) 775-4789

Circolo
161 Sutter Street (Crocker Galleria)
San Francisco, CA   94104
(415) 362-0404

Cuisine Cusine (see page 304)

Domaine Chandon
1 California Drive
Yountville, CA   94599
(707) 944-2892

Donatello
501 Post Street
San Francisco, CA   94102
(415) 441-7182

Enoteca Lanzone
601 Van Ness Avenue
San Francisco, CA   94102
(415) 928-0400

Ernie's
847 Montgomery Street
San Francisco, CA   94133
(415) 397-5969

Flea Street Café
3607 Alameda de las Pulgas
Menlo Park, CA   95025
(415) 854-1226

Fleur de Lys
777 Sutter Street
San Francisco, CA   94109
(415) 673-7779

Fog City Diner
1300 Battery Street
San Francisco, CA   94111
(415) 982-2000

Fournou's Ovens
Stanford Court
905 California Street
San Francisco, CA   94108
(415) 989-3500

Fourth Street Grill
1820 Fourth Street
Berkeley, CA   94710
(415) 849-0526

The French Room
Four Seasons Clift Hotel
495 Geary Street
San Francisco, CA   94102
(415) 775-4700

Greens
Fort Mason, Building A
San Francisco, CA   94123
(415) 771-6222

Harbor Village
4 Embarcadero Center, Lobby Level
San Francisco, CA   94111
(415) 781-8833

Harry's Bar and American Grill
500 Van Ness Avenue
San Francisco, CA   94102
(415) 86-HARRY

Hayes Street Grill
320 Hayes Street
San Francisco, CA   94102
(415) 863-5545

Hong Kong Flower Lounge Restaurant
1671 El Camino Real
Millbrae, CA   94030
(415) 878-8108

Il Fornaio Gastronomia Italiana
1265 Battery Street
San Francisco, CA   94111
(415) 986-0100

Jack's Restaurant
615 Sacramento Street
San Francisco, CA   94111
(415) 986-9854

Jean Pierre Moullé (see page 304)

John Ash & Co.
4330 Barnes Road
Santa Rosa, CA   95403
(707) 527-7687

Jordan Winery
P.O. Box 878
Healdsburg, CA   95448
(707) 433-6955

Ken Hom (see page 304)

Kuleto's Italian Restaurant
221 Powell Street
San Francisco, CA   94102
(415) 397-7720

La Lanterna
799 College Avenue
Kentfield, CA   94904
(415) 258-0144

Lalime's
1329 Gilman Street
Berkeley, CA   94706
(415) 527-9838

The Lark Creek Inn
234 Magnolia Avenue
Larkspur, CA   94939
(415) 924-7767

Lascaux Bar and Rotisserie
248 Sutter Street
San Francisco, CA   94108
(415) 391-1555

L'Avenue Bistro
3854 Geary Boulevard
San Francisco, CA   94118
(415) 386-1555

Le Castel
3235 Sacramento Street
San Francisco, CA   94115
(415) 921-7115

Le St. Tropez
126 Clement Street
San Francisco, CA   94118
(415) 387-0408

Le Trou Restaurant Français
1007 Guerrero
San Francisco, CA   94117
(415) 550-8169

Lipizzaner
1242 4th Street
San Rafael, CA   94901
(415) 459-2202

The Maltese Grill
20 Annie Street
San Francisco, CA   94105
(415) 777-1955

Manora's Thai Cuisine
1600 Folsom Street
San Francisco, CA   94103
(415) 861-6224

Masa's
648 Bush Street
San Francisco, CA   94108
(415) 989-7154

Meadowood
900 Meadowood Lane
St. Helena, CA   94574
(707) 963-3646

Miramonte Restaurant and Country Inn
1327 Railroad Avenue
St. Helena, CA   94574
(707) 963-3970

muchacha's
4238 18th Street
San Francisco, CA   94114
(415) 861-8234

Mustards Grill
7399 St. Helena Highway
Napa, CA   94558
(707) 944-2424

Narsai David (see page 304)

Piatti Ristorante
6480 Washington Street
Yountville, CA   94599
(707) 944-2070

Postrio
545 Post Street
San Francisco, CA   94102
(415) 776-7825

RAF Centrogriglia
478 Green Street
San Francisco, CA   94133
(415) 362-1999

Regina's
490 Geary Street
San Francisco, CA   94102
(415) 885-1661

Remillard's
127 Sir Francis Drake Boulevard
Larkspur, CA   94939
(415) 461-3700

Restaurant 231 Ellsworth
231 South Ellsworth Street
San Mateo, CA   94401
(415) 347-7231

Santa Fe Bar and Grill
1310 University Avenue
Berkeley, CA   94702
(415) 841-4740

Silks
222 Sansome Street
San Francisco, CA   94104
(415) 986-2020

Square One
190 Pacific Avenue
San Francisco, CA   94111
(415) 788-1110

Stars
150 Redwood Alley
San Francisco, CA   94102
(415) 861-7827

Tadich Grill
240 California Street
San Francisco, CA   94111
(415) 391-2373

Timberhill Ranch
35755 Hauser Bridge Road
Cazadero, CA   95421
(707) 847-3258

Tortola
3640 Sacramento Street
San Francisco, CA   94118
(415) 929-8181

Tra Vigne
1050 Charter Oak Avenue
St. Helena, CA   94574
(707) 963-4444

Trader Vic's
20 Cosmo Place
San Francisco, CA   94109
(415) 776-2232

Vivande
2125 Fillmore Street
San Francisco, CA   94115
(415) 346-4430

Washington Square Bar & Grill
1707 Powell Street
San Francisco, CA   94133
(415) 982-8123

Wu Kong Restaurant
1 Rincon Center, 101 Spear Street
San Francisco, CA   94105
(415) 957-9300

Yank Sing
427 Battery Street
San Francisco, CA   94111
(415) 362-1640

Zola's
395 Hayes Street
San Francisco, CA   94102
(415) 864-4824

Zuni Café
1658 Market Street
San Francisco, CA   94102
(415) 552-2522

Caterers/Chefs/Cooking Schools

Cuisine Cuisine
Dan Bowe and Jane Fehon, Co-owners
P.O. Box 884841
San Francisco, CA   94188
(415) 863-8166

Jean Pierre Moullé
1231 Henry Street
Berkeley, CA   94709
(415) 526-6596

Ken Hom
P.O. Box 4303
Berkeley, CA   94704
(415) 843-5579

Narsai David
350 Berkeley Park Boulevard
Berkeley, CA   94707
(415) 527-7900

Acknowledgments

The San Francisco Symphony Cookbook Steering Committee wishes to express its deepest appreciation to the many people who generously contributed their time, talents, and expertise to this project. Without the help and support of the following individuals and businesses, this cookbook could never have become a reality.

RECIPE TESTERS

Pat Baker
Susie Brown
Mary Chiu
Suzie Cronholm
Lois Gundlack
Loni Kuhn, Cook's Tours
Olive Lawton
Mary Lonergan, Just Cooks
Lynne LoPresto
Jacqueline Mallorca

Betty Studer Miller
Claudette Nicolai
Ernita O'Brien, Just Cooks
Sue Ohrenschall
Agnes Shapiro
Gretchen Stone
Mary Tilden
Michelle Winchester
Sharon Woo
Heidi Zellerbach

COMMITTEE MEMBERS

Design:

Judy Pryor
Lydia Titcomb

Finance:

Donna Ellis
Cynthia Sperry Harris

Marketing—Planning:

Lynn Brown
Robert LeBow
Barbara L. Moore
Gary Schweikhart
Sylvia Wilkerson

Marketing—Sales and Public Relations:

Usha Burns
Lynn Jason Cobb
Ann Cosby
Coleen Ehrlich
Barbara Glynn
Alice Hodge
Gabrielle Jackson
Betsy Riley
Sandra Farish Sloan
Martha Sullivan
Kristine Taylor
Barbara Tuffli

Production:

Harline Hurst

Recipes:

Claudia Kersevan
Mary Lonergan
Joselyn Mercier
Reddie Nichols
Agnes Shapiro
Mary Tilden
Sandra Velasco
Michelle Winchester
Gloria Wong
Heidi Zellerbach

AND VERY SPECIAL THANKS TO:

Larry Banka
Biordi Art Imports, San Francisco
Chris Bliss
Patty Gessner
Paulette Goodrich
Jeanne Harris
Louise Hohenthal
Claudia Kersevan
Sally Ketchum
George Lucas
Lena Martelli
Robin McKee
Joselyn Mercier
Liz Meyer

Barbara Moore
David Neuman
Sue Ohrenschall
William O'Meara
Reddie Nichols
Ann Seymour
Agnes Shapiro
Sandra Velasco
Mary Margaret Ward
Robert Ward
Michelle Winchester
Gloria Wong
Heidi Zellerbach

Maître Cuisinier de France René Verdon

Robert F. Ohrenshall

Primo Angeli, Inc.

Afternoon tea, 8–12
Aioli, 45
  Sun-Dried Tomato, 47
  Tomato, 104
Almond(s)
  Biscotti (Almond Dipping Cookies),
    264
  Biscuit Tortoni, 230
  Blueberry-Almond Tart, 204–5
  Crust, Lemon Tart with, 173–74
  Filet of Sole Amandine, 254–55
  Fresh, Assorted Figs with Raspberries
    and, 287
  in Hazelnut Soufflé with Crème
    Anglaise, 197
  Praline Mousse with a Caramel
    Crown, 241–42
  Toasted, Fresh Peaches and Peach Ice
    Cream with Caramel Sauce and,
    235
Almond Oil Vinaigrette, 203
Amaretto
  in Fruit and Light Mascarpone, 76–
    77
  in Hazelnut Soufflé with Crème
    Anglaise, 197
  Mousse, 241–42
Anchovies
  on Celery Victor, 137
  Tapenade, 102
  Tapenade Toast, 63
Appetizers
  Baked Buffalo Mozzarella, 103
  Baked Chèvre with Sun-Dried
    Tomatoes and Basil, 154
  Bruschetta (Roman Garlic Bread), 217–
    18
  Ceviche with Scallops, 57

Chili-Orange Cold Noodles, 65–66
Crenshaw Melon with Prosciutto
  Sauce and Fried Parsley, 5
Crepes with Radicchio, 23–24
Crisp Corn Cakes with Prawns in Red
  Bell Pepper Sauce, 164–65
Crostini of Wild Mushrooms, 169
Dungeness Crab Enchiladas, 52–53
Eggplant with Ginger Butter, 210
Fresh Crab with Orange Dressing,
  266–67
Fresh Tomato and Herb Tarts,
  281–82
Golden Shrimp Puffs, 120
Green Beans and Pecorino, 285–86
Grilled Marinated Shiitake Mush-
  rooms with Red Onion Jam, 106–7
Grilled Pasilla Peppers with Salsa,
  239–40
Grilled Quail Stuffed with Figs and
  Prosciutto, 171–72
Grilled Vegetables with Sun-Dried
  Tomato Aioli, 46–47
Involtini di Melanzane (Eggplant Rolls
  with Goat Cheese), 218–19
Mussels Baked with Cream, 140–41
Onion Tart Bonne Femme, 61
Peppered Oysters on Toast, 232
Pickled Beets, 160–61
Pizzetta con Aglio (Pizza with Olive
  Oil and Roasted Garlic), 262–63
Popier Sod (Crab Rolls with Tamerind
  Sauce), 191–92
Quesadilla of Smoked Chicken,
  198–99
Rice Paper Shrimp Rolls, 150–51
Roquefort Custards with Sautéed
  Chard, 180–81

Appetizers (*cont.*)
  Scallops with Tomato and White
    Wine, 20–21
  Sicilian-Style Eggs, 269
  Steamed Artichokes with Potato-Garlic
    Puree, 92–93
  Stuffed Squash Blossoms, 229
  Tapenade Toast, 63
  Thai Beef Salad, 26–27
  Timberhill Prosciutto Roll, 256
  Tuna Tartare, 29–30, 147
  See also Pasta; Salad(s); Soup(s)
Apple(s)
  Baked Rome Beauty, 265
  Brie Puff with Sautéed Apples and
    Caramel Sauce, 6–7
  Butternut Squash Soup with Apples
    and Fresh Thyme, 109–10
  Caramelized, Crème Brulée and,
    102
  -Cranberry Crisp, 167–68
  Fritters, 268
Apricot(s)
  Crisp, 127
  Custard, with Raspberry Coulis, 62
  -Ginger Ice Cream, 73
  in Dried Fruit and Malaga Compote,
    162
  Soufflé, 271
Artichoke(s)
  in Chopped Vegetable Salad, 225
  Noisette of Lamb with, 24–25
  Soup, with Hazelnuts and Cognac,
    178
  Steamed, with Potato-Garlic Puree,
    92–93
Asian pears, Chinese Pear Apple Warm
    Compote with Candied Ginger à la
    Mode, 152–53
Asparagus
  in Dungeness Crab and Avocado
    Salad, 199–200
  Grilled Swordfish with Asparagus
    Salad, 100–2
  Roast Chicken Breast with New Pota-
    toes, Asparagus, Spinach, and Aioli,
    44–45
  in Salade Gourmande, 13–14
Avocado(es)
  in Chopped Vegetable Salad, 225
  Cream Sauce, 75

Dungeness Crab and Avocado Salad,
    199–200
  in Timberhill Prosciutto Roll, 256

Bagnat, Grilled Duck Breast with, 148
Balsamic Onions, Grilled Chicken
    Spiedini with, 230
Balsamic Vinaigrette, 222
Banana Rolls, Crispy, 121
Basil
  Baked Chèvre with Sun-Dried Toma-
    toes and, 154
  Bruschetta (Roman Garlic Bread), 217–18
  in *Capellini al Pomodoro Naturale*
    (Pasta with Fresh Tomato), 134
  Grilled Prawns with Fresh Tomato,
    Lemon, and Basil Sauce, 107–8
  Linguini with Roasted Peppers, Basil,
    Pine Nuts, and Niçoise Olives, 117
  Mayonnaise, 251
  Orange Sorbet with Basil Cream, 149
  Pecan-Pesto Sauce, Rabbit with, 39–40
  Pesto Sauce, 103–4
  Spicy Tomato Soup with Lime-Basil
    Crème Fraîche, 53–54
  Tomato-Basil Sauce, Sea Bass en Pap-
    illote with, 37
Bean curd. *See* Tofu
Beans. *See* Green beans; Legumes
Béchamel Sauce, 296
Beef
  Filet Mignon Mathurin, 61–62
  Filet of Beef in Herb and Mustard
    Butter, 141
  Filet of Beef Marchand de Vin, with
    Parisian Potatoes, 90–91
  Flank Steak Quesada, 260
  Glaze, 293
  Grilled Flank Steak and Fresh Horse-
    radish–Tomato Relish, 30–31
  Mandarin, 279–80
  Manzo Salmistrato (Polenta with
    Corned Beef Hash), 133
  Marinated Skirt Steak with Tomato
    Aioli, 104
  Roast Filet of, with Calvados and
    Chanterelles, 176
  Sautéed Minute Steak with Confit of
    Onion and Boiled Red Potatoes,
    234–35
  Stock, 293

Beef (*cont.*)
Thai Beef Salad, 26–27
Beer, Tender Squab Marinated in, 128
Beer Batter, for Stuffed Squash Blossoms, 229
Beets, Pickled, 160–61
Bell peppers
Bell Pepper Cream Sauce, 222
broiling and peeling, 291
Chilled Tomato and Red Bell Pepper Soup, 100
Crab Cake Salad with Sweet Red Pepper Sauce, 221–22
in Goat Cheese Salad, 72
Grilled Paillard of Chicken with Red Bell Pepper Coulis, 113–14
Linguini with Roasted Peppers, Basil, Pine Nuts, and Niçoise Olives, 117
Penne with chicken and, 42
Pollo al Peperoni (Chicken with Red and Yellow Bell Peppers), 123–24
Red Bell Pepper Sauce, Crisp Corn Cakes with Prawns in, 164–65
in Roast Duck Salad, 119–20
in Roasted Eggplant Soup, 143
roasting and peeling, 291
Benedictine-Orange Sabayon, 91
Berries
Bacca di Sottobosco alla Crema Fresca (Berries with Crème Fraîche), 134
Fresh Fruit with Champagne Zabaglione, 155
Peach and Blackberry Summer Pie with Cinnamon Ice Cream, 227–28
Vanilla Wafers with Fresh Berries and Champagne Sabayon, 252–53
Warm Berry Gratin, 118
See also specific kinds
Beverages
Root Beer Float, 105
Tiziano (Champagne Cocktail), 132
Biscotti (Almond Dipping Cookies), 264
Biscotti di Niccioli, 156
Biscuits
Cream, with Poached Fresh Fruit and Raspberry Sauce, 114–15
Shortcake, for Peach and Blackberry Summer Pie with Cinnamon Ice Cream, 227–28
Biscuit Tortoni, 230
Bitter greens. *See* Greens

Black bean(s)
Grilled Pork Loin with Black Beans, Pickled Onions, and Tomatillo Salsa, 211–12
Soup, with Lime Cream, 259–60
Blackberries. *See* Berries
Blueberries
Blueberry-Almond Tart, 204–5
Cream Biscuits with Poached Fresh Fruit and Raspberry Sauce, 114–15
Lemon Cake with Crème Anglaise and, 48
Nectarine-Blueberry Crisp, 45
Peach-Blueberry Upside Down Cake, 31–32
See also Berries
Boning poultry, 291
Breads
Bruschetta (Roman Garlic Bread), 217–18
Tapenade Toast, 63
Brie Puff with Sautéed Apples and Caramel Sauce, 6–7
Brown Sauce, 296–97
Butter
clarifying, 291–92
Ginger, Eggplant with, 210
Herb and Mustard, Filet of Beef in, 141
Tarragon, and Potatoes, Roast Poussin with, 282
Buttercream, Raspberry, 183, 184
Butternut Squash Soup, 175
with Apples and Fresh Thyme, 109–10

Cabbage, Braised Napa, with Creamy White Sauce, 276
Cake(s)
Chocolate Decadence, 50–51
Date and Walnut, with Orange Buttercream, 11–12
Genoise, for *Tiramisú,* 135, 136
Ginger and Pear, 213
Lemon, with Crème Anglaise and Blueberries, 48
Linzer Torte, 186–87
Orange-Pecan, 108
Peach-Blueberry Upside Down, 31–32
Peach Shortcake, 215–16
Pistachio Meringue with Raspberry Buttercream, 183–84
Steve's Chocolate-Walnut Torte, 111

Calamari
   cleaning, 69–70
   Salad, 69
Calvados and Chanterelles, Roast Filet
      of Beef with, 176
Caper(s)
      Pan-Fried Chicken Cutlets with,
         21–22
   Penne alla Puttanesca (Pasta with Ol-
      ives, Capers, and Tomato Sauce),
      122–23
   Scallops of Breast of Fowl with Lemon
      and, 270
   Vinaigrette, 75
Caramel Crown, Almond Praline
      Mousse with, 241–42
Caramel Sauce, 7
   Brie Puff with Sautéed Apples and,
      6–7
   and Toasted Almonds, Fresh Peaches
      and Peach Ice Cream with, 235
Cassata all'Italiana, 84–85
Cassis Sauce, Lemon Mousse with,
      37–38
Caviar, Salad with Salmon and, 202–3
Celery
   in Chopped Vegetable Salad, 225
   Puree, 226–27
   Victor, 137
Ceviche with Scallops, 57
Champagne
   Cocktail (*Tiziano*), 132
   Sabayon, 252, 253
   Vinaigrette, 247–48
   Zabaglione, Fresh Fruit with, 155
Chanterelles. *See* Mushroom(s)
Chard
   Ruby, Creole Shrimp Steamed in,
      18–19
   Sautéed, with *Quatre Épices*, 181
Chardonnay Scallion Butter Sauce,
      Grilled Jumbo Shrimp with (*Spiedini
      di Gamberi*), 263–64
Cheddar cheese, in Grilled Pasilla Pep-
      pers with Salsa, 239–40
Cheese. *See specific kinds*
Cherries
   Chocolate Bread Pudding with, 224
   Clafoutis, 35
Chicken
   boning, 291

Breast of, with Mustard Sauce and
      Creamy Polenta, 155
Galletto al Forno (Baby Chicken Baked
      in Terracotta), 134–35
Grilled, and Fresh Horseradish-
      Tomato Relish, 30–31
Grilled, Spiedini, with Balsamic
      Onions, 230
Grilled Paillard of, with Red Bell
      Pepper Coulis, 113–14
Mascotte, 138
Mole, with Baked Mexican Green
      Rice, 207–9
Pan-Fried Chicken Cutlets with
      Capers, 21–22
with Pear-Cream Sauce, 6
Penne with Chicken and Bell
      Peppers, 42
Penne with Chicken, Garlic, and
      Sun-Dried Tomatoes, 86
Pollo al Mattone (Grilled Chicken with
      Sage and Rosemary), 4
Pollo al Peperoni (Chicken with Red
      and Yellow Bell Peppers), 123–24
Roast, with Goat Cheese and Lemon-
      Garlic Jalapeño Sauce, 93–94
Roast Chicken Breast with New
      Potatoes, Asparagus, Spinach, and
      Aioli, 44–45
Sautéed Hazelnut Chicken Breasts,
      Viennese-Style, 34
Scallops of Breast of Fowl with Lemon
      and Capers, 270
Smoked, Quesadilla of, 198–99
Stock, 294
See also Poultry
Chicory. *See* Greens
Chili-Orange Oil, 66
Chili peppers
   Grilled Pasilla Peppers with Salsa,
      239–40
   Lemon-Garlic Jalapeño Sauce, 94
Chocolate
   Bread Pudding with Cherries, 224
   Decadence Cake, 50–51
   Flan with Hazelnut Praline, 19
   Gioia Mia (Chocolate Tart in a Pecan
      Crust), 71–72
   Mocha Custards, 260–61
   Mocha Pots de Crème, 22
   Pears in Velvet, 200–1

Chocolate (*cont.*)
  Poached Pears with White Chocolate
    and Raspberries, 258
  Semifreddo con Noce (Frozen Nut and
    Chocolate Cream), 220
  Soufflé, 245–46
  Soufflé Glacé au Chocolat, 237–38
  Steve's Chocolate-Walnut Torte, 111
  White Chocolate Mousse, 190
Chowder, Wild Rice and Corn, 231
Cilantro Dressing, for Mongolian Lamb
    Chops, 268
Cinnamon Ice Cream, 228
Citrus Vinaigrette, 195
Clafoutis, 35
Clams. *See* Shellfish
Clarifying butter, 291–92
Coconut, fresh, in Siam Gems, 192–93
Coconut Empanades, 59–60
Cognac, Artichoke Soup with Hazelnuts
    and, 178
Compote
  Blood Orange and Strawberry, 64
  Chinese Pear Apple Warm Compote
    with Candied Ginger à la Mode,
    152–53
  Dried Fruit and Malaga, 162
Cookies
  Biscotti di Niccioli, 156
  Biscotti (Almond Dipping Cookies),
    264
  Brown Sugar and Ginger Fingers, 11
  Empire, 10
  Sesame and Lemon Bars, 9–10
  Shortbread, 162–63
  Vanilla Wafers, 252, 253
Corn
  Lobster, Scallops, and Clams with
    Corn and Ginger Cream, 244–45
  Wild Rice and Corn Chowder, 231
Corned Beef Hash, Polenta with (*Manzo
    Salmistrato*), 133
Cornish game hens. *See* Poultry
Cornmeal
  Crisp Corn Cakes with Prawns in Red
    Bell Pepper Sauce, 164–65
  Fig and Cornmeal Tart, 55–56
  See also Polenta
Court Bouillon, 15
Couscous with Grilled Lobster, Prawns,
    and Scallops, 79–80

Crab
  Angel Hair Pasta with Crab Meat,
    Hazelnuts, and Lemon, 47
  Braised Tofu Dumplings Stuffed with
    Shrimp and, 129–30
  Crab Cake Salad with Sweet Red Pep-
    per Sauce, 221–22
  Dungeness Crab and Avocado Salad,
    199–200
  Dungeness Crab Enchiladas, 52–53
  Fresh, with Orange Dressing, 266–67
  Popier Sod (Crab Rolls with Tamarind
    Sauce), 191–92
  in Salad of Mixed Greens with Papaya
    and Macadamia Nuts, 112
Cranberries, Apple-Cranberry Crisp,
    167–68
Cream Biscuits with Poached Fresh
    Fruit and Raspberry Sauce, 114–15
Crème Anglaise, 297
  Ginger, 146
  Hazelnut Soufflé with, 197
Crème Brûlée and Caramelized Apples,
    102
Crème Caramel, Orange-Rum, 40
Crème Fraîche, 297
  Berries with (*Bacca di Sottobosco alla
    Crema Fresca*), 134
  Lime-Basil, 54
  in Warm Berry Gratin, 118
Crenshaw Melon with Prosciutto Sauce
    and Fried Parlsey, 5
Crepes
  with Radicchio, 23–24
  Sweet Shanghai, with Red Bean
    Paste, 277
Croutons, 98, 101
Curried Prawns (*Goong Chu Chee*), 192
Custards, mousses, and puddings
  Almond Praline Mousse with a
    Caramel Crown, 241–42
  Apricot Custard with Raspberry
    Coulis, 62
  Chocolate Bread Pudding with
    Cherries, 224
  Chocolate Flan with Hazelnut
    Praline, 19
  Crème Brûlée and Caramelized
    Apples, 102
  Floating Island with Raspberries, 142
  Fried Cream with Rum, 138–39

Custards, mousses, and puddings (*cont.*)
Grand Marnier Mousse with Strawberry Coulis, 15–16
Lemon Custard, for Tart Doryn, 42–43
Lemon Mousse with Cassis Sauce, 37–38
Mexican Flan, 209
Mocha Custards, 260–61
Mocha Pots de Crème, 22
Orange-Rum Crème Caramel, 40
Pastry Cream, for Blueberry-Almond Tart, 204
Roquefort Custards with Sautéed Chard, 180–81
Tangerine Custard Meringue, 95–96
Thai Pumpkin Custard, 27–28
White Chocolate Mousse, 190
See also Crème Anglaise; Sabayon; Zabaglione

Dandelion greens. *See* Greens
Date(s)
and Parmesan Cheese, 289
Paste, for Sweet Shanghai Crepes, 277
and Walnut Cake with Orange Buttercream, 11–12
Desserts
Apple-Cranberry Crisp, 167–68
Apple Fritters, 268
Apricot Crisp, 127
Apricot Soufflé, 271
Assorted Figs with Raspberries and Fresh Almonds, 287
Bacca di Sottobosco alla Crema Fresca (Berries with Crème Fraîche), 134
Baked Figs Chartreuse, 274
Baked Rome Beauty Apples, 255
Blood Orange and Strawberry Compote, 64
Brie Puff with Sautéed Apples and Caramel Sauce, 6–7
Chinese Pear Apple Warm Compote with Candied Ginger à la Mode, 152–53
Chocolate Soufflé, 245–46
Clafoutis, 35
Cream Biscuits with Poached Fresh Fruit and Raspberry Sauce, 114–15
Crispy Banana Rolls, 121
Dates and Parmesan Cheese, 289

Dried Fruit and Malaga Compote with a Shortbread Cookie, 162–63
Elegant Orange Slices, 280
Fragole con Strega (Strawberries with Strega liqueur), 159
Fragole Pazze (Strawberries with Balsamic Vinegar), 265
Fresh Strawberries with Raspberry Coulis, 282–83
Fruit and Light Mascarpone, 76–77
Goat Cheese Gâteau, 179
Hazelnut Soufflé with Crème Anglaise, 197
Il Rustico de Pera (Pear Dessert), 25
Lemon Cake with Crème Anglaise and Blueberries, 48
Lemon Tart with Almond Crust, 173–74
Nectarine-Blueberry Crisp, 45
Peach and Blackberry Summer Pie with Cinnamon Ice Cream, 227–28
Pears in Velvet, 200–1
Pistachio Meringue with Raspberry Buttercream, 183–84
Poached Pears with White Chocolate and Raspberries, 258
Raspberries and Sour Cream, 177
Siam Gems, 192–93
Steve's Chocolate-Walnut Torte, 111
Strawberries with Sour Cream and Rum Sauce, 232
Taro with Tapioca, 131
Tart Doryn, 42–43
Tiramisú (Layered Rum Cream Dessert), 135–36
Vanilla Wafers with Fresh Berries and Champagne Sabayon, 252–53
Warm Berry Gratin, 118
See also Cake(s); Cookies; Custards, mousses, and puddings; Frozen desserts; Pastry; Tarts
Dessert sauces
Basil cream, 149
Berry Sauce, 220
Caramel, 7, 235
Cassis Sauce, 38
Marsala Sabayon, 25
Vanilla Cream, 32
Duck
Duck Breast Orientale, 257

Duck (*cont.*)
  Glaze, 295
  Grilled Duck Breast with Bagnat, 148
  Petaluma, with Pomegranate Sauce
    and Basmati Rice, 240–41
  Roast Duck Salad, 119–20
  Sautéed Duck Breast with Creamy
    Polenta, 161–62
  Scallops of Breast of Fowl with Lemon
    and Capers, 270
  Smoked Duck Breast Salad, 78–79
  Stock, 294–95

Eggplant
  Flambéed in Marc, 182–83
  with Ginger Butter, 210
  Involtini di Melanzane (Eggplant Rolls
    with Goat Cheese), 218–19
  Roasted Eggplant Soup, 143–44
Eggs, Sicilian-Style, 269
  See also Soufflé(s)
Empanadas, Coconut, 59–60
Enchiladas
  Dungeness Crab, 52–53
  Seafood, with Salsa Verde, 58–59
Endive, Belgian
  Bay Shrimp with Endive and Sesame
    Oil, 233–34
  in Chicken with Pear-Cream Sauce, 6
  in Salad with Salmon and Caviar,
    202–3
  with Watercress and Papaya, 185
  See also Greens; Salad(s)
Escarole. *See* Greens

Fennel
  Fennel, Pear, and Walnut Salad,
    287–88
  Insalata all'Arancia (Salad with Or-
    anges and Fennel), 122
  Medallions of Salmon with, 14–15
Feta, Scallops and Prawns Sautéed with
    Greek Olives and, 186
Fig(s)
  Assorted, with Raspberries and Fresh
    Almonds, 287
  Baked Figs Chartreuse, 274
  and Cornmeal Tart, 55–56
  Grilled Quail Stuffed with Figs and
    Prosciutto, 171–72
  Roasted, with Vanilla Ice Cream, 284

Fish
  Filet of Sole Amandine, 254–55
  Halibut in Parchment with Ginger
    Mushrooms, 126–27
  Sea Bass en Papillote with Tomato-
    Basil Sauce, 37
  Stock, 295
  See also Salmon; Swordfish; Tuna
Flageolets. *See* Legumes
Flan. *See* Custards, mousses and
    puddings
Floating Island with Raspberries,
    142
Frisée, 289
Fritters, Apple, 268
Frosting, Orange Buttercream, 12
Frozen desserts
  Apricot-Ginger Ice Cream, 73
  Biscuit Tortoni, 230
  Cassata all'Italiana, 84–85
  Cinnamon Ice Cream, 228
  Fresh Peaches and Peach Ice Cream
    with Caramel Sauce and Toasted
    Almonds, 235
  Lime-Rum Ice Cream, 68
  Orange Sorbet with Basil Cream,
    149
  Roasted Figs with Vanilla Ice Cream,
    284
  Semifreddo con Noce (Frozen Nut and
    Chocolate Cream), 220
  Soufflé Glacé au Chocolat, 237–38
  Whiskey Ice Cream with Fresh Peach
    Marmalade, 81
Fruit
  Dried Fruit and Malaga Compote with
    a Shortbread Cookie, 162–63
  Fresh Fruit with Champagne
    Zabaglione, 155
  and Light Mascarpone, 76–77
  See also Desserts; *specific fruits*

Garlic
  Bruschetta (Roman Garlic Bread),
    217–18
  Fresh Scallops with Garlic Sauce,
    276
  Lemon-Garlic Jalapeño Sauce, 94
  Mashed Potatoes, 55
  New Potato and Garlic Puree,
    167

Garlic (*cont.*)
  Penne with Chicken, Garlic, and Sun-Dried Tomatoes, 86
  and Pepper Prawns, 27
  Pizzetta con Aglio (Pizza with Olive Oil and Roasted Garlic), 262–63
  Potato-Garlic Puree, Steamed Artichokes with 92–93
  Roasted, Swordfish with Lime, Tequila, and, 110–11
  Rouille Sauce, 80
  Soup, 38–39
  Spicy Tomato Soup with Lime-Basil Crème Fraîche, 53–54
  Swordfish with Sesame Oil, Ginger, and, 248
  See also Aioli
Gazpacho, 214
Genoise, for *Tiramisú,* 135, 136
Ginger
  Alaskan Salmon with Ginger and Black Pepper, and Celery Puree, 226–27
  Apricot-Ginger Ice Cream, 73
  Brown Sugar and Ginger Fingers, 11
  Butter, Eggplant with, 210
  Chinese Pear Apple Warm Compote with Candied Ginger à la Mode, 152–53
  Cream, Lobster, Scallops, and Clams with Corn and, 244–45
  Crème Anglais, 146
  and Pear Cake, 213
  Swordfish with Sesame Oil, Ginger, and Garlic, 248
Glaze(s)
  Beef, 293
  Duck, 295
  Baked Chèvre with Sun-Dried Tomatoes and Basil, 154
  Gâteau, 179
  in *Involtini di Melanzane* (Eggplant Rolls with Goat Cheese), 218–19
  Mixed Bitter Greens with Goat Cheese and Wild Scallion Blossom Vinaigrette, 165–66
  Red and Yellow Tomato Salad with Goat Mozzarella, Pancetta, and Fried Okra, 250–51
  Roast Chicken with Goat Cheese and Lemon-Garlic Jalapeño Sauce, 93–94

Salad, 72
  Warm, with Pecans and Greens, 125–26
Gorgonzola cheese, Grilled Quail Stuffed with Figs and, 171–72
Grapefruit
  in Dungeness Crab and Avocado Salad, 199–200
  Honey Grapefruit Dressing, 200
  sectioning, 292
Green beans
  in Chopped Vegetable Salad, 225
  and Pecorino, 285–86
  in Salade Gourmande, 13–14
  in Salad with Salmon and Caviar, 202–3
  Summer Beans and Cherry Tomatoes with Lemon and Tarragon, 116–17
  Warm Bay Scallops and French Green Bean Salad, 96–97
Green peppers. *See* Bell peppers
Greens
  Mixed Bitter Greens with Goat Cheese and Wild Scallion Blossom Vinaigrette, 165–66
  Salad of Bitter Greens, 289
  Salad of Mixed Greens with Papaya and Macadamia Nuts, 112
  Vintage Quail with Bitter Greens and Polenta with White Truffles, 288–89
  Warm Goat Cheese with Pecans and, 125–26
  Warm Salad of Winter Greens with Pancetta, 144
  See also Salad(s); *specific greens*

Halibut in Parchment with Ginger Mushrooms, 126–27
Hash, Corned Beef, Polenta with (*Manzo Salmistrato*), 133
Hazelnut(s)
  Angel Hair Pasta with Crab Meat, Hazelnuts, and Lemon, 47
  Artichoke Soup with Hazelnuts and Cognac, 178
  in Biscotti di Niccioli, 156
  Chocolate Flan with Hazelnut Praline, 19
  in Linzer Torte, 186–87

Hazelnut(s) (*cont.*)
  Sautéed Hazelnut Chicken Breasts,
    Viennese-Style, 34
  Semifreddo con Noce (Frozen Nut and
    Chocolate Cream), 220
  Soufflé, with Crème Anglaise, 197
Hearts of Palm Salad, Oven-Dried
  Tomatoes and, 74
Herb and Mustard Butter, Filet of Beef
  in, 141
Honey Grapefruit Dressing, 200
Honey-Mustard Vinaigrette, 243–44
Horseradish-Tomato Relish, Fresh,
  30–31

Ice cream. *See* Frozen desserts
Icing, Orange Buttercream, 12

Jack cheese
  in Dungeness Crab Enchiladas, 52
  Flank Steak Quesada, 260
  in Grilled Pasilla Peppers with Salsa,
    239–40
  Grilled Polenta with Sonoma Jack
    Cheese, 145
Jalapeño peppers. *See* Chili peppers
Jam, Red Onion, 107

Kale. *See* Greens
Kiwi fruit, Fruit and Light Mascarpone,
  76–77

Lamb
  Campagna-Style Lamb Chops in
    Parchment, 170
  Chops, with Herbed Potato Crust,
    196–97
  Grilled Lamb Steaks, 215
  Marinated Roast Rack of Lamb, Oku,
    273
  Mongolian Lamb Chops, 267–68
  Noisettes of, with Artichokes, 24–
    25
  Roast Leg of, with Red Currant
    Sauce, 181–82
Legumes
  Black Bean Soup with Lime Cream,
    259–60
  Grilled Pork Loin with Black Beans,
    Pickled Onions, and Tomatillo
    Salsa, 211–12

Penne, Flageolets, and Caviar, 272
Roast Salmon with French Lentils and
  Saffron Sauce, 251–52
Lemon
  Angel Hair Pasta with Crab Meat,
    Hazelnuts, and, 47
  Cake, with Crème Anglaise and
    Blueberries, 48
  Custard, for Tart Doryn, 42–43
  -Garlic Jalapeño Sauce, 94
  Grilled Prawns with Fresh Tomato,
    Lemon, and Basil Sauce, 107–8
  Meyer Lemon Tartlets, 248–49
  Mousse, with Cassis Sauce, 37–38
  Scallops of Breast of Fowl with Lemon
    and Capers, 270
  sectioning, 292
  Sesame and Lemon Bars, 9–10
  Tart, with Almond Crust, 173–74
Lime
  Ceviche with Scallops, 57
  Cream, Black Bean Soup with,
    259–60
  -Rice Pilaf, 215
  -Rum Ice Cream, 68
  sectioning, 292
  Soy-Lime Dressing, 41–42
  Spicy Tomato Soup with Lime-Basil
    Crème Fraîche, 53–54
  Swordfish with Lime, Tequila, and
    Roasted Garlic, 110–11
Linzer Torte, 186–87
Lobster
  Couscous with Grilled Lobster,
    Prawns, and Scallops, 79–80
  Lobster, Scallops and Clams with
    Corn and Ginger Cream, 244–45
  Warm Lobster Salad with Citrus
    Vinaigrette, 194–95

Mâche. *See* Greens
Malaga, Dried Fruit and Malaga Com-
  pote with a Shortbread Cookie,
    162–63
Mandarin Beef, 279–80
Mango
  in Dungeness Crab and Avocado
    Salad, 199–200
  Vinaigrette, 207
Marinade, Soy-Ginger, 127
Marsala Sabayon, 25

Mascarpone
  in Baked Figs Chartreuse, 274
  Cream, for *Tiramisú,* 135, 136
  Light, Fruit and, 76–77
Mayonnaise, Basil, 251
  See also Aioli
Meats. *See specific kinds*
Melon, Crenshaw, with Prosciutto
  Sauce and Fried Parsley, 5
Meringue, Tangerine Custard, 95–
  96
Mocha Custards, 260–61
Mocha Pots de Crème, 22
Mousses. *See* Custards, mousses, and
  puddings
Mozzarella cheese
  Baked Buffalo Mozzarella, 103
  Fresh Tomato and Mozzarella Salad,
  33
  in Stuffed Squash Blossoms, 229
Mushroom(s)
  *Fettucine con Funghi, Prosciutto, e
  Panna* (Noodles with Mushrooms,
  Ham, and Cream), 157–58
  Fresh Shiitake, Salad of, 30
  Ginger, Halibut in Parchment with,
  126–27
  Grilled Shiitake, with Red Onion Jam,
  106–7
  Grilled Swordfish with Porcini Vinai-
  grette, 172–73
  Grilled Veal Steak with New Potato
  and Garlic Puree and Wild Onion–
  Chanterelle Compote, 166–67
  Morel, Free-Range Veal Loin with,
  283–84
  Pork Ragout with Balsamic Vinegar
  and Cèpes, 189–90
  Roast Filet of Beef with Calvados and
  Chanterelles, 176
  in Salade Gourmande, 13
  Tortellini with Morels and Parmesan,
  89–90
  in Veal Bauletto, 87
  Wild, Crostini of, 169
Mussels
  Baked with Cream, 140–41
  Zimino con Capellini (Steamed Mussels
  and Clams with Angel Hair Pasta),
  219–20
Mustard greens. *See* Greens

Mustard Sauce
  and Creamy Polenta, Breast of
  Chicken with, 155
  Escalopes of Turkey with, 50
  Herb-Marinated Salmon with, 283
Mustard Vinaigrette, 225

Napa cabbage, Braised, with Creamy
  White Sauce, 276
Nectarine-Blueberry Crisp, 45

Okra, Fried, Red and Yellow Tomato
  Salad with Goat Mozzarella,
  Pancetta, and, 250–51
Olives
  Niçoise, Linguini with Roasted
  Peppers, Basil, Pine Nuts, and, 117
  Penne alla Puttanesca (Pasta with Ol-
  ives, Capers, and Tomato Sauce),
  122–23
  Scallops and Prawns Sautéed with
  Greek Olives and Feta, 186
  in Tapenade, 63, 102
Onion(s)
  Balsamic, Grilled Chicken Spiedini
  with, 230
  Grilled Veal Steak with New Potato
  and Garlic Puree and Wild Onion–
  Chanterelle Compote, 166–67
  Pickled, 211–12
  Red Onion Jam, 107
  Sautéed Minute Steak with Confit of
  Onion and Boiled Red Potatoes,
  234–35
  Soup, 44
  Tart Bonne Femme, 61
  Tuna Steaks with Onion Marmalade,
  179
  Veal Medallions with Onion Marma-
  lade in Port Wine Sauce, 223
  Wild Scallion Blossom Vinaigrette, 166
Orange(s)
  Benedictine-Orange Sabayon, 91
  Blood Orange and Strawberry Com-
  pote, 64
  Buttercream, 12
  -Coconut Filling, for Empanadas, 59–60
  Dressing, Fresh Crab with, 266–67
  in Dried Fruit and Malaga Compote,
  162
  Elegant Orange Slices, 280

Orange(s) (*cont.*)
  Fruit and Light Mascarpone, 76–77
  Insalata all'Arancia (Salad with Oranges and Fennel), 122
  -Pecan Cake, 108
  -Rum Crème Caramel, 40
  Sorbet, with Basil Cream, 149
  sectioning, 292
Oysters, Peppered, on Toast, 232

Palm. *See* Hearts of Palm Salad
Pancetta
  in *Galletto al Forno* (Baby Chicken Baked in Terra-cotta), 134–35
  in Grilled Chicken Spiedini with Balsamic Onions, 230
  Red and Yellow Tomato Salad with Goat Mozzarella, Pancetta, and Fried Okra, 250–51
  Saddle of Veal with, 84
  in *Spiedini di Gamberi* (Grilled Jumbo Shrimp with Chardonnay Scallion Butter Sauce), 263–64
  in Tuna Steaks with Onion Marmalade, 179
  Warm Salad of Winter Greens with, 144
Papaya
  Belgian Endive with Watercress and, 185
  Fruit and Light Mascarpone, 76–77
  Salad of Mixed Greens with Papaya and Macadamia Nuts, 112
Parmesan cheese
  Dates and, 289
  Tortellini with Morels and, 89–90
Parsley, Fried, Crenshaw Melon with Prosciutto Sauce and, 5
Parsnips, Pear-Parsnip Soup, 36–37
Pasta
  Agnollotti with Fresh Sage, 70–71
  Angel Hair, with Crab Meat, Hazelnuts, and Lemon, 47
  Capellini al Pomodoro Naturale (Pasta with Fresh Tomato), 134
  Chili-Orange Cold Noodles, 65–66
  Fettucine con Funghi, Prosciutto, e Panna (Noodles with Mushrooms, Ham, and Cream), 157–58
  Fresh, 71
  Fresh Egg, 83

Linguini with Roasted Peppers, Basil, Pine Nuts, and Niçoise Olives, 117
Linguini with Sea Scallops and Sun-Dried Tomatoes, 72–73
Penne, Flageolets, and Caviar, 272
Penne alla Puttanesca (Pasta with Olives, Capers, and Tomato Sauce), 122–23
Penne Arrabiata (Penne with Hot Chili–Fresh Tomato Sauce), 3
Penne with Chicken and Bell Peppers, 42
Penne with Chicken, Garlic, and Sun-Dried Tomatoes, 86
Pumpkin Tortelli, 82–83
Tortellini with Morels and Parmesan, 89–90
Zimino con Capellini (Steamed Mussels and Clams with Angel Hair Pasta), 219–20
Pastry
  American Tea Scones, 8–9
  Coconut Empanadas, 59–60
  Pastry Shell (Pâte Brisée), 298
  Pâte Brisée Tartlet Shells, 249
  Pâte Sablée, 204
  Pâte Sucrée, 201
  See also Tarts
Pastry Cream, for Blueberry-Almond Tart, 204
Peach(es)
  and Blackberry Summer Pie with Cinnamon Ice Cream, 227–28
  -Blueberry Upside Down Cake, 31–32
  Cream Biscuits with Poached Fresh Fruit and Raspberry Sauce, 114–15
  Fresh Fruit with Champagne Zabaglione, 155
  Fresh Peaches and Peach Ice Cream with Caramel Sauce and Toasted Almonds, 235
  Shortcake, 215–16
  Whiskey Ice Cream with Fresh Peach Marmalade, 81
Pear(s)
  Chicken with Pear-Cream Sauce, 6
  Cream Biscuits with Poached Fresh Fruit and Raspberry Sauce, 114–15

Pear(s) (*cont.*)
  in Dried Fruit and Malaga Compote, 162
  Fennel, Pear, and Walnut Salad, 287–88
  Ginger and Pear Cake, 213
  Il Rustico de Pera (Pear Dessert), 25
  -Parsnip Soup, 36–37
  Poached, with White Chocolate and Raspberries, 258
  Poached Winter, with Ginger Crème Anglaise, 145–46
  in Velvet, 200–1
  Warm Bosc Pear and Pecan Cream Tart, 99
  Watercress and Pear Salad, 243–44
Pear Apple, Chinese, Warm Compote with Candied Ginger à la Mode, 152–53
Pecan(s)
  Gioia Mia (Chocolate Tart in a Pecan Crust), 71–72
  Orange-Pecan Cake, 108
  -Pesto Sauce, Rabbit with, 39–40
  Warm Bosc Pear and Pecan Cream Tart, 99
  Warm Goat Cheese with Pecans and Greens, 125–26
Pecorino, Green Beans, and 285–86
Peppers. *See* Bell peppers; Chili peppers
Persillade, in Red Currant Sauce, 181, 182
Pesto. *See* Basil
Pickled Beets, 160–61
Pickled Onions, 211–12
Pies. *See* Tarts
Pine nuts, Linguini with Roasted Peppers, Basil, Pine Nuts, and Niçoise Olives, 117
Pistachio Meringue with Raspberry Buttercream, 183–84
Pizzetta con Aglio (Pizza with Olive Oil and Roasted Garlic), 262–63
Polenta, 39
  with Corned Beef Hash (*Manzo Salmistrato*), 133
  Creamy, Sautéed Duck Breast with, 161–62
  Grilled, with Sonoma Jack Cheese, 145
  Rabbit with Polenta and Pecan-Pesto Sauce, 39–40

Vintage Quail with Bitter Greens and Polenta with White Truffles, 288–89
Pomegranate Sauce, 240–41
Pork
  Grilled Pork Loin with Black Beans, Pickled Onions, and Tomatillo Salsa, 211–12
  Marinated Pan-Fried Pork Chops, 121
  Ragout, with Balsamic Vinegar and Cèpes, 189–90
Port
  Scaloppine di Vitello all'Opporto e Pepe Verde (Scallops of Veal with Port and Green Peppercorns), 158
  Veal Medallions with Onion Marmalade in Port Wine Sauce, 223
Potato(es)
  Boiled Red, Sautéed Minute Steak with Confit of Onion and, 234–35
  in Celery Puree, 226–27
  in Corned Beef Hash, 133
  Finnish, Salt-Roasted, 286–87
  Garlic Mashed, 55
  -Garlic Puree, Steamed Artichokes with, 92–93
  Lamb Chops with Herbed Potato Crust, 196–97
  New Potato and Garlic Puree, 167
  Parisian, 91
  Roast Chicken Breast with New Potatoes, Asparagus, Spinach, and Aioli, 44–45
  Roast Poussin with Tarragon Butter and, 282
  Smoked Salmon and New Potato Salad, 236–37
Poultry
  Aromatic Chicken Soup, 17
  boning, 291
  Escalopes of Turkey with Mustard Sauce, 50
  Five-Spice Roast Squab with Rice Wine–Butter Sauce, 151–52
  Galletto al Forno (Baby Chicken Baked in Terra-cotta), 134–35
  Grilled Quail Stuffed with Figs and Prosciutto, 171–72
  Roasted Szechwan Pepper-Salt Quail, 67–68

Poultry (*cont.*)
  Roast Poussin with Tarragon Butter
    and Potatoes, 282
  Scallops of Breast of Fowl with Lemon
    and Capers, 270
  Squab with Quince, 237
  Tender Squab Marinated in Beer, 128
  Vintage Quail with Bitter Greens and
    Polenta with White Truffles, 288–
    89
  See also Chicken; Duck
Praline Mousse, Almond, with a
  Caramel Crown, 241–42
Prawns. *See* Shrimp or prawns
Prosciutto
  Crenshaw Melon with Prosciutto
    Sauce and Fried Parsley, 5
  Fettucine con Funghi, Prosciutto, e
    Panna (Noodles with Mushrooms,
    Ham, and Cream), 157–58
  Grilled Quail Stuffed with Figs and,
    171–72
  in Oven-Dried Tomatoes and Hearts
    of Palm Salad, 74
  Timberhill Prosciutto Roll, 256
  in Veal Bauletto, 87
Provolone cheese, Pumate-Provolone
  Salad, 247–48
Prunes, in Dried Fruit and Malaga
  Compote, 162
Puddings. *See* Custards, mousses, and
  puddings
Pumate. *See* Tomato(es), sun-dried
Pumpkin
  Thai Pumpkin Custard, 27–28
  Tortelli, 82–83

Quail. *See* Poultry
Quesadilla of Smoked Chicken, 198–99
Quince, Squab with, 237

Rabbit
  with Polenta and Pecan-Pesto Sauce,
    39–40
  Roulades, with Garlic Mashed Pota-
    toes, 54–55
Radicchio
  Crepes with, 23–24
  Grilled Swordfish with Porcini Vinai-
    grette, Served on a Bed of Sautéed
    Spinach and, 172–73

  See also Greens
Raspberries
  Apricot Custard with Raspberry Cou-
    lis, 62
  Assorted Figs with Raspberries and
    Fresh Almonds, 287
  Berry Sauce, 220
  Cream Biscuits with Poached Fresh
    Fruit and Raspberry Sauce,
    114–15
  Floating Island with, 142
  Fresh Strawberries with Raspberry
    Coulis, 282–83
  Pistachio Meringue with Raspberry
    Buttercream, 183, 184
  Poached Pears with White Chocolate
    and, 258
  and Sour Cream, 177
  Warm Berry Gratin, 118
  See also Berries
Red Bean Paste, Sweet Shanghai Crepes
  with, 277
Red currant jelly
  in Duck Breast Orientale, 257
  Roast Leg of Lamb with Red Currant
    Sauce, 181–82
Red Onion Jam, 107
Red peppers. *See* Bell peppers
Relish(es)
  Fresh Horseradish-Tomato, 30–31
  Pickled Beets, 160–61
  Pickled Onions, 211–12
  See also Salsa
Rice
  in Aromatic Chicken Soup, 17
  Baked Mexican Green, 208–9
  Basmati, 76
    Petaluma Duck with Pomegranate
      Sauce and, 240–41
  Lime-Rice Pilaf, 215
  Timberhill Prosciutto Roll, 256
  Wild Rice and Corn Chowder, 231
Rice Wine–Butter Sauce, Five-Spice
  Roast Squab with, 151–52
Root Beer Float, 105
Roquefort cheese
  in Grilled Pasilla Peppers with Salsa,
    239–40
  Roquefort Custards with Sautéed
    Chard, 180–81
Rouille Sauce, 80

Rum
  Fried Cream with, 138–39
  in Lemon Mousse with Cassis Sauce,
    37–38
  Lime-Rum Ice Cream, 68
  Orange-Rum Crème Caramel, 40
  Strawberries with Sour Cream and
    Rum Sauce, 232
  in *Tiramisú*, 135

Sabayon
  Benedictine-Orange, 91
  Champagne, 252, 253
  Marsala, 25
Saffron Sauce, Roast Salmon with
    French Lentils and, 251–52
Sage, Fresh, Agnollotti with, 70–71
Salad(s)
  Asparagus, Grilled Swordfish with,
    100–2
  Bay Shrimp with Endive and Sesame
    Oil, 233–34
  Belgian Endive with Watercress and
    Papaya, 185
  Calamari, 69
  Celery Victor, 137
  Chopped Vegetable, 225
  Crab Cake, with Sweet Red Pepper
    Sauce, 221–22
  Dungeness Crab and Avocado,
    199–200
  Fennel, Pear, and Walnut, 287–88
  of Fresh Shiitake Mushrooms, 30
  Fresh Tomato and Mozzarella, 33
  Goat Cheese, 72
  Green, with Mango Vinaigrette, 206–7
  Green, with Sesame and Walnut Oil
    Dressing, 152
  Hearts of Romaine, 254
  House Smoked Salmon, 188–89
  Insalata all'Arancia (Salad with
    Oranges and Fennel), 122
  Oven-Dried Tomatoes and Hearts of
    Palm, 74
  Pumate-Provolone, 247–48
  Red and Yellow Tomato, with Goat
    Mozzarella, Pancetta, and Fried
    Okra, 250–51
  Roast Duck, 119–20
  Salade Gourmande, 13–14
  with Salmon and Caviar, 202–3

Scallop, 49–50
  Smoked Duck Breast, 78–79
  Smoked Salmon and New Potato,
    236–37
  Summer Beans and Cherry Tomatoes
    with Lemon and Tarragon, 116–17
  Thai Beef, 26–27
  Thai Prawn, 41–42
  Tossed Bean Curd, 275
  Warm Bay Scallops and French Green
    Bean, 96–97
  Warm Lobster, with Citrus
    Vinaigrette, 194–95
  Watercress and Pear, 243–44
  See also Greens
Salad dressings
  Almond Oil Vinaigrette, 203
  Balsamic Vinaigrette, 222
  Basil Mayonnaise, 251
  Caper Vinaigrette, 75
  Champagne Vinaigrette, 247–48
  Chili-Orange Oil for, 66
  Citrus Vinaigrette, 195
  Dijon Mustard Vinaigrette, 49–50
  French Dressing, 137
  Honey Grapefruit Dressing, 200
  Honey-Mustard Vinaigrette, 243–44
  Lemon-Tarragon Vinaigrette, 117
  Lemon Vinaigrette, 101
  Mango Vinaigrette, 207
  Mustard Vinaigrette, 225
  Red Wine Vinaigrette, 64, 234
  Sesame, 119–20
  Sesame and Walnut Oil, 152
  Sherry-Shallot Vinaigrette, 126
  Soy-Lime, 41–42
  Vinaigrette with Almonds, 98
  Vinaigrette with Fresh Herbs, 251
  Walnut Dressing, 185
  Wild Scallion Blossom Vinaigrette,
    166
  See also Salad(s)
Salmon
  Alaskan, with Ginger and Black Pep-
    per, and Celery Puree, 226–27
  with Avocado Cream Sauce, 75
  Braised in Vernaccia, 286–87
  Charcoal-Grilled, Vinaigrette, 64
  Herb-Marinated, with Mustard Sauce,
    283
  House Smoked Salmon Salad, 188–89

Salmon (*cont.*)
  Medallions of, with Fennel, 14–15
  Roast, with French Lentils and Saf-
    fron Sauce, 251–52
  Salad with Salmon and Caviar, 202–3
  Smoked Salmon and New Potato
    Salad, 236–37
Salsa, 199, 239–40
  Tomatillo, 212
  Verde, 59
Sauce(s)
  Avocado Cream, 75
  Bagnat, 148
  Béchamel, 296
  Bell Pepper Cream, 222
  Brown, 297–98
  Cilantro Dressing, for Mongolian
    Lamb Chops, 268
  Creoja, 101
  Lemon-Garlic Jalapeño, 94
  for Mongolian Lamb Chops, 267–68
  Mustard, 50, 155, 283
  Pecan-Pesto, Rabbit with, 39–40
  Pesto, 103–4
  Pomegranate, 240–41
  Port Wine, Veal Medallions with
    Onion Marmalade in, 223
  Rouille, 80
  Seasoning, for Mandarin Beef,
    279–80
  Sorrel, Veal Chops with, 203
  Tamarind, Crab Rolls with (*Popier
    Sod*), 191–92
  Tomatillo, 53
  Tomato, 71, 123
    for *Involtini di Melanzane*, 218–19
  White, 24
  See also Aioli: Dessert sauces; Salsa
Sausage, Chinese pork, in *Popier Sod* (Crab
  Rolls with Tamarind Sauce), 191–92
Scallop(s)
  Ceviche with, 57
  Couscous with Grilled Lobster,
    Prawns, and Scallops, 79–80
  Fresh, with Garlic Sauce, 276
  Linguini with Sea Scallops and
    Sun-Dried Tomatoes, 72–73
  Lobster, Scallops, and Clams with
    Corn and Ginger Cream, 244–45
  and Prawns, Sautéed with Greek
    Olives and Feta, 186

Salad, 49–50
Seafood Enchilada with Salsa Verde,
  58–59
with Tomato and White Wine, 20–21
Warm Bay, and French Green Bean
  Salad, 96–97
Scones, American Tea, 8–9
Sea Bass en Papillote with Tomato-Basil
  Sauce, 37
Seafood. *See* Fish; Shellfish; *specific kinds*
Sesame Dressing, 119–20
Sesame and Lemon Bars, 9–10
Sesame and Walnut Oil Dressing, 152
Shellfish
  Couscous with Grilled Lobster,
    Prawns, and Scallops, 79–80
  Lobster, Scallops and Clams with
    Corn and Ginger Cream, 244–45
  Mussels Baked with Cream, 140–41
  Peppered Oysters on Toast, 232
  Seafood Enchilada with Salsa Verde,
    58–59
  Warm Lobster Salad with Citrus
    Vinaigrette, 194–95
  Zimino con Capellini (Steamed Mussels
    and Clams with Angel Hair Pasta),
    219–20
  See also Crab; Scallops; Shrimp or
    prawns
Sherry-Shallot Vinaigrette, 126
Shiitake mushrooms. *See* Mushroom(s)
Shortbread Cookies, 162–63
Shortcake, Peach, 215–16
Shortcake Biscuits, for Peach and Black-
  berry Summer Pie with Cinnamon
  Ice Cream, 227–28
Shrimp or prawns
  Bay Shrimp with Endive and Sesame
    Oil, 233–34
  Braised Tofu Dumplings Stuffed with
    Shrimp and Crab, 129–30
  Couscous with Grilled Lobster,
    Prawns, and Scallops, 79–80
  Creole Shrimp Steamed in Ruby
    Chard, 18–19
  Crisp Corn Cakes with Prawns in Red
    Bell Pepper Sauce, 164–65
  Garlic and Pepper Prawns, 27
  Golden Shrimp Puffs, 120
  Goong Chu Chee (Curried Prawns),
    192

Shrimp or prawns (*cont.*)
  Grilled Prawns with Fresh Tomato,
    Lemon, and Basil Sauce, 107–8
  Phoenix, 278–79
  in *Popier Sod* (Crab Rolls with Tama-
    rind Sauce), 191–92
  Prawns with Walnuts, 130
  Rice Paper Shrimp Rolls, 150–51
  Scallops and Prawns Sautéed with
    Greek Olives and Feta, 186
  Seafood Enchilada with Salsa Verde,
    58–59
  Shrimp Paste, for Phoenix Shrimp,
    279
  Spiedini di Gamberi (Grilled Jumbo
    Shrimp with Chardonnay Scallion
    Butter Sauce), 263–64
  Thai Prawn Salad, 41–42
Sole, Filet of, Amandine, 254–55
Sonoma Jack cheese, Grilled Polenta
  with, 145
Sorrel Sauce, Veal Chops with, 203
Soufflé(s)
  Apricot, 271
  Chocolate, 245–46
  Glacé au Chocolat, 237–38
  Hazelnut, with Crème Anglaise, 197
Soup(s)
  Aromatic Chicken, 17
  Artichoke, with Hazelnuts and
    Cognac, 178
  Beef Stock, 293
  Black Bean, with Lime Cream, 259–
    60
  Butternut Squash, 175
    with Apples and Fresh Thyme,
      109–10
  Chicken Stock, 294
  Chilled Tomato and Red Bell Pepper,
    100
  Duck Stock, 294–95
  Fish Stock, 295–96
  Garlic, 38–39
  Gazpacho, 214
  Onion, 44
  Pear-Parsnip, 36–37
  Roasted Eggplant, 143–44
  Spicy Tomato, with Lime-Basil Crème
    Fraîche, 53–54
  Veal Stock, 294
  Wild Rice and Corn Chowder, 231

Sour cream
  Raspberries and, 177
  and Rum Sauce, Strawberries with,
    232
Soy-Ginger Marinade, 127
Soy-Lime Dressing, 41–42
Spinach
  in Agnollotti with Fresh Sage, 70–71
  Grilled Swordfish with Porcini Vinai-
    grette, Served on a Bed of Sautéed
    Spinach and Radicchio, 172–73
  Roast Chicken Breast with New Pota-
    toes, Asparagus, Spinach, and Aioli,
    44–45
  Sautéed Spinach and Radicchio,
    Grilled Swordfish with Porcini
    Vinaigrette Served on a Bed of,
    172–73
  Veal Medallion Sauté with Watercress
    and Spinach Sauce, 98
  in Warm Salad of Winter Greens with
    Pancetta, 144
Spread. *See* Tapenade
Squab. *See* Poultry
Squash
  Butternut Squash Soup, 175
    with Apples and Fresh Thyme,
      109–10
  Stuffed Squash Blossoms, 229
  Stuffed Zucchini, 270–71
Squid. *See* Calamari
Stocks, 293–96
Strawberries
  Berry Sauce, 220
  Blood Orange and Strawberry
    Compote, 64
  Cream Biscuits with Poached Fresh
    Fruit and Raspberry Sauce,
    114–15
  Fragole con Strega (Strawberries with
    Strega liqueur), 159
  Fragole Pazze (Strawberries with Bal-
    samic Vinegar), 265
  Fresh, with Raspberry Coulis, 282–83
  Fruit and Light Mascarpone, 76–77
  Grand Marnier Mousse with Straw-
    berry Coulis, 15–16
  with Sour Cream and Rum Sauce,
    232
  with Zabaglione, 170
  See also Berries

Streusel, for Peach and Blackberry Summer Pie with Cinnamon Ice Cream, 227, 228
Sushi, Timberhill Prosciutto Roll, 256
Swordfish
    Grilled, with Asparagus Salad, 100–2
    Grilled, with Porcini Vinaigrette, Served on a Bed of Sautéed Spinach and Radicchio, 172–73
    with Lime, Tequila, and Roasted Garlic, 110–11
    with Sesame Oil, Ginger, and Garlic, 248

Tamarind Sauce, Crab Rolls with (Popier Sod), 191–92
Tangerine Custard Meringue, 95–96
Tapenade, 102
Tapenade Toast, 63
Taro with Tapioca, 131
Tarragon Butter and Potatoes, Roast Poussin with, 282
Tarts
    Blueberry-Almond, 204–5
    Fig and Cornmeal, 55–56
    Fresh Tomato and Herb, 281–82
    Gioia Mia (Chocolate Tart in a Pecan Crust), 71–72
    Meyer Lemon Tartlets, 248–49
    Onion Tart Bonne Femme, 61
    Tart Doryn, 42–43
    Warm Bosc Pear and Pecan Cream, 99
Techniques, 291–92
Teleme cheese, Flank Steak Quesada, 260
Tofu
    Braised Tofu Dumplings Stuffed with Shrimp and Crab, 129–30
    in Popier Sod (Crab Rolls with Tamarind Sauce), 191–92
    Tossed Bean Curd Salad, 275
Tomatillo(es)
    Salsa, 212
    in Salsa Verde, 59
    Sauce, 53
Tomato(es)
    -Basil Sauce, Sea Bass en Papillote with, 37
    Bruschetta (Roman Garlic Bread), 217–18

Capellini al Pomodoro Naturale (Pasta with Fresh Tomato), 134
Chilled Tomato and Red Bell Pepper Soup, 100
in Chopped Vegetable Salad, 225
Fresh Tomato and Herb Tarts, 281–82
Fresh Tomato and Mozzarella Salad, 33
Gazpacho, 214
Grilled Prawns with Fresh Tomato, Lemon, and Basil Sauce, 107–8
Horseradish-Tomato Relish, 30–31
Oven-Dried, and Hearts of Palm Salad, 74
Penne alla Puttanesca (Pasta with Olives, Capers, and Tomato Sauce), 122–23
Red and Yellow Tomato Salad with Goat Mozzarella, Pancetta, and Fried Okra, 250–51
in Salsa, 199, 239–40
Sauce, 71, 123
in Sicilian-Style Eggs, 269
Spicy Tomato Soup with Lime-Basil Crème Fraîche, 53–54
Summer Beans and Cherry Tomatoes with Lemon and Tarragon, 116–17
sun-dried
    Baked Chèvre with Sun-Dried Tomatoes and Basil, 154
    in Grilled Duck Breast with Bagnat, 148
    in Involtini di Melanzane (Eggplant Rolls with Goat Cheese), 218–19
    Linguini with Sea Scallops and, 72–73
    Penne with Chicken, Garlic, and, 86
    Pumate-Provolone Salad, 247–48
    in Rice Paper Shrimp Rolls, 150–51
    in Salsa, 199
    in Stuffed Squash Blossoms, 229
    Sun-Dried Tomato Aioli, 47
    Tomato Aioli, 104
Toppings
    for Apple-Cranberry Crisp, 167, 168
    Crème Fraîche, 297
    Lime-Basil Crème Fraîche, 54
    Streusel, 227, 228
Tortes
    Linzer, 186–87
    Steve's Chocolate-Walnut, 111

Tuna
  Steaks, with Onion Marmalade, 179
  Tartare, 29–30, 147
Turkey. *See* Poultry

Vanilla Wafers, 252, 253
Veal
  Bauletto, 87
  Chops, with Sorrel Sauce, 203
  Free-Range Veal Loin with Morel
    Mushrooms, 283–84
  Glaze, 294
  Grilled Veal Steak with New Potato
    and Garlic Puree and Wild Onion–
    Chanterelle Compote, 166–67
  Medallion, Sauté with Watercress and
    Spinach Sauce, 98
  Medallions, with Onion Marmalade in
    Port Wine Sauce, 223
  Saddle of, with Pancetta, 84
  *Scaloppine di Vitello all'Opporto e Pepe
    Verde* (Scallops of Veal with Port
    and Green Peppercorns), 158
  Stock, 294
Vegetables, Grilled, with Sun-Dried To-
  mato Aioli, 46–47
  See also Greens; Salad(s); *specific
    vegetables*
Vinaigrettes. *See* Salad dressings

Walnut oil
  Sesame and Walnut Oil Dressing, 152
  Walnut Dressing, 185
Walnuts
  Date and Walnut Cake with Orange
    Buttercream, 11–12

Fennel, Pear, and Walnut Salad,
    287–88
  in Grilled Quail Stuffed with Figs
    and, 171–72
  Prawns with, 130
  Semifreddo con Noce (Frozen Nut and
    Chocolate Cream), 220
  Steve's Chocolate-Walnut Torte,
    111
Watercress
  Belgian Endive with Watercress and
    Papaya, 185
  in *Insalata all'Arancia,* 122
  and Pear Salad, 243–44
  Veal Medallion Sauté with Watercress
    and Spinach Sauce, 98
  See also Greens
Whiskey Ice Cream with Fresh Peach
    Marmalade, 81
White chocolate
  Mousse, 190
  Poached Pears with White Chocolate
    and Raspberries, 258
White Sauce, 24
Wild Rice and Corn Chowder, 231
Winter Greens. *See* Greens

Zabaglione
  Champagne, Fresh Fruit with,
    155
  Chilled, 88
  Strawberries with, 170
  for *Tiramisú,* 135, 136
Zucchini
  Stuffed, 270–71
  Stuffed Squash Blossoms, 229